The ADA Mandate
for Social Change

The ADA Mandate for Social Change

edited by

Paul Wehman, Ph.D.
Professor of
Physical Medicine and Special Education
Rehabilitation Research and Training Center
Virginia Commonwealth University
Richmond

·P·A·U·L·H·
BROOKES
PUBLISHING C.º

Baltimore • London • Toronto • Sydney

Paul H. Brookes Publishing Co.
P.O. Box 10624
Baltimore, Maryland 21285-0624

Typeset by The Composing Room of Michigan, Inc., Grand Rapids, Michigan.
Manufactured in the United States of America by
The Maple Press Company, York, Pennsylvania.

Library of Congress Cataloging-in-Publication Data
The ADA mandate for social change /   edited by Paul Wehman.
    p.   cm.
  Includes bibliographical references and index.
  ISBN 1-55766-117-0
  1. Handicapped Government policy—United
States. 2. Handicapped—United States—Economic
conditions. 3. Handicapped—United States—Social
conditions. 4. Handicapped—Legal status, laws, etc.—United
States. 5. Handicapped—Services for—United
States. 6. United States. Americans with Disabilities Act
of 1990.
I. Wehman, Paul.
HV1553.A595   1993
362.4′0973—dc20   92-31810
                                                   CIP

British Library Cataloguing-in-Publication data are available from the British
Library.

Contents

Contributors

About the Editor

Paul Wehman, Ph.D., Professor of Physical Medicine and Special Education, Rehabilitation Research and Training Center, Virginia Commonwealth University, 1314 West Main Street, Post Office Box 2011, Richmond, Virginia 23284-2011

Paul Wehman is Professor at the Department of Physical Medicine and Special Education, Medical College of Virginia, Virginia Commonwealth University. Internationally recognized for his service and scholarly contributions in the fields of special education, psychology, and vocational rehabilitation, Dr. Wehman is the recipient of the 1990 Joseph P. Kennedy, Jr., Foundation Award in Mental Retardation. He also was presented in October 1992 with the Distinguished Service Award from the President's Committee on Employment for Persons with Disabilities. He is the author or editor of over 100 books, research monographs, journal articles, and chapters in the areas of traumatic brain injury, mental retardation, supported employment, and special education. Specific research interests include transition from school to work and supported employment.

About the Authors

Karen Barrett, M.S., C.R.C., Work Adjustment Specialist, National Center for Disability Services, 201 I.U. Willets Road, Albertson, New York 11507-1599

Karen Barrett is the Work Adjustment Specialist on a Rehabilitation Services Administration funded Traumatic Brain Injury project. She worked previously as a state vocational rehabilitation counselor and as an employment specialist for the Association for Retarded Citizens and the Rehabilitation Research and Training Center, Virginia Commonwealth University. Ms. Barrett has background knowledge and experience in the area of supported employment and has an extreme amount of expertise in task analyzing various training program components and in developing job modification strategies for persons with severe disabilities. She has presented on the employment needs and job accommodation issues of persons with TBI at the National Head

Injury Annual Conference and the National Rehabilitation Association Conference. Ms. Barrett holds a Master's degree in Rehabilitation Counseling from Virginia Commonwealth University.

David F. Bateman, Ph.D., The University of Kansas, Beach Center on Families and Disability, Bureau of Child Research, 3111 Haworth Hall, Lawrence, Kansas 66045

David F. Bateman is an assistant professor in the Division of Psychology and Special Education, Teachers College at Emporia State University, Emporia, Kansas. He has spoken widely on advocacy and policy issues relating to individuals with disabilities and their families. He serves on numerous national boards and commissions. He is also very active in monitoring special education legislation in Kansas and coordinating statewide lobbying and education efforts, particularly for the Council for Exceptional Children.

Robert Bogdan, Ph.D., Professor of Special Education and Sociology, Syracuse University, School of Education, Special Education Programs, 805 South Crouse Avenue, Syracuse, New York 13244-2280

Robert Bogdan is a Professor of Special Education and Sociology at Syracuse University. He received his Ph.D. in sociology from Syracuse in 1971. He is also a Senior Researcher at the Center on Human Policy. His current interests include the sociology of disability and qualitative research methods. His books include *Qualitative Research for Education* with Sari Knopp Biklen, *Introduction to Qualitative Research* with Steve Taylor, and *Freak Show*. He teaches courses in qualitative research methods and the sociology of disability.

Shirley K. Chandler, M.S., C.R.C., Department of Rehabilitation Science, University of Texas Southwestern Medical Center, School of Allied Health, 5323 Harry Hines Boulevard, Dallas, Texas 75235-9088

Shirley K. Chandler is employed by the Department of Rehabilitation Science, The University of Texas Southwestern Medical Center at Dallas, as a Research Associate and Instructor. Prior to her current position, she was an Instructor and Training Associate for the Rehabilitation Research and Training Center on Supported Employment, Virginia Commonwealth University, where she was involved in a Community-Based Instructor educational program for special education teachers. Ms. Chandler is currently involved in several research projects including a study on the vocational decision-making patterns of individuals with traumatic brain injury, client empowerment issues for rehabilitation counselors, and substance abuse prevention for youth. Ms. Chandler is a Ph.D. candidate in Urban Services at Virginia Commonwealth University. She holds an M.S. degree in Rehabilitation Counseling and an M.S. degree in Special Education from Syracuse University.

Thomas Czerlinsky, Ph.D., Department of Rehabilitation Science, University of Texas Southwestern Medical Center, School of Allied Health, 5323 Harry Hines Boulevard, Dallas, Texas 75235-9088

Thomas Czerlinsky is an Associate Professor and Director of Research at the Department of Rehabilitation Science, The University of Texas Southwestern Medical Center at Dallas. Prior to his current position, he held the position of Research Scientist at the Research and Training Center on New Directions for Facilities, University of Wisconsin-Stout, where he was involved in projects on school to work transition and vocational decision making for persons with disabilities. His research interests include client empowerment, vocational decision making, community reintegration for persons with chronic mental illness, and traumatic head injury. He holds a Ph.D. in Experimental Social Psychology from the University of Virginia, and an M.A. in Rehabilitation Counseling from New York University. He also received a postdoctoral fellowship in Biobehavioral Neuropsychopharmacology at Boston University Medical School.

Charles Wm. Harles, J.D., Executive Director, Inter-National Association of Business, Industry, and Rehabilitation (I-NABIR), Post Office Box 15242, Washington, DC 20003

Charles Wm. Harles, Esq., is Executive Director of the Inter-National Association of Business, Industry, and Rehabilitation (I-NABIR). It is the association that represents Projects With Industry (PWI) programs. He is also President of Harles & Associates, a Washington-based consulting firm on disability and rehabilitation issues. Mr. Harles has also served as General Counsel of Goodwill Industries of America and as Associate Director of the National Association of Rehabilitation Facilities. Mr. Harles earned his undergraduate and law degrees from the University of North Carolina at Chapel Hill. He is a member of the Bar of the District of Columbia and North Carolina. He is also a member of the American Bar Association and the Federal Bar Association.

John Kregel, Ed.D., Associate Director, Rehabilitation Research and Training Center, Virginia Commonwealth University, 1314 West Main Street, Post Office Box 2011, Richmond, Virginia 23284-2011

John Kregel is currently a Professor of Special Education and the Associate Director of the Rehabilitation Research and Training Center on Supported Employment at Virginia Commonwealth University in Richmond. Dr. Kregel has had 8 years of direct experience in conducting policy analysis and attitudinal and benefit-cost research. Dr. Kregel is the author/editor of three books as well as author or co-author of over 20 journal articles, numerous book chapters, research monographs, and other publications on developmental disabilities and supported employment. His particular area of interest lies in analyzing federal and state policies and service delivery systems to identify obstacles to independence and productivity on the part of individuals with developmental disabilities. Recent activities have focused on an analysis of government policies to promote employment, personal assistant services, and transition from school to work.

Craig Michaels, M.A., C.R.C., Senior Coordinator of Special Rehabilitation Projects, National Center for Disability Services, 201 I.U. Willets Road, Albertson, New York 11507-1599

Craig Michaels is the Senior Coordinator of Special Projects within the Career and Employment Institute at the National Center for Disability Services in Albertson, New York. He is responsible for the conceptualization, implementation, and management of a variety of research and demonstration programs in the areas of transition, employment, post-secondary services, learning disabilities, and traumatic brain injury. Mr. Michaels has published and lectured extensively on adult issues and the full inclusion of persons with disabilities. He has completed his doctoral studies at New York University in Special Education and is currently completing his dissertation, which is focused on differences in curriculum ideologies as they relate to the transition planning process.

Bonnie Milstein, J.D., Director of the Community Watch Program, Mental Health Law Project, 1101 15th Street, NW, Suite 1212, Washington, DC 20005

Bonnie Milstein is the Director of the Community Watch Program for the Mental Health Law Project of Washington, DC. A civil rights and poverty lawyer for 20 years, Ms. Milstein began her career as a legal services lawyer in Connecticut. She pursued her advocacy of low income people at the ACLU Prison Project in Washington, DC, the General Counsel's Office of the United States Department of Health, Education, and Welfare and Health and Human Services, and the Center for Law and Social Policy.

For the past 10 years, Ms. Milstein has focused most of her efforts on civil rights aspects of health, housing, and disability law. She has worked to expand the Fair Housing Act to protect adults and children with disabilities, to increase funding for the Maternal and Child Health Block Grant, and to provide technical assistance to advocates around the country on traditional and disability civil rights law.

Sherril Moon, Ed.D., Associate Professor of Special Education, Department of Special Education, University of Maryland, 1308 Benjamin Building, College Park, Maryland 20742-1121

Sherril Moon is an Associate Professor of Special Education in the secondary, transition, and severe disabilities areas at the University of Maryland. She has worked as a special educator, adult service provider, teacher trainer, and researcher in transition and supported employment. She has provided inservice training to educational and adult service agencies and employers across the country. Sherril currently works with several school systems, revamping their community-based curricula for students with severe disabilities and developing their transition procedures. She has written text-books, articles, monographs, and curriculum guides in the areas of transition and community living for persons with severe disabilities.

Paola Nappo, M.S.Ed., C.R.C., Project Manager, National Center for Disability Services, 201 I.U. Willets Road, Albertson, New York 11507

Paola Nappo is the Project Manager on a Rehabilitation Services Administration funded Traumatic Brain Injury project at the National Center for Disability Services. She has worked as a job coach and as a case manager for the supported employment program at the National Center. Ms. Nappo has experience in working with individuals with developmental disabilities, TBI, and their families. Ms. Nappo is currently the Vice-President of the Long Island Rehabilitation Association and is the former Secretary/Treasurer of the Long Island Rehabilitation Counseling Association. She has also been the monitor for the Certification of Rehabilitation Counselor's Exam. Ms. Nappo holds a Master's degree in Rehabilitation Counseling from Hofstra University.

Debra A. Neubert, Ph.D., Assistant Professor of Special Education, Department of Special Education, University of Maryland, 1308 Benjamin Building, College Park, Maryland 20742-1121

Debra A. Neubert is an Associate Professor of Special Education who is currently teaching coursework in the secondary and transition area. She has been a vocational evaluator, a project director of a federal research grant investigating the impact of time-limited transition services on young adults with disabilities, and an inservice trainer to special and vocational educators in the State of Maryland. Dr. Neubert has also conducted a research study of post-secondary outcomes for individuals exiting one of the largest school districts in the country. She is actively involved in national, state, and local transition efforts, and she is widely published in the areas of transition and vocational education for at-risk students and those with mild disabilities.

Wendy Parent, M.S., Research Associate, Rehabilitation Research and Training Center on Supported Employment, Virginia Commonwealth University, 1314 West Main Street, Post Office Box 2011, Richmond, Virginia 23284-2011

Wendy Parent is a Research Associate at the Rehabilitation Research and Training Center on Supported Employment at Virginia Commonwealth University. She has worked previously to provide supported employment services for school-age youth and adults with mental retardation, cerebral palsy, and traumatic brain injury. Ms. Parent has presented nationally on vocational rehabilitation and supported employment for individuals with disabilities and has published extensively on these topics. She is interested in vocational integration and consumer empowerment issues related to supported employment implementation. Ms. Parent is currently a doctoral candidate at Virginia Commonwealth University.

R. G. Rayfield, M.A., Research Associate, Virginia Commonwealth University, Rehabilitation Research and Training Center, 1314 West Main Street, Post Office Box 2011, Richmond, Virginia 23284-2011

R. G. Rayfield is currently a Research Associate at the Rehabilitation Research and Training Center (RRTC) on Supported Employment, Virginia Commonwealth University (VCU). His background in providing hands-on and programmatic services to disadvantaged populations began in the late 1960s at Bell Labs where he spearheaded an entry-level engineering program for intercity minority youth. For the past 2 decades he has provided a variety of programmatic, supervisory, and management services to persons with severe disabilities as well as to at-risk youth in metropolitan Chicago and New Orleans. He has served on numerous social services planning committees and has designed and developed a number of consumer training manuals. At present he is in the process of petitioning for candidacy in VCU's doctorate program.

Ronald Reynolds, Ph.D., Department of Recreation, Parks, and Tourism, Virginia Commonwealth University, 923 West Franklin Street, Post Office Box 2015, Richmond, Virginia 23284

Ronald Reynolds received his Ph.D. from the University of Illinois in 1973. Since then he has taught at three major universities and served as Special Projects Officer for the Recreation Council for the Disabled in Nova Scotia, Canada. He has been editor of the *Journal of Leisurability* and the *Therapeutic Recreation Journal*. Dr. Reynolds has authored dozens of articles and book chapters. He has co-authored two major textbooks on therapeutic recreation and has developed a study guide for the National Certification examination in therapeutic recreation with Dr. Gerald O'Morrow. Dr. Reynolds is currently a Professor and Coordinator of Therapeutic Recreation in the Department of Recreation, Parks, and Tourism at Virginia Commonwealth University, Richmond.

Donald A. Risucci, Ph.D., Assistant Chairman for Education and Research, Department of Surgery, North Shore University Hospital, Assistant Professor of Psychology in Surgery, Cornell University Medical College, 300 Community Drive, Manhasset, New York 11030

Donald A. Risucci is the Assistant Chairman for Education and Research in the Department of Surgery at North Shore University Hospital, Manhasset, NY, and Assistant Professor of Psychology in Surgery at Cornell University Medical College. His current research interests include: personality and neuropsychological evaluation of surgical residents and clerks; statistical and methodological issues in evaluation; and multivariate statistical modeling of surgical risks, outcomes, and decision making. He has published research in each of these areas, as well as in the areas of child neuropsychology, cardiopulmonary resuscitation, gynecology, traumatic brain injury, and healthcare quality assurance. Dr. Risucci is on the editorial board of the *Journal of*

Developmental and Behavioral Pediatrics and is also currently a statistical consultant for the Division of Special Education, Bureau of Cooperative Educational Services (BOCES) of Nassau County.

Leonard S. Rubenstein, J.D., Executive Director, Mental Health Law Project, 1101 15th Street, NW, Suite 1212, Washington, DC 20005-2765

Leonard S. Rubenstein is Executive Director of the Mental Health Law Project, a national nonprofit public interest law firm in Washington, DC. He graduated from Harvard Law School in 1975 and has been lead counsel in a number of major cases concerning rights of persons with mental disabilities and has also written extensively in the field. His articles have appeared in publications including the *American Journal of Psychiatry, Harvard Civil Rights–Civil Liberties Law Review, International Journal of Law and Psychiatry,* and the *New York Times.* He was co-founder of and serves on the Board of Directors of the Washington Legal Clinic for the Homeless, is a member of the American Bar Association's Commission on Mental and Physical Disability Law, is a member of the District of Columbia Bar Legal Ethics Committee, and is Adjunct Professor of Law in the Public Interest Scholars Program at Georgetown University Law Center. He has also served on the National Board of Directors of the American Civil Liberties Union.

Steven J. Taylor, Ph.D., Professor and Director, Center.on Human Policy, Syracuse University, 200 Huntington Hall, Syracuse, New York 13244-2340

Steven J. Taylor is a Professor of Special Education and Director of the Center on Human Policy at Syracuse University. He also directs the Research and Training Center on Community Integration. His current interests include social policy and disability, the sociology of disability, community integration, and qualitative research methods. Dr. Taylor is the author or co-author of more than 45 chapters and articles and six books, including *Life in the Community: Case Studies of Organizations Supporting People with Disabilities* and *Introduction to Qualitative Research Methods.*

Ann P. Turnbull, Ed.D., The University of Kansas, Beach Center on Families and Disability, Bureau of Child Research, 3111 Haworth Hall, Lawrence, Kansas 66045

Ann P. Turnbull is a Professor of Special Education and Co-Director of the Beach Center on Families and Disability at The University of Kansas at Lawrence. She received her Ed.D. from the University of Alabama, her M.Ed. from Auburn University, and her B.S. Ed. from the University of Georgia. Dr. Turnbull is the author of numerous books and articles on disabilities, with a special focus on families, the integration of people with disabilities into the mainstream of school and community life, and the individualization of their education. In addition, she has co-edited *Parents Speak Out: Then and Now,* and has co-authored *Disability and the Family: A Guide to Decisions for Adulthood* and *Families, Professionals, and Exceptionality: A Special*

Partnership. In 1990 Dr. Turnbull received the Rose Kennedy Leadership Award. She has three children, one of whom, Jay, has mental retardation. He is a young adult who is currently working, living, and socializing in typical community settings.

H. Rutherford Turnbull, III, LL.B., LL.M., The University of Kansas, Beach Center on Families and Disability, Bureau of Child Research, 3111 Haworth Hall, Lawrence, Kansas 66045

H. Rutherford Turnbull, III is Professor of Special Education and Law, Senior Research Associate of the Institute for Life Span Studies, and Co-Director of the Beach Center on Families and Disability at The University of Kansas at Lawrence. Mr. Turnbull is Chairman, American Bar Association Commission on Mental and Physical Disability Law; Past-President, American Association on Mental Deficiency; former Secretary, Association for Retarded Citizens, United States; former Director, Foundation for Exceptional Children; and former Treasurer, The Association for Persons with Severe Handicaps. In 1988 he worked as a special counsel at the U.S. Subcommittee on Disability Policy as a Kennedy Public Policy Fellow. Mr. Turnbull has been an active parent advocate based on his experiences as the father of Jay Turnbull, who has mental retardation and autism.

Michael J. Ward, Ph.D., U.S. Department of Education, Office of Special Education Programs, Mary Switzer Building, 400 Maryland Avenue, SW, Washington, DC 20024

Michael J. Ward is the Chief of the Secondary Education and Transition Services branch at the Office of Special Education Programs, the U.S. Department of Education. Before holding this position, he was a rehabilitation counselor for adults with developmental disabilities in Brooklyn, New York.

Dr. Ward grew up in Brooklyn, where he attended public schools. Recently, he completed his doctorate in special education at the University of Maryland. Dr. Ward has cerebral palsy and uses a wheelchair.

Pamela S. Wolfe, Ph.D., Assistant Professor, Department of Educational and School Psychology and Special Education, The Pennsylvania State University, 212A Cedar Building, University Park, Pennsylvania 16802-3109

Pamela S. Wolfe is an Assistant Professor in the Department of Educational and School Psychology and Special Education at The Pennsylvania State University. Dr. Wolfe has worked with individuals with moderate and severe disabilities in a variety of school and post-school settings and has written on topics such as supported employment, developmental disabilities, instructional methodology, and sexuality and disability. She is interested in aspects of school and community integration, as well as advocacy issues for individuals with severe disabilities.

Foreword

Michael J. Ward

P_{rior} to the 20th century, societal attitudes reflected the view that persons with disabilities were "unhealthy, defective, and deviant," requiring "special institutions, services, care, and attention in order to survive" (Funk, 1987). In fact, for centuries, society as a whole treated these people as objects of pity and fear. They were viewed as incapable of participating in or contributing to society. The national policy that grew out of such attitudes emphasized the reliance of individuals with disabilities on welfare and charitable organizations.

Even today, many people assume that children with disabilities are segregated from their peers who do not have disabilities because they cannot learn or because they need special help or protection. Similarly, for many, the absence of persons with disabilities in the work force is obvious proof that they, in fact, are discriminated against (Funk, 1987).

Despite efforts exerted through public policy in the 1950s and early 1960s to integrate persons with disabilities into community programs, societal attitudes had an isolating effect on this population, forcing them to identify with and participate in groups of their own kind. Goffman (1963) wrote that the relationship of such people to informal and formal community organizations made up of their own kind is crucial to the self-concepts of group members; however, the author's book was written long before it was recognized that persons with disabilities could use organizations to improve their social status, and thus reduce the stigmatizing effects of segregation and isolation.

Fortunately, the social and political climate of the civil rights reform movement of the 1960s greatly influenced the disability rights movement. The role of persons with disabilities shifted from passive dependence to active involvement. Rather than being recipients of philanthropy, these individuals were becoming active participants in a far-reaching civil rights movement that challenged the stigmas associated with other denigrated groups, such as ethnic minorities, gays, and persons who are elderly. This shift in attitude raised the consciousness of these groups to the point where "the minority group is no longer one for whom pleas, reforms, and changes are made by others, but where they themselves (those in the movement) are instrumental in provoking change" (Thomas, 1982, p. 6). Persons with disabilities began to understand that, among their rights, they had freedom of choice and freedom to belong to and take part in society (Funk, 1987).

During the civil rights movement of the 1960s, local independent living centers emerged across the country. Weiner (1986) defines an independent living center as "a community-based program that has substantial disabled citizens' involvement and leadership that provides directly, or coordinates indirectly through referral, those services necessary to assist disabled individuals to increase self-determination and to minimize dependence" (p. 6). One of the first such centers was the Center for Independent Living, established in 1964 at the University of California at Berkeley. Its impact was far-reaching. Not only did it provide a wide range of services to the community it served, but it was created by persons with disabilities to meet their own needs. Thus, the center became the symbol of all that those with disabilities could achieve, given the chance, and gave momentum and credibility to the independent living movement and the concept of self-determination.

The acquiring of self-determination is not limited to persons with physical disabilities. People First and United Together are two disability consumer organizations made up of persons with mental retardation and their aides. Although their disabilities often make it difficult for persons with mental retardation to clearly express their needs, these organizations offer evidence that these persons can learn to help manage an advocacy organization, and make decisions that affect their lives. Self-advocacy cannot be reserved for the "elite" among individuals with disabilities. Persons with mental disabilities who cannot communicate well can and should be encouraged to contribute in self-advocacy groups. With time and help, they, too, can learn the skills they need to participate in issues that affect their lives.

WHAT IS SELF-DETERMINATION?

Self-determination has been defined in a variety of ways: as "the determination of one's own fate or course of action without compulsion: free will" (*The American Heritage Dictionary,* 1976); and as "decision according to one's own mind and will" (*Webster's New World Dictionary,* 1972). A common element in both definitions is the importance of people taking control over what affects their lives, without undue external influence.

Self-determination refers both to the attitudes that lead people to define goals for themselves and to their ability to take the initiative to achieve those goals. Acquitting the personal characteristics that lead to self-determination is a developmental process that begins in early childhood and continues throughout the adult life. While it is important for all people to acquire these traits, it is a critical—and often more difficult—goal for persons with disabilities. They must first shatter the pervasive stereotypes, which imply that they cannot, or perhaps should not, practice self-determination.

The traits underlying self-determination include self-actualization, assertiveness, creativity, pride, and self-advocacy. The terms "self-actualization" and "assertiveness," borrowed from modern psychology, are important in the development and personal growth of all individuals. Self-actualization refers to a person realizing his or her potential and living his or her life accordingly. Assertiveness is being able to express your needs clearly and directly and to act and speak out with self-confidence (Des Jardins, 1986). Creativity is the ability to be innovative, to move beyond stereotyped images and expectations. Pride in oneself and one's abilities is a trait that translates into feeling good about the contributions one can make to society. Self-advocacy, an essential component of self-determination, refers to the ability to act on one's own behalf. This concept is an outgrowth of the grass roots disability movement that began in the 1970s, a movement that has given people with disabilities the right and power to take necessary, but often unpopular, actions to ensure that their basic civil rights and socioeconomic needs are addressed. For people with disabilities, self-advocacy is "running risks, challenging rules, and acquiring resources" (Varela, 1986, p. 245).

Achieving self-determination, to borrow a concept from Gestalt psychology, is definitely "more than the sum of its parts." It requires not only that persons with disabilities develop inner resources, but also that society support and respond to them. Self-determination is a lifelong interplay between the individual and society, in which the individual accepts risk-taking as a fact of life and in which society, in turn, bases an individual's worth on ability, not disability.

Persons with disabilities who want to achieve self-determination need to learn how to trust and respect themselves. They also need to learn to identify their rights and needs and to find the most appropriate ways of communicating these privileges to others. Most important, people with disabilities must acquire a sense of political purpose and an understanding of their rights, responsibilities, and the democratic process (Williams & Shoultz, 1984).

ADOLESCENCE: THE CRITICAL
STAGE FOR SELF-DETERMINATION

Manus and Manus (1983) discuss the theory that adolescence is a phase in which young adults, both with and without disabilities, test their own knowledge, try out new roles, and rely on peer groups, rather than on their families, for support. Generally, it is a phase in which young people challenge parental authority in order to assert independence and gain control over their lives as a necessary part of successful movement into adulthood.

Many young persons with disabilities have difficulty with this process of transition for several reasons. First, it is difficult for adolescents to be psychologically and emotionally independent from their parents when they are dependent on them for meeting their basic physical needs. Second, although peers without disabilities may encourage and reinforce the expression of differences, a disability may be a difference that they find unacceptable.

Some of the barriers that young adults with disabilities face are, in fact, found within the family structure. One such obstacle is that these young persons are not being given "the right to fail" (i.e., the opportunity to experience failure, to make mistakes). It is vital that all adolescents be allowed to "absorb the pain of failure, to react immediately to failure or to delay and react to failure later" (Manus & Manus, 1983). As children with disabilities become older, they should be given more responsibility and more support so that they can make their own decisions, even when parents feel that such decisions are not always the best ones. Young people with disabilities need to learn that it is acceptable to fail and start over again. Failure can provide important opportunities for problem solving, decision making, and responding creatively to difficult situations. By being allowed to fail and to make mistakes, young people with disabilities can begin to develop an understanding of their abilities and limitations.

Parents and other adults can do much to encourage children with disabilities to exercise independence and self-determination. Children need to be included in making decisions that affect the whole family; for example, what car the family will purchase, or how family time will be spent. As early as possible, children should make decisions about basic issues that directly affect them—what clothes to wear, or even how their bedroom furniture is arranged.

Parents should also encourage their children to perform household chores that are within their capabilities. It has been said that parents should never do anything for their children that their children can do for themselves. This is especially sound advice for parents reluctant to assign chores or responsibilities to their child with disabilities in the belief that he or she is already overwhelmed and should avoid anything that would make life more difficult. While doing chores may take longer for some persons with disabilities, most are not in any overwhelming physical discomfort. An important point for parents to remember is that children challenge their parents in a sincere and necessary attempt to become independent adults. For young persons with disabilities, this conflict may be more difficult or prolonged, but it is just as necessary for them as it is for all young adults.

CONCLUSION

The Americans with Disabilities Act (ADA) provides the unique opportunity to enhance self-determination, choice, and greater freedom for all the men, women, and children with disabilities in the United States. The ADA will be a vehicle that will create opportunity in the workplace, as well as increased accessibility to movie theaters, shopping malls, transportation lines, and telecommunication systems. The question of whether or not American society has the will, compassion, and sensitivity to make these issues a reality remains. In *The ADA Mandate for Social Change,* Wehman and his contributors begin to wrestle with this question.

REFERENCES

American Heritage Dictionary. (1976). Boston, MA: Houghton Mifflin.

Des Jardins, C. (1986). Assertiveness is/is not. In F. Weiner (Ed.), *No apologies: A guide to living with a disability, written by the real authorities—people with disabilities, their families and friends* (pp. 122–123). New York: St. Martin's Press.

Funk, R. (1987). Disability rights: From caste to class in the context of civil rights. In A. Gartner & T. Joe (Eds.), *Images of the disabled, disabling images* (pp. 7–30). New York: Praeger.

Goffman, E. (1963). *Stigma: Notes on the management of spoiled identity.* Englewood Cliffs, NJ: Prentice Hall.

Manus, G.I., & Manus, M.L. (1983). Psychosocial needs. In *Programming adolescents with cerebral palsy and related disabilities* (pp. 34–35). New York: United Cerebral Palsy Associations, Inc. and Cathleen Lyle Murray Foundation.

Thomas, D. (1982). *The experience of handicap.* New York: Methuen & Co., Ltd.

Varela, R.A. (1986). Risks, rules, and resources: Self-advocacy and the parameters of decision making. In J.A. Summers (Ed.), *The right to grow up: An introduction to adults with developmental disabilities* (pp. 245–254). Baltimore: Paul H. Brookes Publishing Co.

Webster's New World Dictionary. (1972). Springfield, MA: Merriam-Webster Inc.

Weiner, F. (1986). *No apologies: A guide to living with a disability, written by the real authorities—people with disabilities, their families and friends.* New York: St. Martin's Press.

Williams, P., & Shoultz, B. (1984). *We can speak for ourselves.* Bloomington: Indiana University Press.

Introduction

I feel fortunate to have been among the more than 3,000 people who were in attendance on the White House lawn July 26, 1990, to witness the signing of the Americans with Disabilities Act (ADA). Even more inspiring is that by July 26, 1991, exactly one year after the ADA was signed, employment regulations regarding implementation had been issued, making the ADA a reality. A broad, far-reaching mandate, the ADA will involve not only employers, but also those persons who design various public accommodations, telecommunication systems, and public transportation systems. All aspects of public life will be affected, enabling persons with disabilities to achieve equal access in American society.

Essentially civil rights legislation for persons with disabilities, the ADA guarantees the rights of full inclusion into the mainstream of American life. While there have been some improvements toward integration during the last decade, segregation and discrimination of individuals with disabilities continues to be a pervasive social problem. The opportunities of full inclusion created by the ADA should transform the quality of life for all persons in society.

But how do Americans feel about persons with disabilities? Does American society support such wide-reaching legislation? A poll conducted by Louis Harris and Associates in 1991, which sampled the attitudes of American society toward people with disabilities, provides some answers to these questions.

The Louis Harris poll was revealing and positive. For example, 98% of the individuals questioned believe that *all* people, regardless of one's ability, should have an opportunity to participate in the mainstream of society. Furthermore, there was a strong sentiment toward increased employment of people with disabilities; 92% polled believed that employment of persons with disabilities would be economically beneficial to society. Americans seem to feel that people with disabilities have "underused potential" in the workplace.

While it is difficult to know why those Americans polled feel the way they do, it is encouraging to see the strong trend toward acceptance. These positive findings, however, seem to contradict the opinions of many professionals in the disability field and others who have suggested that American society will not be supportive of including people with disabilities in the work force. For example, 77% polled said they feel pity for individuals with disabilities; yet 92% feel admiration for individuals who have "overcome" the demands of a disability. If the ADA is to be implemented with any degree of success, attitudes such as these must change.

The ADA lays a foundation for increased physical as well as attitudinal accessibility in America for people with disabilities. This accessibility will manifest itself with increased mobility throughout the community and with the right to a fair chance at a decent job. The ADA will help to galvanize society in the empowerment of people with disabilities as they seek their rightful place in the community.

There is little question, then, that with the passage of the ADA and the recent documentation of attitudes the general population has toward persons with disabilities, the opportunity for inclusion seems to be greater than ever before. A discrepancy remains, however, between societal attitude and action. As noted above, the ADA will be the force to move the ideas of equality into action. The material in this book will help to outline several key issues—legal implications, physical accessibility, transportation options, employment opportunities, and recreation—within the context of the ADA that stimulate community action for full inclusion.

The following sections provide a concise summary of the specific titles within the ADA and serve as a forerunner to the rest of the book. The various provisions of the ADA that relate to employment and access to public services are briefly discussed. Pages xxiv–xxvi offer an overview of the law and highlight the key components. The reader may find it helpful to refer to these pages throughout the discussion. In addition, the chapters of the book address a number of specific and important issues in the disability field, many of which are specifically tied into the implementation of the ADA. All issues are vital to securing equality and choice for individuals with all types of disabilities.

DEFINITION OF DISABILITY

Before practices can be deemed discriminatory on the basis of disability, one must first define disability. The ADA defines a person with a disability as follows:

1. *A physical or mental impairment that substantially limits one or more of an individual's major life actitivies* (e.g., specific physical or developmental disabilities, drug addiction, alcoholism, specific learning disabilities, HIV infection). A condition is considered an impairment for purposes of the ADA even if medicine or a prosthetic device completely controls the condition's symptoms. An impairment is only considered to substantially limit the ability of a person if it significantly restricts the ability to perform a class or range of jobs. Environmental, cultural, or economic disadvantages are not considered to be impairments.
2. *A record of such an impairment.* This provision protects persons who have recovered from a disabling condition and persons who have been misclassified as having such a condition. For example, if one had experienced a heart attack and was hospitalized, he or she could not be fired due to absence from work.
3. *Being regarded as having such an impairment.* This provision protects persons whose condition does not substantially limit their major life activities, but who may be treated if the condition were to become limiting. For example, this may include persons who are burn victims, who have controllable diabetes or epilepsy, or whose back X-ray shows an abnormality although no symptoms are present.

These three definitions are very important aspects of the ADA and employment. By definition they establish a broad set of protections for as many people with disabilities as possible.

EMPLOYMENT OPPORTUNITIES AND THE ADA

The aspects of the law that prohibit discrimination are likely to be the most controversial, as well as provide the greatest source of litigation and disgruntlement on the part of employers. Clearly, there will be some challenges to the definitions described above and questions concerning how people with disabilities are able to perform a given job. In the disability field, it is imperative that professionals work closely with businesses to remove the significant levels of anxiety, misplaced or otherwise, that are present as a result of the ADA's passage. There needs to be a spirit of collaboration and not an adversary environment. The business community's attitude—negative or receptive— toward the ADA and the employment of persons with disabilities remains to be seen.

Qualification

The ADA explicitly protects a person from exclusion from employment when that exclusion is based solely on the person's disability. A "qualified individual with a disability"—that is, a person who has the necessary skills, education, and/or other job-related requirements and who can perform the job with or without reasonable accommodation—cannot be excluded from employment because of his or her disability. In addition, employers may not alter their personnel policies and practices when such alterations are made solely on the basis of an applicant's or employee's disability. Such personnel policies and practices include job application procedures, hiring, advancement, discharge, compensation, training, sick leave and other leaves of absence, job assignment, and other common terms of employment. An employer also may not limit, segregate, or classify applicants or employees based on their disability in ways that would adversely affect them.

The issue of "essential functions" must also be clarified. The essential functions of a position must be fundamental, not marginal, job duties. For instance, a function is considered to be essential if the position exists to perform that specific duty. The employer exercises his or her own judgment in determining what functions are essential to the job. Determining factors include: a job description that the employer created before seeking to fill the position, the amount of time devoted to the function, the consequences of not requiring performance of the function, and the work experience of others who hold or who have held the position.

Reasonable Accommodation

Not only must employers eliminate discriminatory practices regarding hiring and promoting of individuals with disabilities, but employers must also provide "reasonable accommodation." A reasonable accommodation is a modification or adjustment made to the job application process, the work environment, the operational practices, and/or the conditions affecting the employee's ability to enjoy the benefits and privi-

Highlights	Effective Date	Regulations/Enforcement
Title I: Employment		
• Employers may not discriminate against a person with a disability in hiring or promotion if the individual is otherwise qualified for the job.	• All employers with 25 or more employees must comply, effective July 26, 1992.	• Equal Employment Opportunity Commission (EEOC), Attorney General. Private right of action, remedies, and procedures set forth in Title VII of the Civil Rights Act of 1964.
• Employers can ask about a person's ability to perform a job, but cannot inquire if a person has a disability or require a person to take tests that tend to screen out persons with disabilities.	• All employers with 15–24 employees must comply, effective July 26, 1994.	• Complaints may be filed with the EEOC. Available remedies include back pay and court orders to stop discrimination.
• Employers are required to provide "reasonable accommodation" to individuals with disabilities. This includes steps such as job restructuring and equipment modification, unless an undue burden would result.		
Title II: Public Entities		
• New public transit buses must be accessible to individuals with disabilities.	• After August 26, 1990.	• Individuals may file complaints with the U.S. Department of Transportation concerning public transportation and with other federal agencies to be designated by the U.S. Attorney General concerning matters other than public transportation. Individuals may also file a private lawsuit.
• Unless an undue burden would result, transit authorities must provide comparable paratransit or other special transportation services to individuals with disabilities who cannot use fixed-route bus services.	• By January 26, 1992.	
• Existing rail systems must have one accessible car per train.	• By July 26, 1995.	
• Newly ordered rail cars must be accessible.	• For those ordered after August 26, 1990.	• Remedies are the same as
• New bus and train stations must be accessible.		

available under Section 505 of the Rehabilitation Act of 1973. Court may order entity to make facilities accessible, provide auxiliary aids or services, modify policies, and pay attorneys' fees.

- "Key stations" in rapid, light, and commuter rail systems must be made accessible.
  - By July 26, 1993, with extensions up to 20 years for commuter rail and up to 30 years for rapid and light rail.

- All existing Amtrak stations must be made accessible.
  - By July 26, 2010.

Title III: Public Accommodations

- Private entities (e.g., restaurants, hotels, and retail stores) may not discriminate against individuals with disabilities.
  - Effective January 26, 1992.

- Unless an undue burden would result, auxiliary aids and services must be provided to individuals with vision or hearing impairments or to other individuals with disabilities.

- If removal is readily achievable, physical barriers in existing facilities must be removed. If not, alternative methods of providing the services must be offered, if they are readily achievable.
  - Effective January 26, 1992.

- All new construction and alterations of facilities must be accessible.
  - Facilities designed and constructed for first occupancy after January 26, 1993.

- State and local governments may not discriminate against individuals with disabilities.

- All government facilities, services, and communications must be accessible consistent with the requirements of Section 504 of the Rehabilitation Act of 1973.
  - Individuals may file complaints with the U.S. Attorney General. Individuals may also file a private lawsuit.
  - Remedies are the same as available under Title II of the Civil Rights Act of 1964. Court may order an entity to make facilities accessible, provide auxiliary aids or services, modify policies, and pay attorneys' fees.

(continued)

(continued)

Highlights	Effective Date	Regulations/Enforcement
Title IV: Telecommunications		
• Companies offering telephone service to the general public must offer telephone relay services to individuals with hearing impairments who use telecommunication devices (TDDs) or similar devices.	• Effective on July 26, 1993, for provision of relay services.	• Individuals may file complaints with the Federal Communications Commission.
Title V: Miscellaneous Provisions		
• In general, this title depicts the ADA's relationship to other laws, explains insurance issues, prohibits state immunity, provides congressional inclusion, sets regulations by Architectural and Transportation Barriers Compliance Board (ATBCB), explains implementation of each title, and notes amendments to the Rehabilitation Act of 1973.	• By July 26, 1991.	

Adapted from: U.S. Department of Justice, Civil Rights Division, Coordination and Review Section (1990). *Americans with Disabilities Act Requirements Fact Sheet.* Washington, DC: U.S. Government Printing Office.

leges of employment. The employer is exempt from providing a reasonable accommodation if doing so would create an undue hardship. The ADA defines an undue hardship as any significant difficulty or expense incurred upon the employer; that is, in light of the nature and cost, such accommodation would adversely affect the facility itself, the business operation, and the employer's organizational structure. Employers are obliged only to accommodate a known disability; in general, it is the responsibility of the applicant or employee to inform the employer that an accommodation is needed. Even more important to note is that an individual with a disability, if he or she so chooses, is not required to accept an accommodation or other special treatment.

The kinds of modifications and adjustments required may include: making facilities physically accessible, restructuring jobs, modifying schedules, and reassigning persons to vacant positions. Clearly, the issue of reasonable accommodation will have to be negotiated by individuals with disabilities, advocacy groups, rehabilitation counselors, and the business community.

The role of the Equal Employment Opportunity Commission (EEOC) in regard to reasonable accommodation has unquestionably been one of problem-solver and negotiator, as opposed to that of a dictator. The EEOC recommends that the employer first analyze the purpose and essential functions of the job. After this, the employer should consult with the individual about the nature of his or her abilities and limitations, striving to identify and assess potential measures of accommodation.

There is a clear history of implementing reasonable accommodations as exemplified by the Rehabilitation Act of 1973, which mandated that such accommodations be provided by employers who receive federal funds. Presumably, application of the ADA's provisions by the courts will be influenced by previous court decisions involving the Rehabilitation Act, especially in cases involving the determination of reasonable accommodations and undue hardship. Unfortunately, litigation, more so than legislation, will likely prove to be the most effective means of enforcement of the ADA. It is collaboration, communication, and education, however, that will be far more powerful vehicles of change.

The chapters in this volume on supported employment (Chapter 4), job accommodation (Chapter 5), and assistive technology (Chapter 6) more specifically address the issue of reasonable accommodation.

PUBLIC ACCOMMODATIONS

Private entities that provide goods and/or services to the general community must not discriminate against any individual on the basis of a disability. Access to goods and services, as mandated by the ADA applies to a range of public facilities. These facilities include: 1) places of lodging; 2) establishments serving food or drink; 3) entertainment and exhibition facilities (e.g., theaters, auditoriums, sports arenas, stadiums); 4) sales and rental establishments; 5) general service providers (e.g., law offices, funeral homes); 6) hospitals; 7) public transportation terminals; 8) libraries and museums; 9) parks and zoos; 10) private schools; 11) social service centers (e.g., nursing homes, daycare centers); and 12) exercise or recreation facilities (e.g., golf courses, gymnasiums). Private clubs and religious organizations, however, are exempt; therefore, their right to exclude certain individuals because of a disability is reserved.

The provisions also require that public accommodations offer to people with disabilities the "full and equal enjoyment" of the services that they provide to other community members. It is discriminatory not only to provide unequal services to persons with disabilities, but also to offer them services that are different or separate from those provided to the general public.

Public accommodation also entails requirements for physically accessible services and environments. Architectural barriers, communication barriers, and transportation barriers must be remedied from existing facilities in which such removal is readily achievable. As the planning of new facilities and the remodeling of existing facilities proceeds, persons with disabilities must be ensured ready access to, and use of, the facility.

As can be seen, this aspect of the ADA is clearly one of the most extensive provisions. The ADA specifically promotes integration and participation into the community and guarantees inclusion by requiring measures of accessibility. The increased opportunities for persons with disabilities to participate in the mainstream of American society is imperative and is increased substantially as a result of this law. The concepts of public accommodations are addressed in Chapters 10 and 11.

CONCLUSION

The purpose of this introduction is to lay the groundwork for the reader, informing him or her of the purpose and the implications of the ADA as a tool for social change. Both Congress and advocates of the ADA have presented a challenge to American society, employers in business and industry, and individuals with disabilities and their families. The challenge can be either the pursuit of freedom, choice, and opportunity; or, alternatively, the choice to remain in a continuing restrictive mode. As discussed, the Harris poll implies that society, in general, welcomes the full inclusion of individuals with disabilities. If attitudinal resistance is not a major barrier to inclusion, we may need to look elsewhere for an explanation for the lack of opportunities for persons with disabilities. Biklen (1988) and Meyer (1991) suggest that the existing structure of services—not public attitude—may be a major factor in the apparent resistance to change. This leads to the question, "How does the ADA measure up to what individuals with disabilities truly need?"

It is the purpose of this book to provide the concerned professional and consumer with a substantive overview of the issues that need to be raised when trying to understand how the ADA will change society for the entire community of individuals with disabilities.

REFERENCES

Biklen, D. (1988). The myth of clinical judgment. *Journal of Social Issues, 44*(1), 127–140.

Meyer, L.H. (1991). Advocacy, research, and typical practices: A call for the reduction of discrepancies betwen what is and what ought to be, and how to get there. In L.H. Meyer, C.H. Peck, & L. Brown (Eds.), *Critical issues in the lives of people with severe disabilities* (pp. 629–649). Baltimore: Paul H. Brookes Publishing Co.

The ADA Mandate
for Social Change

Part I

Definitions and Expectations of the ADA

The ADA was designed in the hopes that the opportunity for greater inclusion and for increased participation in schools, community settings, and the workplace would be made available to all persons with disabilities. Although there are explicit, detailed regulations that accompany the ADA, the pioneers who drafted the ADA have expectations, hopes, and visions that go beyond these statutes.

The overriding purpose of the ADA is to provide civil rights to the 43 million Americans with disabilities who have been unable to access our communities with the same ease as their peers without disabilities. The ADA was not developed to enforce intrusive regulatory actions meant to hamstring businesses and society as a whole, but merely to promote freedom and choice for persons with disabilities. The achievement of equal rights for all and the abolition of notions related to "separate but equal" are some expectations of the ADA. The law also hopes to abolish the underlying presumption that persons with disabilities are second or third class citizens. Alone, the ADA cannot overcome discriminatory attitudes that are held by many uninformed persons toward persons with disabilities; however, the law is an important vehicle that provides various opportunities for persons willing to use it to their advantage.

In this section, the major titles of the ADA are reviewed and specific information regarding these titles is also presented. In addition, issues related to equality, quality of life, and consumer choice are also discussed in great depth. In the 1990s, the concept of consumerism, the active role that persons with disabilities have in the planning and implementation of disability programs, will play an increasingly important role in the disability field.

Chapter 1

Redefining Equality Through the ADA

Leonard S. Rubenstein and Bonnie Milstein

The Americans with Disabilities Act (ADA) is the latest civil rights law in a quarter-century stream of legislation designed to end discrimination against people who, up to this point, have been disenfranchised from participation in American life, impoverished by this exclusion, and devalued by society. Since the 1960s, the preeminent value contained in civil rights legislation has been equality, a familiar principle mandating that people in like circumstances be treated alike, regardless of such characteristics as race, sex, religion or, now, disability.

The principle of equality is powerful; however, it is also limiting. It demands that the person seeking inclusion be "similarly situated" to others, so that he or she can participate without changes in the environment. From this principle, the common catchphrases of equality were developed, such as the "level" playing field (which assumes everyone can run), "equal opportunity" (which assumes that everyone can take the test) and, in the context of racial discrimination, "color blind" rules. In other words, according to the traditional idea of equality, differences should be irrelevant. That is why even slight deviations from neutral standards in favor of past discrimination victims are controversial, as the debate about affirmative action for racial minorities attests.

For many persons who have disabilities, this common notion of equality is problematic at best, since there are usually apparent differences between them and others. These differences in mobility, in communication, in cognitive capacity, and in emotional stability do not render them similarly situated. Furthermore, the conventional idea of equality—"leveling" the playing field—does not always prove practical. After "leveling," the person may still remain unable to participate because, for example, he or she may not be able to climb the steps or to see the instructions for the test.

The rule of equality tends to accept the exclusion of persons with disabilities as regrettable, but inevitable. Society has viewed as a consequence of fate and not as a matter within its control that many persons with disabilities are unable to enter the physical structures built for everyday life, to board the transportation others use to get from place to place, to use the communication devices others use to talk to one another, and to be accepted into the establishments where others work, entertain themselves, buy food, or seek legal services. The traditional view does not recognize these problems as a violation of the principle of equality. According to that view, the person's characteristics, not unequal treatment, were responsible for his or her exclusion.

Some critics and scholars have argued that the usual understanding of equality, that people should be treated similarly regardless of their differences, is harmful. Not only does it encourage exclusion, but even more perniciously, this concept of equality relies on and reinforces the idea that being treated equally requires acceptance of a preexisting norm or set of standards that may devalue certain people. This is because these differences are socially constructed, not given (Minow, 1990). Even worse, applying the concept of equality to persons with disabilities seems inconsistent with the idea that government has a responsibility to provide benefits and services to certain persons with disabilities on account of their differences. The very notion that a person must be given something "extra" or "different" in order to participate— an attendant, a modified work schedule, an elevator—seems fundamentally at odds with the traditional idea of equality. Put most directly, the need to demand something extra seems to prove that the person is not, after all, equal (Minow, 1990).

The issue, then, is to determine how to reconcile traditional principles of equality with the concept of disability. In conventional social terms, persons with disabilities are often different in a way that precludes—or, more accurately, up until now, has precluded—equal participation in the institutions of social life. How can the law make equality for individuals with disabilities more than just an empty shell?

The ADA, enacted as PL 101-336, directly addresses this problem by expanding society's understanding of equality. The ADA endorses the traditional principle of equality wholeheartedly by outlawing discrimination against similarly situated persons with disabilities in employment, in public services, in transportation, and in public accommodations, from childcare centers to concert halls. It contains simple, declarative statements that describe well-known forms of exclusion as discriminatory. But it also demands more than equal treatment for persons with disabilities. The ADA seeks to promote equality by changing society. It aims to transform institutions and commercial interactions so that a person's disability will not impede full participation. To pursue the metaphor, it not only "levels" the playing field but it requires an accessible route to that field.

The ADA's affirmative message urges that social institutions be examined to determine if and how they have a tendency to exclude. If exclusion is practiced, the institutions—not the person with a disability—must be changed. It thus creates a new, deeper understanding of equality and rejects the traditional approach. It demands that social institutions adapt in order to become accessible to persons with physical and mental disabilities.

Understood in this way, the ADA is a radical piece of legislation. Yet the ADA is the product of the kind of legislative compromise necessary to enact a law of its scope. The ADA does not mandate complete social change (e.g., redefining the meaning of work so that all can participate). There are qualifications for and limitations on the transformation the ADA mandates, and on how the statute defines what can be reasonably imposed on the institutions and private businesses of society. The struggle during the coming years will be to define how seriously and how thoroughly the ADA will be enforced, and to influence the degree to which society, including businesses, legislatures, and the judiciary, will accept the transformations the law requires. Legislatively mandated social change is, after all, notoriously difficult to achieve.

The following chapters examine how the ADA attempts to bring about these changes. The authors do not explore its provisions in depth, but review in broad terms how each Title seeks to accomplish the ADA's goals.

THE CONCEPT OF EQUALITY IN THE ADA

Society is accustomed to thinking that its institutions and physical structures exist as if they represent the natural order of life. People tend to think that doorways and steps, buses and trains, and social practices have developed as they have because they reflect the needs of the general population. But a closer look reveals that there is nothing natural or pre-ordained about buildings, communication services, or social practices. They have evolved to meet the needs of particular groups, to the exclusion of others.

This is true everywhere. Steps are built at a certain height and doors at a certain width, not because some abstract principle establishes their size, but because they are designed to accommodate the needs of the average person. Telephones are designed for people who speak and hear. Social convention silently implies that places of social gathering are meant for those who look "normal." Work schedules are designed for people who do not have any particular medical or childcare needs. Trains and buses are designed for people who are ambulatory and, until the passage of the ADA, it was assumed by many that that was the way they should be designed. Even when technology brings fundamental changes, such as improved communications through computer networks, most employers continue to believe that job applicants must be able to speak "normally" in order to perform a job successfully.

These assumptions have begun to be questioned. For example, some employers now organize work schedules to accommodate the needs of working parents with young children. In the area of transportation, we have learned that systems can and should be made physically accessible.

The ADA confronts society's assumptions with a powerful and even subversive message—social institutions do not have to practice exclusion. This message is not new; in fact, it has been inherent in disability litigation and legislation for the past 20 years, although it has rarely been so boldly articulated on the basis of equality.[1] Yet advocates have commonly eschewed equality theories and instead have asserted some abstract "rights," such as the right to accessible buildings, the right to decision-making authority, or the right to special education services. These "rights," while rooted in equality, tend to be asserted under a less problematic label and, therefore, alleviate the tension between the two conflicting ideas of equality.

The ADA tackles the equality issue directly, constituting a non-discriminatory blueprint, as well as a blueprint for social change that will make true equality possible for persons with disabilities. Its regulations assure that virtually all social institutions, public and private, be required to make the proper changes so that disabilities will not be an obstacle to equal opportunity. For example, if a train has a lift, it will not matter if a person is unable to climb the steps to reach the train. In the same respect, if an elevator has braille numbers, a blind person will not be impeded. As the ADA proclaims, a person's disability does not have to be a barrier to equal participation.

Unlike other laws, the ADA does not represent the traditional "balancing" of one interest against another (although that certainly was part of the ADA's evolution). Rather, it is an exquisite compromise between the mandate that society adopt more inclusive policies and practices and the acceptance of the financial and administrative limits of reaching that goal. Its method is to build on the concept of *reasonable accommodation,* a familiar but minimally enforced concept that has its origins in the regulations of the Rehabilitation

---

[1]Section 504 of the Rehabilitation Act, 29 U.S.C. §794, enacted in 1973, established some of the general principles on which the ADA is based. Section 504 prohibits the use of any federal financial assistance for activities that discriminate on the basis of disability. Thus, universities that accept federal student loans or research grants have been required, since 1977, to make their programs and their structures accessible to students, faculty, employees, and visitors. 45 C.F.R. 84. The ADA significantly expands the principles of Section 504.

Act of 1973. (There is no reference to reasonable accommodation in Section 504 of the Rehabilitation Act itself, but it has appeared in all regulations interpreting that law.) Reasonable accommodation powerfully bridges the gap between traditional and more recent concepts of equality by demanding that social institutions adjust to meet the needs of the person with a disability, not the other way around.

Unfortunately, the concept has had a very checkered past. Miserly interpretations of reasonable accommodation have been the judicial norm in education, employment, and elsewhere, especially after the Supreme Court's decision in *Southeastern Community College v. Davis* (1979), which limited accommodations to those that impose no undue financial and administrative burdens on the entity.[2] As a result, in the absence of specific statutory directives to make identifiable changes (e.g., removal of architectural barriers), few courts have required institutions to make significant adjustments to existing conditions and practices.

The most notable example of the limitations placed on the concept of reasonable accommodation by the court system has been in employment discrimination law. One of the most significant accommodations an employer can make for an employee with a disability, particularly one who experiences an exacerbation of a medical condition on a particular job, is to reassign the employee to another job. Regulations issued by the Equal Employment Opportunity Commission contemplate such reassignment (29 C.F.R. §1613. 704[b]); however, the courts have almost uniformly struck down the regulations and held that the employer has no such duty.[3] Recently, however, reasonable accommodation was given explicit statutory recognition in the Fair Housing Amendments Act of 1988.[4] Now, the ADA approaches the idea of reasonable accommodation anew, and introduces such related concepts as "reasonable modification" and "readily achievable." Together, these two acts can be the engines of change.

Private Employment

The first of the ADA's five titles addresses employment, and like every other part of the law, begins with simple nondiscriminatory principles. It says that an employer, employment agency, labor organization, or joint labor–management committee may not discriminate against any qualified individual with a dis-

---

[2]See, e.g., *Doe v. NYU*, 666 F.2d 761 (2d Cir. 1981); but see *Arline v. Nassau County Board of Education*, 480 U.S. 273 (1987).

[3]See, e.g., *Carter v. Tisch*, 822 F.2d 465 (4th Cir., 1987); *Jasany v. U.S.P.S.*, 755 F.2d 1244 (6th Cir. 1985).

[4]Pub. L. No. 90-284, 82 Stat. 73 (codified at 42 U.S.C. §§ 3601–3617). See Note, *The Impact of Federal Antidiscrimination Laws on Housing for People with Mental Disabilities*, 59 Geo. Wash. L. Rev. 413 (1991); Milstein, B., Pepper, B., & Rubenstein, L. (1989, June). *The Fair Housing Amendments of 1988: What it Means for People with Mental Disabilities*. Clearinghouse Review 128.

ability with regard to any term, condition, or privilege of employment. It also affirms the employer's duty to provide reasonable accommodations to workers. This duty includes:

> (A) making existing facilities used by employees readily accessible to and usable by individuals with disabilities; and
> (B) job restructuring, part-time or modified work schedules, reassignment to a vacant position, acquisition or modification of equipment or devices, appropriate adjustment or modifications of examination, training materials or policies, the provision of qualified readers or interpreters, and other similar accommodations for individuals with disabilities. (ADA, Sec. 101[9] 1990)

This approach of defining by example is consistent with Section 504 of the Rehabilitation Act, whose original regulations are the source for this definition. This definition also proves effective should there be the necessity to tailor any particular reasonable accommodation to its unique factual context.

The possible accommodations are known, but what is the scope and what are the limitations of reasonable accommodation? How far does an employer have to go? What, indeed, does "reasonable" mean? The ADA adopted the answers that were developed in the Section 504 regulations, which imposed greater burdens on those entities most able to afford them.[5] These entities were determined by examining whether or not making the accommodations would create "undue hardship" to the entity by "requiring significant difficulty or expense." It is important to note that undue hardship takes into consideration four factors: 1) the nature and cost of the accommodation; 2) the overall financial resources of the facility or facilities involved in providing reasonable accommodation; 3) the overall financial resources and size (measured by number of employees, type, and location of its facilities) of the covered entity; and 4) the type of operation of the covered entity, including composition of its work force and other factors.

Therefore, since prosperous employers will not experience undue hardship, they will be expected to lead the way in accommodation. The House Judiciary Committee Report on the ADA illustrated this intent. The Committee approved a Section 504 case (*Nelson v. Thornburgh,* 1983) requiring a state agency to provide readers, braille forms, and even computers that store information in braille to welfare department employees since the cost of adopting these accommodations would not be significant to a multimillion dollar agency. As a result, the agency was able to serve a greater number of

---

[5]The same approach is reflected in the effective dates of the employment sections. The business community succeeded in convincing Congress and the Administration that the financial burdens of the law would force small companies out of business. The business lobbyists succeeded in limiting the obligations of the law to those employers with 15 or more employees, and by giving these smaller employers twice the amount of lag time before the law would apply to them. Thus, Title I goes into effect 2 years after July 13, 1992, covering all employers with 25 or more employees. On July 13, 1994, 4 years after the effective date, the law covers all employers with 15 or more employees. Sections 101(5) and 108.

beneficiaries, and therefore, fulfill its own mission. Although small employers would not be required to take these steps, they are not completely free of responsibility. Undue hardship, not hardship alone, is required to escape the obligation to change—an obligation described by the House Judiciary Committee as "significant," not minimal or moderate. An employer cannot claim undue hardship, for example, if a third party, such as a vocational rehabilitation agency, pays for the costs of an accommodation (House Education and Labor Committee Report, 1990).

The concept of reasonable accommodation appears elsewhere in the employment provisions of the ADA, even when no explicit reference to the term is made. For example, one of the definitions of discrimination in employment is as follows:

> failing to select and administer tests concerning employment in the most effective manner to ensure that, when such test is administered to a job applicant or employee who has a disability that impairs sensory, manual, or speaking skill, such test results accurately reflect the skills, aptitude, or whatever other factor of such applicant or employee that such test purports to measure, rather than reflecting the impaired sensory, manual, or speaking skills of such employee or applicant (except where such skills are the factors that the test purports to measure). (ADA, Sec. 102[7], 1990)

On one hand, this section embodies, as clearly as any section of the ADA, its overarching goal—that employers look beyond the physical or mental disabilities of applicants and employees to their ability and willingness to perform the specific job. For example, the ADA prohibits employers from requiring dyslexic applicants to take reading exams. Instead, it requires employers to devise exams that test the skills that the job requires, rather than the skills that a test may require. The concept of reasonable accommodation requires both sensitivity and creativity. It is founded on the American notions of fairness and sound business practices.

On the other hand, this and other provisions of the ADA just as clearly state a limitation—the employer gets to decide what skills are essential to perform a job as long as the selection criteria are job-related and consistent with business necessity, and subject to reasonable accommodation (ADA, Sec. 103[a]). Thus, the ADA does not alter the definition of competitive work, leaving supported employment opportunities limited for persons with disabilities. The ADA travels a major distance, but it cannot be measured in light years.

Services by Public Entities

Title II of the ADA addresses public services provided by state and local government and public transportation. The first part, relating to public services, fills in the gaps that were left by Section 504, which prohibits discrimination by entities receiving federal financial assistance. Title II specifies that no department, agency, special purpose district, or other instrumentality of a state or local government may discriminate against a qualified person with a disability.[6] This title, like Title III (public accommodations), uses the phrase "reasonable modification" rather than "reasonable accommodation," although the two terms have similar meanings. The public service obligation requires reasonable modifications of "rules, policies, or practices, the removal of architectural, communication, or transportation barriers, or the provision of auxiliary aids and services" (ADA, Sec. 201[2], 1990).

For access to programs and services, a related but stricter rule applies. Section 204[b] of the ADA requires the standards for public services to be consistent with the Section 504 regulations for federally conducted programs. The Department of Justice regulations followed this statutory requirement by adopting the rule that state and local governments are not required to take any action that they can demonstrate "would result in a fundamental alteration in the nature of a service, program, or activity or in undue financial and administrative burdens" (*Federal Register,* July 26, 1991). However, such a demonstration must be made, in writing, by the head of the agency "after considering all resources available for use in the funding and operation of the service, program or activity" (*Federal Register,* July 26, 1991). Furthermore, the agency is required to find another method to ensure that "individuals with disabilities receive the benefits or services provided by the public entity" (*Federal Register,* July 26, 1991). Governments, too, can be relieved of obligation to accommodate people with disabilities, but only if they can demonstrate the extreme cost of providing it.

Transportation

The transportation provisions in Title II are the precise accommodations Congress will require to render transportation physically accessible for persons with disabilities.[7] The provisions outline specific requirements applicable to public transportation provided by public transit authorities (Title II, Subtitle B) who are subject to an undue burden limitation. The obligation to provide paratransit for individuals who cannot use mainline accessible transportation is also included.

The limits on accessibility modifications are based more on time than on

---

[6]Section 504 of the Rehabilitation Act, modeled after the Civil Rights Act of 1964, addresses the problem of discrimination through the use of federal funds. In other words, only those who receive or benefit from such funds are bound by the non-discrimination obligations of Section 504. The ADA, on the other hand, applies regardless of whether the covered entity receives or benefits from federal funds. In view of the scope and liberal interpretation of federal financial assistance, the vast majority of services offered by public entities will be covered by both Section 504 and the ADA.

[7]Title II took effect 18 months after July 13, 1990, becoming law on January 13, 1992, except that all new buses purchased after August 13, 1990 are to be accessible.

dollar cost.[8] These regulations were the subject of a long and complex debate. For example, Amtrak and other rail companies receive Federal funds and, therefore, have been obligated to meet the demands of Section 504 for several years. They have failed to comply. Nonetheless, the ADA grants Amtrak and other intercity rail systems up to 20 years to make all of their stations accessible. It allows commuter rail systems up to 20 years, and the systems are required to modify only the "key" stations. Civil rights advocates are dismayed at this leniency.

The Congressional debate on reasonable accessibility accommodation in public transportation has also touched many nerves, and illustrates the compromises made to balance the needed transformations against their costs. For example, Congressman William Lipinski's (D–IL) amendment would have required only one accessible car per train, with a bathroom and dining facility, in commuter rail systems. The issue arose in the House Public Works and Transportation Committee and in the subsequent hearings held by the House Energy and Commerce Committee. It was finally resolved in the floor vote conducted by the House. The House ultimately rejected the Congressman's amendment in order to avoid segregation of persons with disabilities into a single car on the train. The House was also convinced that the logistical problems of providing a single car "might prove just as costly as purchasing a fleet of new accessible cars" (Bureau of National Affairs [BNA], 1990, p. 57).

The transportation section also requires other adjustments. The most reasonable modification principle in transportation requires that vehicles become accessible to people with mobility impairments and people who use wheelchairs. This can be achieved through the provision of mechanical or electric lifts, and elevators, which can be installed in stations. The ADA also requires reasonable modifications that provide access to people with vision impairments, mental retardation, and other disabilities so that they, too, can have equal access. The law itself does not provide specific definitions or descriptions of these reasonable modifications; however, the House Judiciary Report emphasizes the need for a "strong commitment from a transit authority's management team," and "adequate training of maintenance personnel and bus operators, sensitivity training of all personnel which stresses the importance of providing transportation, and creative marketing strategies" (House Education and Labor Committee Report, II, at 87, 1990.). Minds, if not hearts, must adjust:

> A public transit authority should develop training sessions to familiarize bus operators with the services that individuals with disabilities may need. For example,

---

[8]Public entities are only required, however, to provide special transportation or paratransit services available to those who cannot use accessible public transportation to the extent that "providing such services does not impose . . . an undue financial burden." Section 223(c)(4).

assuring that people with vision impairments get off at the correct stop, training bus drivers how to use the lift in a bus, and developing a program which would assist people with mental retardation in how to use the transportation system. Transit authorities should also be required to have written materials available in a format accessible to people with vision impairments and to make TDD numbers available to persons with hearing and communication impairments. (House Education and Labor Committee Report, II, at 89, 1990)

The statute also requires that transportation systems be readily accessible. If it is not clear from the words of the statute itself, the legislative history provides both the narrative and the examples that explain that accessibility extends beyond simply the physical requirements. If transportation is to be readily accessible to every qualified person who has a disability, then the transportation systems must try to make all aspects of their system usable by people with both mental and physical disabilities. The system's only defense can be one of undue burden.

Public Accommodations

The most sweeping provisions of the ADA are those affecting public accommodations. This phrase includes virtually all social institutions affecting a person's day-to-day life and all buildings used for commercial purposes. Title III, like much of the ADA, is modeled on parallel provisions of the Civil Rights Act of 1964 (42 U.S.C. § 2000a-3[a]), but vastly expands upon those provisions to require physical and other changes that can generate true equality.

The public accommodations section of the law addresses two kinds of problems: 1) overtly discriminatory practices used against people with disabilities (e.g., a dentist's refusal to treat a person with cerebral palsy, the refusal to serve a person with AIDS in a restaurant); and 2) "benign" practices and structures that tend to exclude. The latter problem can be broken into two categories: 1) policies, rules, and practices; and 2) physical barriers in buildings and privately operated transportation systems. Title III takes a firm stand against overtly discriminatory practices and contains delicate compromises regarding the nature and timing of the required accessibility changes in practices and buildings.

Title III also prohibits discrimination on the basis of disability in 12 types of private entities, ranging from barber shops to zoos,[9] "if the operations of

---

[9]Section 301(7) of the ADA lists 12 categories of entities that are public accommodations. They include:

1. places of lodging
2. bars and restaurants
3. places of exhibition or entertainment (e.g., movie theaters)
4. places of public gathering (e.g., conference centers, auditoriums)
5. stores and shopping centers
6. service establishments including barber shops, laundromats, hospitals, professional offices and others

such entities affect commerce" (ADA, Sec. 302[a], 1990). Adopting the language of Section 504 regulations, the ADA holds the following as discriminatory:

1. Practices that deny a person with a disability[10] the opportunity to "participate in or benefit from goods, services, facilities, privileges, advantages, or accommodations" (Sec. 302[b][1][A][i])
2. Practices that provide an "unequal benefit" in goods, services, facilities, privileges, advantages, or accommodations on the basis of a disability (Sec. 302[b][1][A][ii])
3. Practices that provide benefits in goods, services, facilities, privileges, advantages, or accommodations that, though "equal," are "different or separate from" those provided to other individuals (unless the difference or separation is necessary to provide the person with a benefit that is "as effective" as that provided to others) (Sec. 302[b][1][A][iii]). This obligation exists *even if* separate or different programs exist for the person with a disability (Sec. 302[b][1][C]). For example, if one social center has specific recreation programs for persons with mental illness, the YMCA next door must also admit persons with mental disabilities to their programs.
4. Practices used in eligibility determinations for the use of goods, services, facilities, privileges, advantages, or accommodations that tend to "screen out" a person with a disability (unless it can be shown that the criteria used are "necessary" for the determinations) (Sec. 302[b][2][A])
5. Practices that tend to segregate in the provision of goods, facilities, privileges, advantages, or services. These should be made available to the individual with a disability in "the most integrated setting appropriate to the needs of the individual" (Sec. 302[b][1][B]).[11]

Consistent with the transforming purpose of the ADA, Title III goes even further. It attempts to force affirmative changes in private social institutions and their structures. As for social practices—rules, policies, procedures—the ADA requires both reasonable modification and the provision of auxiliary

7. terminals and depots
8. cultural institutions (e.g., museums, galleries)
9. places of recreation (e.g., amusement parks, zoos)
10. places of education (including all schools from preschool to university)
11. places where social services are offered (e.g., day care centers, homeless shelters, food banks)
12. places for exercise (e.g., bowling alleys, health clubs)

[10]The law also covers "classes" of persons with disabilities and individuals "associated with" a person with a disability, such as a parent, friend, lover, or social services or medical provider.
[11]Although the House Judiciary Committee recognized that "integration is fundamental to the ADA," House Judiciary Committee Report at 56, it is always dangerous to base a law on a person's "needs" rather than his or her choices.

aids. The obligation of reasonable modification is to change policies, practices, and procedures to afford persons with disabilities the opportunity to take advantage of goods, services, facilities, advantages, or accommodations. These practices may range from a dentist who refuses to see a patient in a wheelchair to a theater that prohibits people with mental retardation from attending a performance. Each case may require some adjustment. Unlike the duty of reasonable accommodation in Titles I and II, the obligation of reasonable modification is not explicitly tied to the economic well-being of the entity that has to be changed. In other words, no exception exists for the impecunious.[12]

However, similar to its cousin, reasonable accommodation, the concept of reasonable modification does have limitations. Policies, practices, and procedures must be changed unless doing so would fundamentally alter the nature of the goods, services, and so forth. The phrase "fundamentally alter" is not defined by the ADA, but it is derived from the Supreme Court's decision in *Southeastern Community College v. Davis*. This decision upheld the exclusion of a deaf student from a nursing school on the ground that her admission would require the school to fundamentally alter the nature of the school's program. That is, the school would have had to exempt her from the course on operating room procedures where, because of the face masks, she would be unable to read lips.

The phrase "fundamentally alter" appears extremely narrow, but it is quite subjective and inherently conservative. It is also dynamic in the sense that the more alterations that are made in the social practices mandated by the ADA, the less "fundamental" the modifications sought by persons with disabilities will appear. Thus, the meaning of fundamentally alter will no doubt change over time.

The second change in social practices requires the provision of auxiliary aids to persons with disabilities.[13] These aids may be of any type, but the examples used refer principally to means of communication designed for people with hearing or visual impairments in order to help them purchase goods and conduct other transactions. However, Congress limited the duty of providing auxiliary aids if doing so would either be an undue burden or would fundamentally alter the nature of the program.

Another long-term objective of this part of the ADA is to make the physical accoutrements of social life—private buildings and privately operated transportation systems—accessible to people with disabilities. Initial

---

[12]It is important to note that "reasonable modifications" apply *only* to rules, policies, and procedures. The costly changes more often come with the provision of auxiliary aids or structural alterations. Both of these types of changes are circumscribed by "readily achievable" and "undue burden" standards, which are discussed later in the chapter.

[13]Auxiliary aids are defined in section 3(1). The requirement to provide them is contained in Section 302(b)(2)(iii).

efforts by disability advocates to require retrofit of all existing buildings were defeated. Instead, Congress took a two-prong approach. This approach requires only readily achievable accessibility changes in existing buildings and transit systems, but requires that any alterations to new construction be readily accessible and usable by individuals with disabilities. The result will be like a moving iceberg, slow, almost imperceptible, but relentless.

In order to avoid any confusion between the terms "readily accessible" and "readily achievable," the House Education and Labor Committee Report explains that:

> [t]he phrase "readily accessible to and usable by individuals with disabilities" focusses on the person with a disability and addresses the degree of ease with which an individual with a disability can enter and use a facility; it is access and usability which must be "ready."
>
> "Readily achievable," on the other hand, focuses on the business operator and addresses the degree of ease or difficulty of the business operator in removing a barrier; if barrier-removal cannot be accomplished readily, then it is not required. (Part II, at 110, 1990)

For existing structures, the duty to make changes is fairly minimal, since readily achievable means "easily accomplishable and able to be carried out without much difficulty or expense" (ADA, Sec. 301[9], 1990). This compromise term, sought by the business community with regard to existing facilities, is based on fears that the ADA would require major, expensive structural alterations. Still, it is not without some teeth, since it is further defined identically to the undue burden limitation on reasonable accommodation. As a result, prosperous entities will have to take steps to make physical structures accessible to persons with disabilities. For these entities, significant changes can be expected, or demanded, in the short term. The readily achievable standard is another example of the compromises that were struck to achieve passage of the ADA.

The other half of the compromise incorporates the Section 504 principle that the program, or, in this case, the wares or services being sold, be accessible. Therefore, if the aisles in a store are too narrow to be negotiated by a wheelchair, the owner must either "adjust its layout of display racks and shelves" or train salespersons to bring merchandise to the customer (House Education and Labor Committee Report, Part II, at 110, 1990). In other words, the business need not make unduly expensive changes to the structure of the store, but it must use some creativity in serving its potential customers.

In the future, no such compromises are allowed. All new construction and major renovations must include accessibility features that are described in the standards for accessible design contained in the Justice Department's Accessibility Guidelines for Buildings and Facilities (*Federal Register,* July 26, 1991). The only exception to these guidelines is in the case that the physical features of the space be such that accessibility is "structurally impracticable." Similarly, with some exceptions, newly acquired private transportation services must be made accessible to persons with disabilities. This requirement applies both to vehicles and to the assistance some riders with disabilities may require from the operators and managers of private companies to benefit from the transportation service.

In sum, the ADA does compromise present obligations, but just moderately. At the same time, a future that now seems almost unimaginable can be envisioned. This is a future in which the social and architectural barriers to equality will disappear, the possibility of truly equal treatment is real, and the limits of participation among people are overcome.

Communications

Title IV addresses telecommunications barriers. According to one author, it was "the most non-controversial portion of the ADA" (BNA, 1990, p. 48). Nevertheless, it requires highly specific changes. One of these changes requires the installation of interstate and intrastate relay services in public telephone services. This will allow individuals with hearing and speech disabilities to have the same opportunities for communication as do people who use voice telephone services. Common carriers have 3 years to comply with the requirements of the statute and with the regulations to be issued by the Federal Communications Commission.

CONCLUSION

It would be fair to conclude that the ADA is the Magna Carta for disability rights. Despite its limitations and compromises, the ADA sets an agenda and provides a framework and timetable for massive social change. But like the Magna Carta's deference to nobility rather than to popular sovereignty, it embodies some of the very prejudices it is designed to overcome; therefore, it cannot be embraced without reservation. Most important, the ADA excludes. Some of its exclusions are simply silly, reflecting more about elected representatives than the people it sought to exclude, as in the case of such groups as transvestites. Many other attempts at exclusion accompanied the bill, but only one succeeded—the exclusion of some persons with mental disorders, primarily persons with compulsive disorders, such as kleptomania, that are associated with antisocial behavior. Nothing in the ADA, of course, protects a person with a disability from discrimination on account of criminal or antisocial behavior. However, this blanket exclusion permits discrimination in areas unrelated to the person's behavior; for example, Pete Rose could be kept out of a theater because he is a compulsive gambler.

When the bill was on the Senate floor, Senator William Armstrong (R-CO) proposed allowing employers to exclude individuals with certain mental disabilities from the ADA's protections on "bona fide moral and religious grounds." The amendment was designed so that employers could refuse to hire people they felt were unworthy because of their disabilities, without any determination of the individual's ability to perform the job.

The Bush administration refused to oppose the amendment, and the Senate sponsors only succeeded in limiting it to people with 11 different types of mental disabilities. Consequently, the ADA conveys the message that some disabilities still carry so much stigma and generate so much bias that even conscientious members of Congress felt bound to avoid certain battles. Other efforts in the House to exclude persons with mental illness failed.

People with AIDS fared better by a small margin. During consideration of the bill on the House floor, a conflict similar to that generated by the Armstrong Amendment erupted with introduction of an amendment by Congressman Jim Chapman (D-TX) that would have permitted employers to remove employees who tested positive for the HIV virus from jobs in which the handling of food is required (BNA, 1990). Like Senator Armstrong, Representative Chapman did not hide the purpose of his amendment. He understood that the medical community, including the Centers for Disease Control, believed there was no possibility of contracting the HIV virus through food. He argued that his amendment was based not on reality but on perception. In other words, he sought to justify the very discrimination that the ADA intended to eliminate. Again, the Bush administration was silent, but the provision was dropped in the House and Senate conference on the bill.

Even the ADA signing ceremony was tinged with irony. The idea of replacing paternalism with equality, of substituting social change for individual adaptation to existing norms and practices, is hard for many to accept. At first, some White House officials insisted that the ceremony be limited to a minimal number of persons with disabilities. They were concerned about not being able to obtain enough ambulances to accommodate the large numbers. This belief—that people with disabilities are sick, frail invalids whose medical needs justify their exclusion from mainstream America—is the very belief that the ADA was supposed to overcome.

Ultimately, the Administration agreed to the presence of more than 3,000 participants with disabilities, making the ceremony one of the largest in the history of the White House. This participation should have conveyed the true message of the ADA.

REFERENCES

Americans with Disabilities Act, PL 101-336. (July 26, 1990). 42 U.S.C. 12101, et seq: *Federal Register, 56*(144), 35544–35756.
Bureau of National Affairs. (1990, August). *The Americans with Disabilities Act: A practical and legal guide to impact, enforcement, and compliance.* 57.
Civil Rights Act of 1964, PL 88–352. (1964). 42 U.S.C.
Federal Register. (July 26, 1991). 56(144), 35720. 28 C.F.R. 35.150 [a][3].

House Education and Labor Committee Report, H.R. Rep. No. 101-485(II), 101st
Cong., 2d Sess. at 68–69 (1990).

Minow, M. (1990). *Making all the difference: Inclusion, exclusion, and American law.*
Ithaca, NY: Cornell University Press.

Nelson v. Thornburgh, 567 F.Supp. 369 (E.D. Pa. 1983) cited at House Judiciary
Committee Rpt., H.R. Rep 101-485 (111), 101st Cong. 2d Sess. at 41.

Southeastern Community College v. Davis. 442 U.S. 397 (1979).

U.S. Department of Justice. Accessibility guidelines for buildings and facilities. 28
C.F.R. Part 36, Appendix A. *Federal Register.* (July 26, 1991). *56*(144), 35605.

29 C.F.R. §1613.704 [b].

Chapter 2

Quality of Life
and Consumer Choice

Wendy Parent

The Americans with Disabilities Act (ADA) has increased the availability of choices for persons with disabilities to include the same opportunities that are typically available to their peers without disabilities. Specifically, the act gives "civil rights protection to individuals with disabilities that are like those provided to individuals on the basis of race, sex, national origin, and religion. It guarantees equal opportunity for individuals with disabilities in employment, public accommodations, transportation, state and local government services, and telecommunications" (U.S. Department of Justice, nd, p.1). In essence, this legislation has removed many of the external barriers that have often interfered with the ability of individuals who have disabilities to express their choices, to exert control over their lives and to achieve empowerment.

For example, in the area of employment, the ADA prevents discrimination of a qualified individual with a disability if he or she is able to perform the essential functions of a job with or without reasonable accommodation; therefore employment opportunities for persons with disabilities can now be based upon individual choice and merit rather than on the lack of knowledge or the potential misconceptions of employers. Similarly, access to the community, including public accommodations, commercial facilities, and transportation can now be determined by the individual with a disability rather than by external factors such as availability, accessibility, or attitudes. For persons with disabilities, the ability to exercise choice in a variety of situations is perhaps one of the most important accomplishments and one of the greatest benefits of the ADA.

The purpose of this chapter is to describe the importance of choice, control, and empowerment to quality of life for individuals with disabilities and to job satisfaction, a major component of overall quality of life and an anticipated outcome of the ADA. Suggestions that were developed to assist rehabilitation professionals in maximizing the choices that are available to individuals with disabilities and in taking full advantage of the opportunities presented by the ADA are also discussed. First, in order to facilitate understanding, quality of life is reviewed relative to its definition, measurement, research findings, and by the implications it has for human services. Second, job satisfaction is examined by including definitions, measurement, and research involving individuals with and without disabilities. Finally, the impact of the ADA on consumer choice is addressed.

IMPORTANCE OF CHOICE

Choice is a highly valued prerogative that reflects the autonomy, identity, and independence of an individual (Condeluci, 1991; Guess, Benson, & Siegel-Causey, 1985). Brigham defines choice as "the opportunity to make an uncoerced selection from two or more alternative events, consequences, or responses" (cited in Bannerman, Sheldon, Sherman, & Harchik, 1990, p. 80); therefore, in order to make a choice, not only is it important to have knowledge of the various alternatives, but also to have the chance to express or follow through with the chosen alternative. The opportunity for an individual to make choices and participate in life decisions improves his or her quality of life and the outcomes achieved, while also positively influencing his or her dignity, self-worth, and independence (Bradley & Bersani, 1990; Condeluci, 1991; Guess et al., 1985).

If individuals are to experience personal satisfaction and quality of life, regardless of whether or not they have a disability, it is critical for them to have the right to make choices, express preferences, and exercise control in their lives (Williams, 1991). For persons without disabilities, the ability to make life choices free from discrimination was established with the passage of the Civil Rights Act of 1964 (Equal Employment Opportunity Commission and the U.S. Department of Justice, 1991). This same right to choice was recently extended to individuals with disabilities with the passage of the ADA. Although the ADA provides a mechanism through which individuals can accomplish their goals, many persons with severe disabilities may still depend upon professionals to provide them with knowledge of the alternatives available to them and to assist them in achieving their desired goals.

THE OPPORTUNITY OF CHOICE
FOR INDIVIDUALS WITH DISABILITIES

Unfortunately, the opportunity to make choices concerning life, work, and recreation has been limited or nonexistent for individuals who have disabilities. It has become increasingly evident that the powerlessness and lack of self-direction often felt by people with disabilities are more frequently related to the attitudes and practices of caregivers, service providers, funding agencies, social institutions, and society, in general, rather than to any limitations or impairments resulting from the disability itself (*Consumer Focus Group,* 1991; West & Parent, 1992). For example, some individuals may never have been provided with more than one choice, decision-making skills may never have been taught, adequate information about alternatives may never have been made available, decisions may have been made by professionals who feel they know best, or capabilities and self-assertions may have been ignored or underestimated.

Choices made by persons with disabilities have often been based upon the avoidance of undesirable alternatives or upon the acceptance of the available rather than on true preferences. Decisions have also frequently been restricted by other external forces, such as agency regulations, lack of accessibility, inadequate supports, or stereotypical attitudes. For example, to avoid sitting at home or attending a sheltered workshop, an individual may agree to work at a particular job that he or she does not really enjoy. An individual may also take a job because the employer was the only person who would hire him or her. In other cases, the rehabilitation professional may have recommended the job as the "only job he or she could do," or it was the only job opening of which the individual was aware, or it was the only job for which the agency could provide the needed assistance and support. With the passage of the ADA, it is hoped that many of these external factors will be eliminated.

One way in which the ADA will help to eliminate external factors is by serving as a vehicle to empower persons with disabilities. The concept of empowerment, which is closely related to choice, is considered to be a process by which people can gain mastery over their lives (Zimmerman & Rappaport, 1988). To empower a person is to provide him or her with the information, skills, or supports that can enable him or her to make choices and decisions regarding his or her life (Conger & Kanungo, 1988). The individualized nature of the importance of empowerment is illustrated by Zimmerman and Rappaport (1988) as follows:

> empowerment is easy to define in its absence; powerlessness, real or imagined; learned helplessness; alienation; loss of a sense of control over one's life. It is more difficult to define positively only because it takes on a different form in different people and contexts. (p. 3)

The limited opportunities for choice that have typically been available to persons with disabilities are likely to negatively affect their feelings of empowerment. For example, an individual may have learned that his or her opinion is meaningless or that others know best whenever he or she expresses a choice, while another individual may be told that his or her preferences are not possible. For persons with disabilities, empowerment is most often realized when external entities, such as society, service providers, or government agencies, relinquish their power and control and allow the individuals to make their own choices. Quality of life is best measured by the power that individuals have to make choices, and their degree of satisfaction with the results of those choices.

QUALITY OF LIFE

Quality of life was first assessed in 1939 with the Hawthorne studies, which aimed at examining the social factors influencing job satisfaction, employee attitudes toward supervision, the nature of the job, and work groups (Cameto, 1990). The emphasis of quality of life research has been on identifying the external factors affecting quality of life and on determining how these factors affect the individual's subjective perceptions of his or her well-being.

The variety of definitions proposed to explain quality of life reflects the complexity and ambiguity of the construct. A common theme throughout these definitions is the importance of individual desires and perceptions in determining what constitutes quality of life. Marinoble and Hegenauer (1988) define a quality adult life as "one in which community environment and individual resources are able to interact in ways that enhance the fullest possible human development of the person" (p. 21). Rice, McFarlin, Hunt, and Near (1985a) suggest that quality of life is the degree to which a person's life experience satisfies his or her wants and needs. These authors define perceived quality of life as "a set of affective (psychological state or feeling) beliefs toward the totality of one's life (overall perceptive quality of life) or toward specific domains of life (e.g., perceived quality of work life or perceived quality of family life)" (p. 297). Emerson (1985) states that quality of life is the "satisfaction of an individual's values, goals, and needs through the actualization of their abilities or lifestyles" (p. 282).

In general, quality of life is considered to be associated with having individual needs met, having control over one's environment, and having the opportunity to make choices. Brown (1988) also states that quality of life can be viewed as the degree to which an individual has control over his or her environment. Mittler (1984) argues that an important constituent of quality of life is the opportunity for an individual to make choices among perceived alternatives. Although a set definition for quality of life has not been determined, it can be concluded from the above definitions that need satisfaction, choice, and autonomy are critical elements if quality of life is to be viewed positively. The ADA ensures that individuals with disabilities have the same opportunities to make choices and to control their lives; therefore, these individuals will experience improved quality of life similar to persons without disabilities.

Measuring Quality of Life

Research suggests that overall quality of life is influenced by satisfaction with multiple life domains. Brief and Hollenbeck (1985) identify these domains as family, health, community, work, and spare time activities. Similarly, general well-being, interpersonal relations, and organizational, occupational, and lei-sure/recreational activity have been determined to be important domains affecting quality of life (Evans, Burns, Robinson, & Garrett, 1985). However, Rice et al. (1985a) recommend a more extensive list of domains including the usual factors of family, work, friendships, free time, and neighborhood as well as transportation, religion, self-esteem, and financial security.

In an attempt to determine a set of domains critical to quality of life, many surveys have been conducted. For example, an analysis of national survey data, collected in 1972 from more than 3,000 American adults, identified 30 quality of life domains (Andrews & Withey, 1974). The domains that accounted for the majority of life satisfaction include: self, family life, money index, amount of fun, house/apartment, family activities, leisure time, spare time activities, national government index, goods and services, health, and job. Flanagan (1978) conducted a similar survey of 3,000 people in the early 1970s. He identified five major components of quality of life from a collection of more than 6,500 critical incidents. These categories include: physical and material well-being; relations with other people; social, community, and civic activities; personal development and fulfillment; and recreation. Despite the variations in life domains, the consistency in the measurement of quality of life indicates that the whole person must be considered when evaluating quality of life outcomes.

In addition to the studies on life domains, numerous national studies have been conducted to assess the overall status of quality of life in America. In general, these findings suggest that most people are satisfied with their quality of life, what they have, and where they live (Taylor, 1987). A national study of 2,164 individuals conducted in 1971 reported similar findings with respondents expressing basic satisfaction with their lives as a whole (Rodgers & Converse, 1975). Interestingly, repeated national studies, which posed a question to people inquiring about their level of happiness with life, indicate a gradual but consistent decline from respondents. The response of "very happy" has more often become one of "pretty happy" or "not too happy" (Rodgers & Converse, 1975). A review of the literature by Zautra and Good-hart (1979) indicates the following general findings from the quality of life research: 1) socioeconomic status is positively related to quality of life, 2) happiness diminishes with age, 3) divorce or separation negatively affects quality of life, and 4) quality of life is rated similarly by both sexes. A more recent study by Mookherjee (1987) of 1,506 adults reported that life satisfaction not only increased with age, but was also significantly influenced by race, marital status, and education.

A variety of factors that positively affect an individual's quality of life have been identified. A 1980 study indicated that respondents mentioned the following as being important to life satisfaction: being able to afford material goods; living well and enjoying peace, security, and happiness; experiencing desired standard of living and living conditions; having necessities of life; and maintaining financial security (Taylor, 1987). Flanagan (1978) asked 2,200 Americans, ages 30, 50, and 70, to rate the importance of 15 quality of life indicators for their personal satisfaction. Factors rated as important by a large number of participants include: maintaining health and personal safety, having/raising children, understanding self, maintaining a close relationship with spouse, having material comforts, working and having close friends. In summary, if an individual is content with many components of his or her life, the individual's feeling of overall satisfaction heightens. Although every person's factors will differ, general categories of factors appear to be consistently identified as offering personal satisfaction. These include: socioeconomic status, interpersonal relationships, psychological well-being, security, and needs satisfaction. It can be assumed that work plays a major role in that it functions as a means for accomplishing many of these goals.

While a positive relationship between job and life satisfaction is reported, the bond is not clearly established. Findings range from a critical relationship to a relationship in which the job only explains a small fraction of overall life satisfaction (Near, Smith, Rice, & Hunt, 1983). One suggestion is that work and nonwork satisfaction are both components of life satisfaction, rather than each one being a separate cause of overall satisfaction (Near et al., 1983). It is likely that the inconsistencies in findings are due to variations in the definitions, instrumentation, methodologies, and populations utilized in studies assessing job and life satisfaction. These inconsistencies limit the conclusions that can be drawn from such research.

Implications of Quality of Life for Individuals with Disabilities

Correlates of life satisfaction for individuals with disabilities have been found to be similar to those for persons who do not have disabilities. A study of 675 persons with disabilities, ages 16–64, was conducted using information obtained in the ICD Survey of Disabled Americans completed in 1986 (Mehnert, Krauss, Nadler, & Boyd, 1990). A variety of questions were asked regarding each individual's life. Life satisfaction was assessed by a global question with a five-point Likert scale response choice. More than half (68%) of the respondents indicated that they were satisfied with their lives in general.

Factors contributing to life satisfaction were determined through analyses of the responses provided by this group (Mehnert et al., 1990). Their findings suggest: 1) younger persons are more satisfied than those who are older, 2) persons with physical disabilities or health impairments are less satisfied than those with mental disabilities or sensory impairments, 3) persons who are working are more satisfied than those who are unemployed, and 4) persons with greater socioeconomic status are more satisfied than those with less household income. When compared to persons who do not have disabilities, the above group was found to experience less life satisfaction. This indicates that a great deal of improvement is necessary if individuals with disabilities are to achieve the level of life satisfaction experienced by their peers. It is likely that the ADA will be a major contributing factor in the accomplishment of this goal.

The issue of quality of life and equal treatment for individuals with disabilities has become increasingly important in recent years due to changing societal values (Goode, 1990). In general, studies measuring quality of life suggest that individuals with disabilities are satisfied with their lives although reports have repeatedly illustrated the need for improvement in certain areas. Marinoble and Hegenaur (1988) interviewed and administered the Quality of Life Survey (an instrument developed by the Education Transition Center, Sacramento, California) to 45 individuals, ages 20–50, who had cerebral palsy, traumatic brain injury, a learning disability, emotional disturbance, a developmental disability, or who were deaf or blind. Overall, the participants rated their quality of life as being fair to very good. Those who worked and had some degree of independence demonstrated a more enhanced self-worth. Although differences were found among individuals, the domains that were reported as needing improvement were interpersonal relationships, environment, and community utilization.

Interviews, observation, and The Quality of Life Questionnaire (Cragg & Harrison, 1984) were used to assess life in the community for nine persons with mental disabilities who had been living alone for a period of at least 12 months (Donegan & Potts, 1988). Their findings indicate that the participants were physically integrated and autonomous. Infrequent use of leisure facilities, participation in few activities within or outside the home, frequent time spent alone, and gaps in their social support network suggest that the individuals were not socially integrated in the community. Similarly, Crapps, Langone, and Swaim (1985) used interview and observation to assess quality of community participation of 15 adults with mental retardation who lived in a group home or intermediate group residence and who attended a sheltered workshop program. Their findings indicate that the individuals spent most of their time at home. Participation in the community was limited to few environments or activities, although self-reports tended to overestimate community participation.

Other studies that have supported these findings did not address reports of dissatisfaction or areas in need of improvement. Weinberg (1985) interviewed 30 adults with physical disabilities. The author reported that approximately half of the respondents were satisfied enough with their lives to indicate that an offer to become able-bodied was either unattractive or partially attractive. Margalit and Cassel-Seidenman (1987) interviewed 34 individuals with cerebral palsy, 16 of whom were in a sheltered workshop and 10 of whom were employed. The authors reported levels of life satisfaction and a sense of coherence within the normal range. Amount of support and guidance and feelings of meaningfulness and of manageability and control accounted for individual satisfaction. Cameron, Titus, Kostin, and Kostin (1973) conducted three studies comparing the effects of fixed social status on life satisfaction for adults with physical disabilities, children with mental retardation, and matched control groups. They reported no differences in self-reported life satisfaction between the two groups or between persons who are members of fixed social status. Again, it is likely that differences in what is being measured, populations being assessed, and research methodologies utilized account for the variations in findings that are reported across studies.

Research designed to assess the relationship between service delivery and life satisfaction for persons with disabilities has revealed similar trends in self-reported satisfaction, regardless of the types of services received. Baker and Intagliata (1982) used self-report measures and interviews with 118 individuals with chronic mental illness to assess their quality of life and life satisfaction. The participants reported their greatest satisfaction when out of the hospital, and stated that they were least satisfied with their economic situation, their health, and amount of leisure activities they participated in. Indepth interviews with 20 of these individuals suggested that they were socially isolated, lacked meaningful relationships, led overly restricted lives, and experienced poor economic situations. There is a possibility that response bias and "grateful testimony" might have influenced the positive feelings reported; therefore, the evaluations may not have been accurate reflections of their lives.

A 6-year longitudinal study conducted in Canada of 240 individuals with mental retardation reported that quality of life is negatively affected by gaps between what an individuals needs and wants and what is received across the various life domains, as well as the degree of control experienced by an individual (Brown, Bayer, & MacFarlane, 1988). The results suggest that the participants were happy with their home and community environment and the training and services they received, despite parental and self-reported needs. In addition, the authors reported that the philosophy and programming of service agencies did not seem to be directed toward meeting an individual's needs or toward allowing personal control.

Quality of life has been suggested to be an important outcome measure by which to judge the success of employment services for individuals with disabilities (Sandow, Rhodes, Mank, Ramsing, & Lynch, 1990; Schalock, Keith, Hoffman, & Karan, 1989). The focus of the following studies was on assessing the impact of supported employment on the lives of individuals with disabilities. This assessment was done by comparing the quality of life of persons in sheltered and supported employment situations. Generally, these studies reported improvements in quality of life and higher life satisfaction for those individuals participating in supported employment situations. Inge, Banks, Wehman, Hill, and Shafer (1988) compared quality of life for 20 individuals with mental retardation in supported employment to a matched group of 20 individuals in a sheltered workshop. They reported a significant increase in community participation, social vocational skills, financial outcomes, health measures, and scores on the Adaptive Behavior Scale (Nihira, Foster, Shellhaas, & Leland, 1974) for the individuals in supported employment. These results indicate improved quality of life for persons participating in integrated employment.

Moseley (1988) conducted a qualitative study to assess the quality of life of individuals with severe mental retardation involved in supported employment who were previously in sheltered workshops. He reported that the workers were more satisfied with their competitive employment situation due to factors related to job tasks, better pay, more consistent work, and less distractions. Interestingly, some participants reported that wages were most important, while for others nonwork factors such as the nature of the job were significant to their level of satisfaction. In a related study, Conte, Murphy, and Nisbet (1989) conducted a qualitative study of 35 individuals with mental retardation or a psychiatric disorder to assess the impact of work stations in industry on quality of life. The individuals were reported to earn higher wages, to perform higher status jobs, and to be more integrated as compared to their previous sheltered workshop placement. However, the authors report that the participants earned less than minimum wage, experienced frequent social and physical isolation, and did not complete work tasks in a manner similar to typical jobs. They suggest that very different responses may have been given by respondents had they compared their situations to competitive employment situations.

In summary, individuals with disabilities often report satisfaction with their lives, regardless of their present situation or the types of services they receive. It is likely that this trend is influenced by positive response characteristics common to individuals with severe disabilities, as well as limited experiences with which to compare and few chances for self-expression. While most would agree that opportunities have improved for individuals with disabilities in recent years, the research on quality of life suggests that many areas still need improvement. Inconsistencies in research methodologies such as sample selection, instrumentation, data collection, and operational definitions of constructs limit the inferences that can be made from the studies. However, consistent findings indicate that quality of life is higher for those individuals who are employed and who participate in normal residential, recreational, and community-based environments.

The intent of the ADA is to open the doors to various life domains by eliminating the environmental barriers that often limit free choice in each of these areas. By being aware not only of the factors that contribute to life satisfaction for persons with and without disabilities, but also of the restrictions that typically impede quality of life for persons with disabilities and of the content and ramifications of the ADA, professionals can assist persons with disabilities to experience the benefits of this legislation through informed choice, empowerment, and self-advocacy.

JOB SATISFACTION

The advantages associated with job satisfaction for workers who do not have disabilities and the businesses where they are employed have been clearly documented in business, psychology, and social work literature. Work is reported to be an activity of some importance for people not only because of the economic security it offers, but also for reasons not confined to money, such as self-esteem, independence, social relationships, self-worth, and personal identity (Rice, Near, & Hunt, 1980). These findings suggest that job satisfaction is an important indicator of successful employment and quality services for individuals with disabilities similar to their coworkers who do not have disabilities.

In general, studies show that a careful match between the characteristics of the worker and the environmental attributes of the job is essential for personal satisfaction and employment success (Schalock & Jensen, 1986). Research suggests that job satisfaction has a positive impact on life satisfaction and overall quality of life. This relationship is illustrated by the following statement:

> job satisfaction is an important indicator of the quality of work life, and life satisfaction is an important indicator of the quality of life as a whole. Hence, the job satisfaction relationship is an indicator of the more general relationship between quality of work life and quality of life as a whole. (Rice, McFarlin, Hunt, & Near, 1985b, p. 298)

The policy implications of the relationship between quality of life and job satisfaction indicate that improvements in work will also significantly improve life satisfaction. Therefore, it can be assumed that ending discrimination in employment, as is the intent of the ADA, will allow individuals with disabilities to select jobs that offer satisfaction both at work and in their personal lives.

Numerous definitions of job satisfaction have been proposed. Despite the variations in describing the construct, a general consensus of the interactive effect between the job and the individual can be found. Seashore and Taber (1975) state that job satisfaction is determined by both the characteristics of the job and the job environment, as well as the characteristics of the individual. Conway (1987) describes it as a "feeling or affective state that an employee holds in relation to his or her job" (p. 48). Henne and Locke (1985) consider job satisfaction to be a result of "the perception that one's job fulfills or allows the fulfillment of one's important job values" (p. 222).

Each individual values different components of his or her job. Job satisfaction results when important job values are perceived as being fulfilled, while dissatisfaction occurs when these values are perceived as being unfulfilled. The intensity of satisfaction is expected to vary depending upon the importance that the individual places on the value. Despite individual differences, it is generally assumed that people want similar things from a job. These broad categories include: 1) the work itself, 2) pay and benefits, 3) working conditions, 4) coworkers, 5) supervision, and 6) the organization that a job provides (Henne & Locke, 1985).

Similar definitions reflect the importance of need fulfillment in determining job satisfaction. For instance, Froehlich and Wolins (1960) cite two definitions indicating this relationship. Rosen and Rosen (cited in Froehlich & Wolins, 1960) suggest that job satisfaction "results when people see occurring what they want to occur in a given situation, and that dissatisfaction will tend to result when they do not" (p. 409). Schaffer (cited in Froehlich & Wolins, 1960) states that:

> overall job satisfaction will vary directly with the extent to which those needs of an individual which can be satisfied in a job are actually satisfied; the stronger the need, the more closely will job satisfaction depend on the fulfillment. (p. 409)

It is evident from the above definitions that job satisfaction is individually determined and will vary for different individuals, as well as for the same person, over time.

Measuring Job Satisfaction

Attempts at measuring job satisfaction have primarily involved two major approaches. One approach is that of a global concept of job satisfaction or an overall feeling about one's job (Conway, Williams, & Green, 1987; Evans, 1969; Scarpello & Campbell, 1983). This procedure assumes that individuals form an attitude of either like or dislike toward their job, regardless of the specific factors that may influence their opinion. Scales designed to measure overall satisfaction include Kunin's Faces Scale (Dunham & Herman, 1975),

Hoppock's Job Satisfaction Blank (Hoppock, 1935), and the Brayfield and Rothe scale (cited in Evans, 1969). The following question illustrates a common example of a global measure of job satisfaction: All things considered, how satisfied are you with your job? (Campbell, Converse, & Rodgers, 1976).

In contrast, job facet satisfaction measures focus upon the multiple components of a job that contribute to an individual's feeling about his or her work (Conway et al., 1987; Evans, 1989; Scarpello & Campbell, 1983). This approach is based on the assumption that individuals can like some features of a job and dislike others. Conway et al. (1987) used close-ended items and open-ended questions in a survey of 9,775 public employees in a southwestern state. The results indicated a job satisfaction model with 17 facets, including: promotion, training, supervisor, upper management, organization of work tasks, work stress, work challenge and autonomy, physical work space and equipment, work group, organizational commitment, organizational structure, pay, merit pay, Affirmative Action, benefits, job security, and distribution of staff.

In order to measure job facet satisfaction, multiple instruments have been developed. For example, the Job Perception Scale assesses satisfaction with 21 items across five job facets including work, pay, promotions, supervision, and coworkers (Hatfield, Robinson, & Huseman, 1985). Other job facet scales include the Job Descriptive Index (Roznowski, 1989), the Worker Opinion Survey (Bell & Weaver, 1987), and the Index of Organizational Reaction (Smith, 1976).

Research suggests that the global and job facet approaches do not yield equivalent measures of job satisfaction. Scarpello and Campbell (1983) assessed job satisfaction of 185 employee volunteers in two midwest corporations using two single-question global measures and one job facet measure, the Minnesota Satisfaction Questionnaire (Weiss, Davis, England, & Lofquist, 1967). The reported that the global measures were more complex than the facet measures and that a sum of the job facets may actually neglect major factors related to attitudes of job satisfaction. One explanation for these findings may be that the job facet instrument did not include all of the components that define job satisfaction. These results indicate the significance of valid instrumentation when assessing job satisfaction.

Studies investigating job satisfaction have utilized a variety of methodologies. Data collection techniques typically used include: 1) questionnaires, 2) interviews, 3) rank order studies, 4) sentence completion, and 5) critical incidents (Fournet, Distefano, & Pryer, 1969). The differences in conceptual definitions, assessment approaches, instrumentation, and data collection techniques tend to limit the generalizations and comparisons that can be made from the wealth of studies investigating job satisfaction. The factors generally considered to affect job satisfaction include individual differences, age, education, sex, and occupation level (Fournet et al., 1969). In a similar study, Campbell et al. (1976) surveyed 1,533 people in 1969 and reported the following findings: 1) young persons tend to be less satisfied than those who are considered old, 2) those with more education are less satisfied than those with less education, 3) blacks are less satisfied than whites, and 4) males and females do not show significant differences in their levels of satisfaction. The authors identified four factors as being the most powerful predictors of job satisfaction, including: 1) whether the work is interesting or not, 2) the perceived opportunity to use one's skills, 3) perception of pay, and 4) perception of job security.

Studies examining the relationship between job satisfaction and work performance have reported contradictory findings. Generally, the research indicates correlations between job satisfaction/dissatisfaction and absenteeism, work performance, self-esteem, on-the-job destructive behaviors, work-related drug use, physical health, productivity, job change, and work-related injury. However, this relationship tends to be small and does not support causation (Fournet et al., 1969; Seashore & Taber, 1975). Overall, the research indicates some relationship between absenteeism, turnover, and job satisfaction, but does not support the assumption of a relationship between productivity and satisfaction (Conway, 1987). Brayfield and Crockett (cited in Henne & Locke, 1985) suggest that satisfaction is related to productivity when the worker is motivated to achieve goals that result in rewards. Henne and Locke (1985) argue that poor performance is not a product of dissatisfaction, but rather one response to the dissatisfaction that an individual may choose. A review of the relevant literature indicates that although work performance and productivity are affected by job satisfaction, the importance and intensity of this relationship will vary across jobs and among individual workers.

Implications of Job Satisfaction for Individuals with Disabilities

Few studies have been conducted to study job satisfaction for individuals with disabilities. In general, the findings of these studies suggest that a high level of satisfaction is reported, as a whole, for the members of society who have disabilities (McAfee, 1986). In addition, workers with disabilities tend to express job satisfaction and dissatisfaction for reasons similar to employees without disabilities (McAfee, 1986). These reasons include pay, participation in decisions, profit sharing, leadership behavior, hours, and coworker behaviors. Therefore, since job satisfaction is influenced by the same factors for persons with and without disabilities, it is likely that having similar opportunities for employment (as is possible with the ADA) will lead to equal measures of job satisfaction for both groups.

Rosen, Halenda, Nowakiwska, and Floor (1970) assessed job satisfaction of 92 former residents of Elwyn Institute, Elwyn, Pennsylvania, who were employed in unskilled or semi-skilled blue collar jobs. They reported no significant differences between workers who had mental retardation and other workers with disabilities. When compared to a control group of employees without disabilities, the workers with disabilities were found to be more dissatisfied with their jobs, particularly in the areas of supervision and compensation. Talkington and Overbeck (1975) studied job satisfaction and work performance of 45 women with mental retardation. Supervisor's ratings on 10 important job characteristics indicated that the workers who were satisfied received higher ratings on 7 of the attributes. The authors concluded that work performance was significantly related to job satisfaction. The inferences that can be made from these studies for quality of life are limited since these studies assessed job satisfaction for workers who were not employed in competitive jobs.

Another study assessed job satisfaction of 35 workers with mental retardation who were placed into competitive jobs using the Job Satisfaction Survey (Judd, Woods, Young, & Singleton, 1981), a modified version of the Science Research Association Attitude Survey, in a structured interview. They reported high levels of satisfaction with the work itself, the work groups, and the company. A significant difference was found between full-time and part-time workers regarding satisfaction of pay, with the full-time workers expressing greater satisfaction. Seltzer (1984) assessed job satisfaction of 65 individuals with mild mental retardation using a modified Job Descriptive Index (Smith, Kendall, & Hulin, 1969). Her findings indicate that those persons who were unemployed or in workshops, but who were previously employed, were less satisfied than those who only attended the workshop or who were competitively employed. The author reported this pattern with respect to job tasks, coworkers, and promotions. The content of work and the interpersonal climate of the work setting were identified as the most important aspects of a job with respect to overall satisfaction.

Nisbet and York (1989) attempted to identify indicators for measuring job satisfaction for individuals with severe disabilities through observation and interviews with six persons who had severe mental retardation, their parents, teachers, and employers. Twenty-two factors were identified as being indicators of job satisfaction. Examples of indicators include consistent attendance, positive facial expressions, demonstration of adult-like behavior, communication of positive work aspects on weekends or days off, and verbal or nonverbal expression of job satisfaction at home, school, or other environment. The authors recommend that the presence or absence of these behaviors should be used by service providers as a means of assessing an individual's satisfaction with his or her job. However, these findings may be misleading because they focus on performance indicators that have not been empirically validated as indicators of job satisfaction and, in fact, may actually be creating a different criteria from that typically used to assess workers without disabilities.

Corporate Alternatives, Inc., (1990) has recently completed the second year of a 3-year longitudinal study designed to compare the effects of sheltered and supported employment on 53 individuals who stayed in the sheltered workshop (stayers) and 53 individuals who moved out of the workshop into a supported employment placement (movers). Both groups were interviewed before and after the individuals moved into supported employment. The interview findings suggest that the movers were more satisfied with their present placements. Their families also reported that the individuals were happier in their supported employment situation. Conflicting findings are reported in a study comparing job satisfaction for 50 individuals with mental retardation in a sheltered workshop and 50 individuals with mental retardation in supported employment (Lam, 1986). The Job Satisfaction Scale, adapted by the author from the Minnesota Satisfaction Questionnaire (Weiss et al., 1967), was used to assess job satisfaction. Both groups were found to express a high degree of satisfaction with no significant differences between the sheltered and supported employees. Critics of the research methodology utilized suggest that these conclusions should be interpreted with caution, specifically with regards to sample selection, data collection, validity, and data analyses (Szymanski & Parker, 1987; Wehman, Kregel, Banks, Hill, & Moon, 1987).

A study investigating job satisfaction of persons in supported employment was recently conducted with 18 individuals who were working in the individual placement or enclave models (Test, Alford, & Keul, 1991). There were 17 individuals with mental retardation and an individual with a traumatic brain injury. Four of these individuals had a secondary disability of mental illness, cerebral palsy, or seizures. The Job Satisfaction Questionnaire (Test et al., 1991), containing 13 open-ended questions, was administered during an interview with each of the participants. For the sake of accuracy, responses to 10 of the 13 questions were verified by the job coach who was asked to confirm the participants' answers. The results indicate that the majority of individuals liked both their job and their job coach, and were satisfied with their wages and coworker relationships. Although less than half of the supported employees reported being able to choose their jobs, the majority of consumers stated that they would rather not work elsewhere. Interestingly, more than half of the individuals said that they had friends at work; however, none of the respondents socialized with their coworkers after work hours. Overall, the results of the study suggest a need to improve the quality of supported employment services so that consumers have the opportunity to choose their jobs and develop friendships with their coworkers.

The Rehabilitation Research and Training Center on Supported Employment at Virginia Commonwealth University (Parent & Kregel, 1991) conducted a study to assess job and service satisfaction for 27 individuals with traumatic brain injury, cerebral palsy, and mental retardation who were competitively employed and receiving supported employment services. The majority of respondents reported that they had chosen their jobs alone or with assistance. Most of the workers stated that they liked their job and were satisfied with the services they had received; however, some individuals expressed a desire to change their job or were in need of some type of service. These findings indicate that workers with disabilities can like their jobs and the services that they receive while still desiring a change in some aspect of their job or the opportunity to select a new job. The results suggest that the level of satisfaction experienced by a person is individually determined and will often change over time. Service providers can more readily determine satisfaction by assessing specific aspects of jobs and services, rather than posing global questions that address the individual's entire employment situation. It appears as though most consumers will respond positively to general questions even though specific areas may be unsatisfactory or in need of improvement.

Employed individuals with disabilities, as a group, tend to report satisfaction with their jobs regardless of whether they are in a vocational training, sheltered workshop, or supported employment situation. However, it is not clear whether the individuals are truly satisfied or merely expressing satisfaction with the only choice that they are aware of or were offered. In addition, inconsistencies in research methodologies limit the comparisons and conclusions that can be made from the results of the job satisfaction research. First, instrumentation is often varied and lacks evidence of validity and reliability. Second, small sample sizes across different populations are often assessed. Third, informants other than the individual with a disability are often used for data collection making it difficult to determine the validity of the responses. Fourth, job satisfaction with different types of employment situations that lack operational definition are often selected for investigation.

Overall, the most accurate and effective method of measuring job and life satisfaction of persons with disabilities would be self-reported job assessments. These assessments serve as indicators of the ADA's impact, examine the complex components of quality of life domains, and demonstrate the effectiveness of professionals who assist persons with disabilities to acquire vocations of their choice.

QUALITY OF WORK LIFE

Quality of work life is influenced by the interaction between the characteristics of the workplace and the needs and preferences of the individual. Variations in what constitutes quality of work life differ for each individual, depending upon his or her culture, social class, education, background, personality, and family (Kiernan & Knutson, 1990). Rosenthal (1989) suggests that a variety of factors are considered when an individual judges a job as being good or bad and that these ratings are going to differ depending upon the value placed on each characteristic. These factors include job duties, working conditions, job satisfaction, period of work, job status, and job security. It is assumed that these expectations and attitudes are going to change for the individual and the job over time. This is particularly significant for individuals with disabilities who may not have had the opportunity to choose their jobs and careers, or may not have had any prior work experience by which to formulate expectations or to judge quality.

The emphasis on worker involvement in decision making and problem solving for quality of work life indicates that individuals with disabilities need to be involved in deciding where they want to work and the type of job they would like to have if they are going to experience satisfaction with their jobs, quality of work life, and, ultimately, quality of life (Kiernan & Knutson, 1990). Moseley (1988) suggests that autonomy and control in the development and selection of a job is critical for employment success.

It is assumed that most individuals like certain aspects of a job more than others and, when selecting a job, will trade one attribute for another, such as higher wages for nonmonetary benefits (Rosenthal, 1989). Knowledge of the options and active involvement throughout the job selection process is critical if individuals with disabilities are going to make employment choices that offer personal satisfaction and enhanced quality of life. The ADA intends for individuals with disabilities to be able to choose a job based on their abilities after weighing the alternatives, rather than being forced to compromise their desires. The ability to make choices and exert control over their jobs and careers will allow these individuals to experience quality of life related to job and life satisfaction similar to that experienced by their peers without disabilities.

CONCLUSION

The 1990s have witnessed dramatic changes in rehabilitation services, with greater emphasis being placed on consumer participation and empowerment throughout all phases of service delivery (Emener, 1991; Nichols, 1990). Increased recognition of the importance of choice and control to job satisfaction and overall quality of life for individuals without disabilities has had a major influence on perceptions toward persons with disabilities and the factors thought to contribute to their life satisfaction. Despite this change in attitude, practices have continued to be frequently affected by policy restrictions, limiting funding sources, unavailable services and supports, lack of professional and public awareness, and stereotypical myths and biases. All too often, persons with disabilities are placed in segregated employment, residential, recreational, or community programs because society believes that they would be happier with their own kind or because funding and staff shortages prevent individualized support in normal environments. In addition, professionals or other members of society frequently feel that persons with disabilities are not capable of more independent functioning. Barriers, both physical and attitudinal, also prevent their participation in regular community settings.

The passage of the ADA removes many of the external barriers that have interfered with the achievement of personal goals and life choices for many persons with disabilities. Individuals with disabilities are no longer expected or required to participate in segregated environments or to receive special services unless it is their choice to do so and unless they are provided with adequate information to make an informed selection from the range of alternatives. In fact, "the ADA recognizes that the provision of goods and services in an integrated manner is a fundamental tenet of nondiscrimination on the basis of disability. Providing segregated accommodations and services relegates persons with disabilities to the status of second-class citizens" (Equal Employment Opportunity Commission and the U.S. Department of Justice, 1991, p. III–48).

Although the ADA allows for many opportunities, some individuals with disabilities may require assistance in order to obtain information on available alternatives or desired options. Professionals have ample opportunity to help enable individuals to make choices about their lives, the goals they would like to pursue, and the services and supports they would like to receive.

First, consumers should receive information about all potential options and supports, rather than just what is available or what someone else feels they should know, so that they can make informed choices. The only way that the full impact of the ADA will be realized by persons with disabilities is if a person has knowledge of all possible alternatives and of the skills or supports needed to follow through with a preferred choice. Second, consumers should have the opportunity to choose their jobs, the places they would like to live, the activities in which they would like to participate, the community environments they would like to access, and the friends they would like to have, as well as the opportunity to alter their decisions as preferences, needs, and desires change. Having the ability to control the direction and outcomes in one's life is a critical factor in achieving personal satisfaction and quality of life.

Third, consumers should not only be able to make decisions concerning which options they choose, but also to seek assistance as needed or desired from professionals who are their full and equal partners. The role of service provider becomes one of advocate, support facilitator, information and referral source, or resource coordinator in conjunction with the person who has a disability. The service providers should assist him or her to make choices and follow through to achieve desired goals. Fourth, consumers should be given practical information about the ADA, as well as the how-tos that would enable them to access the careers, homes, community settings, transportation, and supports that they would like to receive. Knowledge is empowering, enabling persons with disabilities to make informed choices that will lead them to experience job and life satisfaction.

Fifth, consumers should be provided with a responsive service delivery system that offers the services and supports needed to take advantage of the opportunities made available by the ADA. Being restricted by professional opinion or agency regulations will prevent persons with disabilities from accomplishing their goals and obtaining the maximum benefits intended by passage of the law.

It is hoped that this landmark legislation will dramatically change the opportunities available to persons with disabilities by eliminating the obstacles that interfere with their pursuit of life goals, namely discrimination and segregation. The ADA is not only comprehensive in scope, but it also encompasses the multiple domains that contribute to improved quality of life for persons with and without disabilities. "In order for people with disabilities to enter the mainstream of America, they must have meaningful opportunities to obtain employment; access to public services and to goods and services offered by private businesses; accessible transportation to reach these jobs, goods, and services; and a means of communicating with employers, businesses, and others" (Feldblum, 1991, p. 105). The ADA addresses all of these interdependent factors so that persons with disabilities can begin to make choices in their lives and achieve their desired outcomes without the external barriers that have typically restricted this population.

REFERENCES

Andrews, F.A., & Withey, S.B. (1974). Developing measures of perceived life quality. *Social Indicators Research, 1,* 1–26.

Baker, F., & Intagliata, J. (1982). Quality of life in the evaluation of community support services. *Evaluation and Program Planning, 5,* 69–79.

Bannerman, D.J., Sheldon, J.B., Sherman, J.A., & Harchik, A.E. (1990). Balancing the right to habilitation with the right to personal liberties: The rights of people with developmental disabilities to eat too many doughnuts and take a nap. *Journal of Applied Behavior Analysis, 23*(1), 79–89.

Bell, R.C., & Weaver, J.R. (1987). The dimensionality and scaling of job satisfaction: An internal validation of the Worker Opinion Survey. *Journal of Occupational Psychology, 60*(2), 147–155.

Bradley, V.J., & Bersani, H.A. (Eds.). (1990). *Quality assurance for individuals with developmental disabilities: It's everybody's business.* Baltimore: Paul H. Brookes Publishing Co.

Brief, A.P., & Hollenbeck, J.R. (1985). Work and the quality of life. *International Journal of Psychology, 20*(2), 199–206.

Brown, R.I. (1988). Quality of life and rehabilitation: An introduction. In R.I. Brown (Ed.), *Quality of life for handicapped people* (pp. 1–6). London: Croom-Helm.

Brown, R.I., Bayer, M.B., & MacFarlane, C. (1988). Quality of life amongst handicapped adults. In R.I. Brown (Ed.), *Quality of life for handicapped people* (pp. 111–140). London: Croom-Helm.

Cameron, P., Titus, D.G., Kostin, J., & Kostin, M. (1973). The life satisfaction of non-normal persons. *Journal of Consulting and Clinical Psychology, 41,* 207–214.

Cameto, R. (1990). Quality of life: Its conceptualization and use as a tool for social policy. In R. Gaylord-Ross, S. Siegel, H.S. Park, S. Sacks, & L. Goetz (Eds.), *Readings in ecosocial development.* San Francisco, CA: San Francisco University.

Campbell, A., Converse, P.E., & Rodgers, W.L. (1976). *The quality of American life.* New York: Russell Sage Foundation.

Condeluci, A. (1991). *Interdependence: The route to community.* Orlando, FL: Paul Deutsch Press, Inc.

Conger, J.A., & Kanungo, R.N. (1988). The empowerment process: Integrating theory and practice. *Academy of Management Review, 13*(3), 471–482.

Consumer Focus Group. (1991, August). Richmond: Virginia Commonwealth University, Rehabilitation Research and Training Center.

Conte, L., Murphy, S.T., & Nisbet, J. (1989). A qualitative study of work stations in industry. *Journal of Rehabilitation, 55*(2), 53–61.

Conway, P.G. (1987). A model of job facet satisfaction. *Journal of Social Work Education, 23*(1), 48–57.

Conway, P.G., Williams, M.S., & Green, J.L. (1987). A model of job facet satisfaction. *Journal of Social Work Education, 23*(1), 48–57.

Corporate Alternatives, Inc. (1990). *Overview of second year longitudinal study of supported employment in Illinois.* Springfield, IL: Author.

Cragg, R., & Harrison, J. (1984). *Living in a supervised home: A questionnaire of quality of life* (pilot version). West Midlands Campaign for People with Mental Handicaps.

Crapps, J.M., Langone, J., & Swaim, S. (1985). Quantity and quality of participation in community environments by mentally retarded adults. *Education and Training of the Mentally Retarded, 20,* 123–129.

Donegan, C., & Potts, M. (1988). People with mental handicaps living alone in the community: A pilot study of their quality of life. *The British Journal of Mental Subnormality, 34*(1), 10–22.

Dunham, R., & Herman, J. (1975). Development of a female faces scale for measuring job satisfaction. *Journal of Applied Psychology, 60*(5), 629–631.

Emener, W.G. (1991). Empowerment in rehabilitation: An empowerment philosophy for rehabilitation in the 20th century. *Journal of Rehabilitation, 57*(4), 7–12.

Emerson, E.B. (1985). Evaluating the impact of deinstitutionalization on the lives of mentally retarded people. *American Journal of Mental Deficiency, 90*(3), 277–288.

Equal Employment Opportunity Commission and the U.S. Department of Justice. (1991). *Americans with Disabilities Act handbook.* Washington, DC: Author.

Evans, D.R., Burns, J.E., Robinson, W.E., & Garrett, O.J. (1985). The quality of life questionnaire: A multidimensional measure. *American Journal of Community Psychology, 13*(3), 305–322.

Evans, M.C. (1969). Conceptual and operational problems in the measurement of various aspects of job satisfaction. *Journal of Applied Psychology, 53,* 93–101.

Feldblum, C.R. (1991). Employment protections. In J. West (Ed.), *The Americans with Disabilities Act: From policy to practice* (pp. 81–110). New York: Milbank Memorial Fund.

Flanagan, J.C. (1978). A research approach to improving our quality of life. *American Psychologist, 33,* 138–147.

Fournet, G.P., Distefano, M.C., & Pryer, M.W. (1969). Job satisfaction: Issues and problems. *Personnel Psychology, 19,* 165–183.

Froehlich, H.P., & Wolins, L. (1960). Job satisfaction as need satisfaction. *Personnel Psychology, 13,* 407–420.

Goode, D.A. (1990). Thinking about and discussing quality of life. In R.L. Schalock (Ed.), *Quality of life* (pp. 41–57). Washington, DC: American Association on Mental Retardation.

Guess, D., Benson, H.A., & Siegel-Causey, E. (1985). Concepts and issues related to choice-making and autonomy among persons with severe disabilities. *Journal of The Association for Persons with Severe Handicaps, 10*(2), 77–86.

Hatfield, J.D., Robinson, R., & Huseman, R.C. (1985). An empirical evaluation of a test for assessing job satisfaction. *Psychological Reports, 56*(1), 39–45.

Henne, D., & Locke, E.A. (1985). Job dissatisfaction: What are the consequences? *International Journal of Psychology, 20*(2), 221–240.

Hoppock, R. (1935). *Job satisfaction.* New York: Harper.

Inge, K.J., Banks, D., Wehman, P., Hill, J.W., & Shafer, M.S. (1988). Quality of life for individuals who are labeled mentally retarded: Evaluating competitive employment versus sheltered workshop employment. *Education and Training in Mental Retardation, 23*(2), 97–104.

Judd, P.A., Woods, J.N., Young, P.L., & Singleton, R.J. (1981). *Job satisfaction of developmentally disabled workers in competitive employment.* Jonesboro, AR: Focus, Inc.

Kiernan, W.E., & Knutson, K. (1990). Quality of work life. In R.L. Schalock (Ed.), *Quality of life* (pp. 101–114). Washington, DC: American Association on Mental Retardation.

Lam, C.S. (1986). Comparison of sheltered and supported work programs: A pilot study. *Rehabilitation Counseling Bulletin, 30*(2), 66–82.

Margalit, M., & Cassel-Seidenman, R. (1987). Life satisfaction and sense of coherence among young adults with cerebral palsy. *Career Development for Exceptional Individuals, 10,* 42–50.

Marinoble, R., & Hegenauer, J. (1988). *Quality of life for individuals with disabilities: A conceptual framework.* Sacramento: California State Department of Education, Education Transition Center.

McAfee, J.K. (1986). The handicapped worker and job satisfaction. *Vocational Evaluation and Work Adjustment Bulletin, 19*(1), 23–27.

Mehnert, T., Krauss, H.H., Nadler, R., & Boyd, M. (1990). Correlates of life satisfaction in those with disabling conditions. *Rehabilitation Psychology, 35*(1), 3–17.

Mittler, P. (1984). Quality of life and services for people with disabilities. *Bulletin of the British Psychological Society, 37,* 218–225.

Mookherjee, H.N. (1987). Perception of life satisfaction in the U.S.: A summary. *Perceptual and Motor Skills, 65,* 218.

Moseley, C.R. (1988). Job satisfaction research: Implications for supported employment. *Journal of The Association for Persons with Severe Handicaps, 13*(3), 211–219.

Near, J.P., Smith, C.A., Rice, R.W., & Hunt, R.G. (1983). Job satisfaction and nonwork satisfaction as components of life satisfaction. *Journal of Applied Social Psychology, 13*(2), 126–144.

Nichols, J.L. (1990). The new decade dawns: The search for quality and consumer empowerment converge. *Journal of Rehabilitation Administration, 14*(3), 69–70.

Nihira, K., Foster, R., Shellhaas, M., & Leland, H. (1974). *AAMD Adaptive Behavior Scale.* Washington, DC: American Association on Mental Deficiency.

Nisbet, J., & York, P. (1989). Indices of job satisfaction of persons with moderate and severe disabilities. *Education and Training in Mental Retardation, 24*(3), 274–280.

Parent, W., & Kregel, J. (1991, November). *Consumer empowerment in supported employment.* Paper presented at The Association for Persons with Severe Handicaps Conference, Washington, DC.

Rice, R.W., McFarlin, D.B., Hunt, R.G., & Near, J.P. (1985a). Organizational work and perceived quality of life: Toward a conceptual model. *Academy of Management Review, 10*(2), 296–310.

Rice, R.W., McFarlin, D.B., Hunt, R.G., & Near, J.P. (1985b). Job importance as a moderator of the relationship between job satisfaction and life satisfaction. *Basic and Applied Psychology, 6*(4), 297–316.

Rice, R.W., Near, J.P., & Hunt, R.G. (1980). The job satisfaction–life satisfaction relationship: A review of empirical research. *Basic and Applied Social Psychology, 1,* 37–64.

Rodgers, W.L., & Converse, P.E. (1975). Measures of the perceived overall quality of life. *Social Indicators Research, 2,* 127–152.

Rosen, M., Halenda, R., Nowakiwska, M., & Floor, L. (1970). Employment satisfaction of previously institutionalized mentally subnormal workers. *Mental Retardation, 8,* 35–40.

Rosenthal, N.H. (1989). More than wages at issue in job quality debate. *Monthly Labor Review, 112*(12), 4–8.

Roznowski, M. (1989). Examination of the measurement properties of the job descriptive index with experimental items. *Journal of Applied Psychology, 74*(5), 805–814.

Sandow, D., Rhodes, L., Mank, D.M., Ramsing, K.D., & Lynch, W.F. (1990). Assuring quality in supported employment. *Journal of Rehabilitation Administration, 14*(1), 20–25.

Scarpello, V., & Campbell, J.P. (1983). Job satisfaction: Are all the parts there? *Personnel Psychology, 36*(3), 577–600.

Schalock, R.L., & Jensen, C.M. (1986). Assessing the goodness of fit between persons and their environments. *Journal of The Association for Persons with Severe Handicaps, 11,* 103–109.

Schalock, R.L., Keith, K.D., Hoffman, K., & Karan, O. (1989). Quality of life: Its measurement and use. *Mental Retardation, 27*(1), 25–31.

Seashore, S.E., & Taber, T.D. (1975). Job satisfaction indicators and their correlates. *American Behavioral Scientist, 18,* 333–368.

Seltzer, M.M. (1984). Patterns of job satisfaction among mentally retarded adults. *Applied Research in Mental Retardation, 5,* 147–159.

Smith, F.J. (1976). Index of organizational reactions. *Catalog of Selected Documents in Psychology, 6*(1), 1–12.

Smith, P.C., Kendall, L.M., & Hulin, C.L. (1969). *Measurement of satisfaction in work and retirement: A strategy for the study of attitudes.* Chicago, IL: Rand McNally.

Szymanski, E.M., & Parker, R.M. (1987). Supported employment research: A commentary. *Rehabilitation Counseling Bulletin, 31*(1), 59–63.

Talkington, L.W., & Overbeck, D.B. (1975). Job satisfaction and performance with retarded females. *Mental Retardation, 13,* 18–19.

Taylor, H. (1987). Evaluating our quality of life. *Industrial Development, 156*(2), 1–4.

Test, D.W., Alford, C.J., & Keul, P. (1991). *Job satisfaction of persons in supported employment.* Unpublished manuscript.

U.S. Department of Justice. (nd). *The Americans with Disabilities Act.* Washington, DC: Author.

Wehman, P., Kregel, J., Banks, D., Hill, M., & Moon, M.S. (1987). Sheltered vs. supported work programs: A second look. *Rehabilitation Counseling Bulletin, 31*(1), 42–53.

Weinberg, N. (1985). Physically disabled people assess the quality of their lives. *Rehabilitation Literature, 45,* 12–15.

Weiss, D.J., Davis, R.V., England, G.W., & Lofquist, L.H. (1967). *Manual for the Minnesota Satisfaction Questionnaire*. Minnesota Studies in Vocational Rehabilitation, Bulletin 22.

West, M.D., & Parent, W.S. (1992). Consumer choice and empowerment in supported employment. In P. Wehman, P. Sale, & W. Parent (Eds.), *Supported employment: Strategies for integrating workers with disabilities* (pp. 29–48). Stoneham, MA: Andover Medical Publishers.

Williams, R.K. (1991). Choices, communication, and control: A call for expanding them in the lives of people with severe disabilities. In L.H. Meyer, C.A. Peck, & L. Brown (Eds.), *Critical issues in the lives of people with severe disabilities* (pp. 543–544). Baltimore: Paul H. Brookes Publishing Co.

Zautra, A., & Goodhart, D. (1979). Quality of life indicators: A review of the literature. *Community Mental Health Review, 4,* 2–10.

Zimmerman, M.A., & Rappaport, J. (1988). Citizen participation, perceived control, and psychological empowerment. *American Journal of Community Psychology, 16*(5), 725–750.

Part II

Implications
of the ADA

Since the ADA is such a broad-ranging legislative mandate for civil rights and equal opportunity for persons with disabilities, it is very tempting to assume that this historic law can "right all the wrongs" that have occurred in the lives of many persons. Unfortunately, the ADA will not right all of the wrongs; however, it does have numerous positive implications. The ADA does imply that greater employment should occur in better-paying jobs; that mobility within and throughout communities should be achieved with greater ease; that more people with disabilities should have access to public and private transportation; and that telecommunication options and alternatives should be greatly improved. Overall, increased access to facilities throughout the United States will allow for greater inclusion of persons with disabilities into the mainstream of society than ever before.

Although the ADA cannot legislatively "make" all of these positive implications become a reality, it can provide a legislative vehicle that will unleash many rehabilitation and behavioral technology advances into the hands of motivated persons with disabilities, advocacy organizations, and concerned service providers and families. It is hoped that the technological advances and improved attitudes toward people with disabilities will take effect in the context of a positive national mandate.

Chapter 3

Employment Opportunities and Career Development

Paul Wehman

There are millions of people with mental, physical, sensory, and health-related disabilities who would like the opportunity to participate in the community and the workplace, but are being denied this opportunity. Some of the reasons for this discrimination include limited expectations and attitudes of professionals in the field, the unwillingness of business to make reasonable accommodations for people with disabilities, lack of sufficient funds for training and placement, and government disincentives to work. However, in the United States today there is a civil rights movement occurring for adults with disabilities who historically have been either unemployed or grossly under-employed. As Michael Ward (Foreword) and Wendy Parent (Chapter 2) indicate, people with disabilities are finally beginning to assert their rights to be included in society. People with disabilities do not just want a job, they want a career. The development and implementation of the Americans with Disabilities Act (ADA) takes a major step toward securing these rights and correcting these injustices.

It is the author's belief that these problems can be overcome and will continue to be overcome dramatically in the future, especially if the United States economy improves and there is a steady increase in job creation. A recent Louis Harris and Associates poll (1986) indicated that two out of three persons with disabilities are not working. These statistics are simply unacceptable, as well as highly inconsistent with the research and innovative practices currently in place in some parts of the country, which illustrate the potential for persons with disabilities in the workplace. Astute professionals, advocates, and persons with disabilities themselves are also aware of the possibilities for this population. Interestingly enough, a more recent survey by the same group reveals that Americans are extremely supportive of people with disabilities working (Louis Harris and Associates, 1991).

The author strongly agrees with the Louis Harris findings and believes that society is not openly opposed to the employment of persons with disabilities. Furthermore, experience suggests that business persons can and will be highly accommodative given sufficient labor demand. However, professionals in the field, such as special educators, rehabilitation counselors, adult basic educators, and vocational evaluators, do not seem to have high vocational expectations for the people they serve who have disabilities. These expectations are shaped by antiquated or inadequate training experience and lack of exposure to the possibilities that the right program can create. In a very real sense, this civil rights movement is a plea to professionals in the field to seriously evaluate their methods of delivering vocational services and creating work opportunities.

This chapter discusses the services that presently exist and how they can be improved as new opportunities are developed. This chapter is based on three themes: 1) the impetus for equal work opportunity promulgated by the ADA, 2) appropriate values of normalization (i.e., real work for real pay with a focus on careers for people with disabilities), and 3) existing research, which provides for an underlying empirical base for the type of adult/vocational service. It is noteworthy to remember that thousands of persons with disabilities each year look for career and work opportunities.

A rationale for work and full employment for people with disabilities is the overriding theme of this chapter. In addressing full employment, numerous types of work options, including consumer driven alliances with local business and industry are described. Also, the combined efforts of different local and state agencies, which can greatly influence vocational outcomes in respective states for persons with disabilities, are discussed.

EMPLOYMENT FOR INDIVIDUALS WITH DISABILITIES: THE IMPACT OF THE ADA

The ADA creates new opportunities for persons with disabilities who wish to enter the labor force. This historic law will have a major impact on persons with disabilities who have previously been unemployed. In a recent article, Patricia Owens (1991) notes:

the ADA is really a straightforward law, best understood in the context of this nation's renewed drive for individuality. People in this era have fought against being limited because they are members of a category—ethnic, racial, or gender. Instead they have insisted on being considered as individuals who pursue their own purposes. Persons with disabilities seeking employment are marked by their purpose. They are looking for an opportunity to do work in exchange for pay. Disability as an entitlement to a fair chance to perform in accordance with abilities deserves an investment in time and money at least comparable to disability as an entitlement to compensation. (p. 21)

The regulations detailing the rules for implementation of the ADA, as noted in the Introduction, were released on July 26, 1991, by the U.S. Equal Employment Opportunity Commission (EEOC).

As of July 26, 1992, under the proposed EEOC regulations, state and local governments and private employers with 25 or more employees, employment agencies, and labor unions are prohibited from discriminating against qualified individuals with disabilities in job application procedures, hiring, firing, advancement, compensation, job training, and other terms, conditions, and privileges of employment. Employers and other covered entities with 15 or more employees will be covered by the regulations after July 26, 1994.

To avoid any confusion or misinterpretation, the ADA defines an individual with a disability as a person who has a physical or mental impairment that substantially limits one or more major life activities, such as caring for oneself, breathing, learning, walking, seeing, hearing, speaking, or working. An individual with a disability can also be a person who has a record of such an impairment, or is regarded as having such an impairment.

To be protected by the nondiscriminatory provisions of the EEOC regulations, an individual with a disability must be qualified and able to perform the essential functions or tasks of the position held or desired, with or without reasonable accommodations. Employers are required to make an accommodation to the known disability of a qualified applicant or employee, if it would not impose an undue hardship as an action requiring significant difficulty or expense. Such factors as an employer's size, financial resources available to the specific site, and the nature and structure of its operations will be considered. The availability of assistance from other sources to offset the cost of the accommodation—such as federal, state, or local tax credits or deductions, and state vocational rehabilitation agencies—will also be taken into consideration.

An analysis of the economic impact of the proposed regulation indicates that reasonable accommodation expenses are normally quite low, with the cost of approximately 70% of such accommodations averaging less than $100. The process of determining an appropriate reasonable accommodation is an informal, interactive, problem-solving technique involving both the employer and the qualified individual with a disability. While significant guidance is provided by the regulations, the dynamics of the process preclude a prescriptive approach to the subject.

Employers cannot ask job applicants about the existence, nature, or severity of a disability, but they can ask about an applicant's ability to perform specific job functions. A job offer may be conditioned on the results of a medical examination, but only if the examination is required for all newly hired employees having similar jobs.

Employees and applicants currently engaging in the illegal use of drugs are not covered by the ADA or its regulations if an employer takes action on the basis of such use. Tests for illegal use of drugs are neither prohibited nor encouraged. Employers may hold illegal drug users and alcoholics to the same performance standards as other employees.

Employers can refuse to assign an individual to a job involving food handling if the individual has an infectious or communicable disease that has been determined by the Secretary of Health and Human Services to be communicable to others through food handling. The infectiousness and communicability of the disease cannot be eliminated by reasonable accommodation. With this provision, individuals with HIV or AIDS are protected from discrimination.

Employers may establish qualification standards that will exclude individuals who pose a direct threat to the health and safety of the individual or others, if the risk cannot be lowered to an acceptable level by reasonable accommodation. However, an employer may not simply assume that a threat exists. Employers are required to establish, through objective, medically supportable methods, that substantial harm could occur in the workplace.

Most persons with disabilities, their families, and professionals have many questions as to how the ADA can help them gain entry into the work force. In Table 3.1, specific questions and answers related to the employment aspects of the ADA can be found.

WORK AND QUALITY OF LIFE

Employment is a major aspect in the lives of people with or without disabilities. Type of employment, amount of money earned, and advancement opportunities directly affect a person's self-perception, society's evaluation of a person, and a person's financial and social freedom. Meaningful work, which pays a fair wage, plays a pervasive part in the quality of life a person enjoys.

Consider more closely some of the previously mentioned points. For example, how much does type of employment affect a person's behavior and the behavior of society toward that person? Frequently, entry-level manual labor is seen as less desirable and more physically straining than office work, assuming the amount of wages are equivalent. However, consider the prospect of a person who is restricted to a developmental adult day program that only serves persons with mental and physical disabilities and does not allow an opportunity for employment. A person in such a limited position might

Table 3.1. Questions and answers about employment under the ADA

Q. **What employers are covered by the ADA, and when is the coverage effective?**

A. The employment provisions apply to private employers, state and local governments, employment agencies, and labor unions. Employers with 25 or more employees will be covered starting July 26, 1992, when the employment provisions go into effect. Employers with 15 or more employees will be covered 2 years later, beginning July 26, 1994.

Q. **What practices and activities are covered by the employment nondiscrimination requirements?**

A. The ADA prohibits discrimination in all employment practices, including job application procedures, hiring, firing, advancement, compensation, training, and other terms, conditions, and privileges of employment. It applies to recruitment, advertising, tenure, layoff, leave, fringe benefits, and all other employment-related activities.

Q. **Who is protected against employment discrimination?**

A. Employment discrimination is prohibited against "qualified individuals with disabilities." Persons discriminated against because they have a known association or relationship with an individual with a disability also are protected. The ADA defines an "individual with a disability" as a person who has a physical or mental impairment that substantially limits one or more life activities, a record of such an impairment, or is regarded as having such an impairment.

The first part of the definition makes clear that the ADA applies to persons who have substantial (as distinct from minor) impairments, and that these must be impairments that limit major life activities such as seeing, hearing, speaking, walking, breathing, performing manual tasks, learning, caring for oneself, and working. An individual with epilepsy, paralysis, a substantial hearing or visual impairment, mental retardation, or a learning disability would be covered, but an individual with a minor, nonchronic condition of short duration, such as a sprain, infection, or broken limb, generally would not be covered.

The second part of the definition would include, for example, a person with a history of cancer that is currently in remission or a person with a history of mental illness.

The third part of the definition protects individuals who are regarded and treated as though they have a substantially limiting disability, even though they may not have such an impairment. For example, this provision would protect a severely disfigured qualified individual from being denied employment because an employer feared the "negative reactions" of others.

Q. **Who is a "qualified individual with a disability"?**

A. A qualified individual with a disability is a person who meets legitimate skill, experience, education, or other requirements of an employment position that he or she holds or seeks, and who can perform the "essential functions" of the position with or without reasonable accommodation. Requiring the ability to perform "essential" functions assures that an individual will not be considered unqualified simply because of inability to perform marginal or incidental job functions. If the individual is qualified to perform essential job functions

(continued)

Table 3.1. (*continued*)

except for limitations caused by a disability, the employer must consider whether the individual could perform these functions with a reasonable accommodation. If a written job description has been prepared in advance of advertising or interviewing applicants for a job, this will be considered as evidence, although not necessarily conclusive evidence, of the essential functions of the job.

Q. Does an employer have to give preference to a qualified applicant with a disability over other applicants?

A. No. An employer is free to select the most qualified applicant available and to make decisions based on reasons unrelated to the existence or consequence of a disabilty. For example, if two persons apply for a job opening as a typist, one a person with a disablity who accurately types 50 words per minute, the other a person without a disability who accurately types 75 words per minute, the employer may hire the applicant with the higher typing speed, if typing speed is needed for successful performance of the job.

Q. What is "reasonable accommodation"?

A. Reasonable accommodation is any modification or adjustment to a job or the work environment that will enable a qualified applicant or employee with a disability to perform essential job functions. Reasonable accommodation also includes adjustments to assure that a qualified individual with a disability has the same rights and privileges in employment as employees who do not have disabilities.

Q. What kinds of actions are required to reasonably accommodate applicants and employees?

A. Examples of reasonable accommodation include making existing facilities used by employees readily accessible to and usable by an individual with a disability; restructuring a job; modifying work schedules; acquiring or modifying equipment; providing qualified readers or interpreters; or appropriately modifying examinations, training, or other programs. Reasonable accommodation also may include reassigning a current employee to a vacant position for which the individual is qualified, if the person becomes disabled and is unable to do the original job. However, there is no obligation to find a position for an applicant who is not qualified for the position sought. Employers are not required to lower quality or quantity standards in order to make an accommodation, nor are they obligated to provide personal use items such as glasses or hearing aids.

The decision as to the appropriate accommodation must be based on the particular facts of each case. In selecting the particular type of reasonable accommodation to provide, the principal test is that of effectiveness (i.e., whether the accommodation will enable the person with a disability to do the job in question).

Q. Must employers be familiar with the many diverse types of disabilities to know whether or how to make a reasonable accommodation?

A. No. An employer is only required to accommodate a "known" disability of a qualified applicant or employee. The requirement generally will be triggered by a request from an individual with a disability, who frequently can suggest

(*continued*)

Table 3.1. (*continued*)

an appropriate accommodation. Accommodations must be made on an individual basis, because the nature and extent of a disabling condition and the requirements of the job will vary in each case. If the individual does not request an accommodation, the employer is not obligated to provide one. If a person with a disability requests, but cannot suggest, an appropriate accommodation, the employer and the individual should work together to identify one. There are also many public and private resources that can provide assistance without cost.

Q. What are the limitations on the obligation to make a reasonable accommodation?

A. The individual with a disability who requires the accommodation must be otherwise qualified, and the disability must be known to the employer. In addition, an employer is not required to make an accommodation if it would impose an "undue hardship" on the operation of the employer's business. "Undue hardship" is defined as "an action requiring significant difficulty or expense" when considered in light of a number of factors. These factors include the nature and cost of the accommodation in relation to the size, resources, nature, and structure of the employer's operation. Where the facility making the accommodation is part of a larger entity, the structure and overall resources of the larger organization would be considered, as well as the financial and administrative relationship of the facility to the larger organization. In general, a larger employer would be expected to make accommodations requiring greater effort or expense than would be required of a smaller employer.

Q. Must an employer modify existing facilities to make them accessible?

A. An employer may be required to modify facilities to enable an individual to perform essential job functions and to have equal opportunity to participate in other employment-related activities. For example, if an employee lounge is located in a place inaccessible to a person using a wheelchair, the lounge might be modified or relocated, or comparable facilities might be provided in a location that would enable the individual to take a break with coworkers.

Q. May an employer inquire as to whether a prospective employee is disabled?

A. An employer may not make a pre-employment inquiry on an application form or in an interview as to whether, or to what extent, an individual is disabled. The employer may ask a job applicant whether he or she can perform particular job functions. If the applicant has a disability known to the employer, the employer may ask how he or she can perform job functions that the employer considers difficult or impossible to perform because of the disability, and whether an accommodation would be needed. A job offer may be conditioned on the results of a medical examination, provided that the examination is required for all entering employees in the same job category regardless of disability, and that information obtained is handled according to confidentiality requirements specified in the Act. After an employee enters on duty, all medical examinations and inquiries must be job-related and necessary for the conduct of the employer's business. These provisions of the law are intended to prevent the employer from basing hiring and employment decisions on unfounded assumptions about the effects of a disability.

(*continued*)

Table 3.1. *(continued)*

Q. Does the ADA take safety issues into account?
A. Yes. The ADA expressly permits employers to establish qualification standards that will exclude individuals who pose a direct threat (i.e., a significant risk) to the health and safety of others, if that risk cannot be lowered to an acceptable level by reasonable accommodation. However, an employer may not simply assume that a threat exists; the employer must establish through objective, medically supportable methods that there is genuine risk that substantial harm could occur in the workplace. By requiring employers to make individualized judgments based on reliable medical evidence rather than on generalizations, ignorance, fear, patronizing attitudes, or stereotypes, the ADA recognizes the need to balance the interests of people with disabilities against the legitimate interests of employers in maintaining a safe workplace.

Q. Can an employer refuse to hire an applicant or fire a current employee who is illegally using drugs?
A. Yes. Individuals who currently engage in the illegal use of drugs are specifically excluded from the definition of a "qualified individual with a disability" protected by the ADA when an action is taken on the basis of their drug use.

Q. Is testing for illegal drugs permissible under the ADA?
A. Yes. A test for illegal drugs is not considered a medical examination under the ADA; therefore, employers may conduct such testing of applicants or employees and make employment decisions based on the results. The ADA does not encourage, prohibit, or authorize drug tests.

Q. Are people with AIDS covered by the ADA?
A. Yes. The legislative history indicates that Congress intended the ADA to protect persons with AIDS and HIV disease from discrimination.

Q. How does the ADA recognize public health concerns?
A. No provision in the ADA is intended to supplant the role of public health authorities in protecting the community from legitimate health threats. The ADA recognizes the need to strike a balance between the right of a person with a disability to be free from discrimination based on unfounded fear and the right of the public to be protected.

Q. What is discrimination based on "relationship or association"?
A. The ADA prohibits discrimination based on relationship or association in order to protect individuals from actions based on unfounded assumptions that their relationship to a person with a disability would affect their job performance, and from actions caused by bias or misinformation concerning certain disabilities. For example, this provision would protect a person who has a spouse with a disability from being denied employment because of an employer's unfounded assumption that the applicant would use excessive leave to care for the spouse. It also would protect an individual who does volunteer work for people with AIDS from a discriminatory employment action motivated by that relationship or association.

Q. Will the ADA increase litigation burdens on employers?
A. Some litigation is inevitable. However, employers who use the period prior to the effective date of employment coverage to adjust their policies and prac-

(continued)

Table 3.1. (*continued*)

tices to conform to ADA requirements will be much less likely to have serious litigation concerns. In drafting the ADA, Congress relied heavily on the language of the Rehabilitation Act of 1973 and its implementing regulations. There is already an extensive body of law interpreting the requirements of the act to which employers can turn for guidance on their ADA obligations. The Equal Employment Opportunity Commission will issue specific regulatory guidance 1 year before the ADA's employment provisions take effect, publish a technical assistance manual with guidance on how to comply, and provide other assistance to help employers meet ADA requirements. Equal employment opportunity for persons with disabilities will be achieved most quickly and effectively through widespread voluntary compliance with the law, rather than through reliance on litigation to enforce compliance.

Q. How will the employment provisions be enforced?
A. The employment provisions of the ADA will be enforced under the same procedures now applicable to race, sex, national origin, and religious discrimination under title VII of the Civil Rights Act of 1964. Complaints regarding actions that occur after July 26, 1992, may be filed with the Equal Employment Opportunity Commission or designated state human rights agencies. Available remedies will include hiring, reinstatement, back pay, and court orders to stop discrimination.

find an entry-level manual position very attractive, not only financially but also socially, in terms of family and community acceptance. The opportunity to make friends who do not have disabilities would be a major advantage of involvement in nonsheltered employment. Therefore, type of employment can be an important factor in self-evaluation.

The amount of earned income is another critical factor that can affect the quality of life. If people with disabilities work for free or volunteer their services all the time, their outlook and society's perceptions of them will be different than if they earn a wage comparable to that earned by workers without disabilities who perform the same job. Generally, the more money a person earns, the more freedom he or she has to purchase desired and/or necessary items in the community and to establish personal independence. A person with a disability who earns $5 per week in a day program or sheltered workshop will probably have a lower perception of him- or herself than a person who earns $190 per week as a micrographics camera operator. Unfortunately, many people with disabilities earn very little money and this becomes a real problem. Wolfe (1980) reports that persons with disabilities, on average, earn $2.55 per hour compared with wages of $4.50 per hour and over for people without disabilities. This type of significant wage discrepancy greatly influences the quality of life of individuals with disabilities.

The opportunity to switch jobs and move to a more favorable work setting, which includes better work conditions, job stability, and increased income, must also be assessed when looking at the importance of employment in the lifestyles of persons with disabilities. Advancement and career mobility are other opportunities that need to be available to people with disabilities. Most important, certain types of jobs in real work settings that yield a decent wage often lead the way to better jobs with more pay.

The astute reader will observe that the word "opportunity" has been used several times already. No one has the right to a job. Jobs are not available for everyone; a person must demonstrate a certain degree of skill and aptitude to gain employment. However, all people should have the opportunity to work if they choose, and society should also extend this opportunity to the thousands of individuals with disabilities who would like to have a career. This is especially the case since there is an abundance of literature since the 1970s that consistently shows the vocational potential of people with disabilities as workers. This literature indicates progressively greater vocational competence on the part of individuals with both mild and severe disabilities. It is unfortunate, however, that there is an enormous schism between what researchers know can be done and what is actually happening. The ADA will begin to help bridge this schism. Several of the most pressing concerns that are related to the employment of individuals with disabilities are discussed in this chapter.

UNEMPLOYMENT: A SERIOUS PROBLEM

In the United States today, the unemployment of persons with disabilities is at an unconscionably high level of 50%–90%. The United States Commission on Civil Rights (1983) reports a level of 50%–75%. This assessment is up from an earlier U.S. Department of Labor estimate in 1977 that reported 59% unemployment for persons with disabilities. As high as these figures seem, similar data in the states of Vermont, Colorado, Virginia, and Maryland seem to corroborate these figures.

In Maryland, for example, a sample of over 1,400 individuals with developmental disabilities was studied with regard to a large number of variables (Smull & Sachs, 1983). Only 7% of these individuals were found to have regular jobs. Similarly, Hill and her colleagues (Hill, Seyfarth, Banks, Wehman, & Orelove, 1987) surveyed 263 parents of adult persons with mental retardation in Virginia. In this study, only 13 of the 263 (5%) parents indicated that their son or daughter was competitively employed, while over one-third indicated no employment of any type for their son or daughter.

Hasazi, Gordon, and Roe (1985) did a follow-up study of recently graduated special education students in Vermont. Through an elaborate telephone interviewing system, it was found that over half of the graduates were not competitively employed. In Virginia, a similar postsecondary follow-up study of 300 young adults with mental retardation between 20 and 24 years old was completed (Wehman, Kregel, & Seyfarth, 1985). The parents of these adults were surveyed by trained interviewers. More than 40% had never held a regular job at any time. Mithaug, Horiuchi, and Fanning (1985) report similar levels of unemployment in the 35%–40% range from the state of Colorado. These studies prove that the current employment of people with disabilities is quite limited, especially in the area of regular job placement. Unfortunately, it seems as if too many professionals and parents are unaware of this high level of unemployment.

THE COSTS OF NOT EMPLOYING PERSONS WITH DISABILITIES

As the seriousness of the unemployment problem for persons with disabilities is considered it will be helpful to review the costs of unemployment to both society and business, and, most important, to individuals with all types of disabilities. It is not difficult to see how the impact of this high level of unemployment can affect thousands of people with and without disabilities. The points that follow address some of the adverse effects that occur when meaningful employment opportunities are not made available to capable persons.

Human Dignity

Human dignity and self-worth of individuals with disabilities are not enhanced if they are not given the opportunity to seek and gain employment. As previously stated, the opportunity and ability to work in a real job, which pays a fair wage, is a major aspect of life, not just for persons with disabilities but for all people. It is apparent after talking with persons with disabilities and their friends that sustained employment is a critical avenue to other successful aspects of life such as health, friendship, self-esteem, and a feeling of purpose. Employment is often the key to improving self-perceptions, reducing feelings of loneliness, and moving toward a richer quality of life (Brolin, 1985).

Family Concerns

The concerns and doubts experienced by families and friends of persons with disabilities must also be considered. These concerns often center around such questions as, "What will happen to my son or daughter after I'm gone?" or "Will my son or daughter be able to get a job after completing school?" These are legitimate and serious questions that sustained employment can help address. While a job may not solve all problems or erase all concerns and doubts, it will be a major step in the right direction. Families need support and assistance in helping individuals with disabilities enter the labor force (Seyfarth, Hill, Orelove, McMillen, & Wehman, 1987; Venn, DuBose, & Merbler, 1977).

Earning Power

As noted earlier, wages for individuals with disabilities are far below average. Earning competitive unsubsidized wages would provide the person with the opportunity to have more independence in his or her lifestyle. Even at minimum wage levels of $4.25/hour, the wage accumulation over time is considerable and allows persons with disabilities to have spending money for housing, meals, and other discretionary items. Often fringe benefits are also made available, such as free uniforms, free meals, better parking conditions, and paid vacation/holiday time. Overall, wages and benefits allow for greater independence on the part of citizens with disabilities and help to improve their quality of life.

Economic Benefits to Society

Wages earned by citizens with disabilities typically flow back into the local and state economy. The impact of this economic benefit should not be minimized. When combined with the taxes, it is apparent that significant reductions in the employment rate for persons with disabilities would quickly become a considerable benefit for state and federal budgets and the general economy.

There are other economic benefits of employment as well. For example, the costs for taxpayers to subsidize restrictive "prevocational" or work adjustment programs, which often do not lead to employment of persons with disabilities who have the potential to work, are significant. In addition to these program costs, the supplemental security income savings can be tremendous for those who are able to work. While it is vitally important to not take social security benefits from persons in need, it is also fiscally and morally necessary to help those who can work to do so. Service agencies, however, need to continue in a direction that fosters joint development of training efforts with industry. These training efforts need to culminate in employment that is not government subsidized.

Impact on Business and Industry

Business and industry lose an excellent labor source when competitive employment opportunities are not made available to citizens with disabilities. For example, an industry in which many coworkers with mental disabilities are employed is the hotel and restaurant industry. In a study conducted by the National Hotel and Restaurant Association in 1983, it was found that the average length of employment for more than 2,000 workers with disabilities was only five months (P. Nelan, personal communication, 1983); yet, data from supported competitive employment efforts in Virginia (Wehman, Hill, et al., 1985) indicated that, for 150 workers with mental disabilities in similar jobs, almost 19 months was the average tenure. Consider the well-known fast food chain of McDonald's Corporation, which had turnover rates of over 175% in 1981. This type of turnover is terribly expensive to business and industry, and can be partially offset by a pool of well-trained workers with disabilities.

Expectations of Family and Friends

The attitudes and expectations of family, friends, professionals, and, above all, citizens with disabilities are negatively influenced when persons with disabilities are continually denied the opportunity to earn decent wages and have a meaningful job. People are often viewed by others in the context of whether or not they have a job, how much money they make, how long they have held their job, what work they do, and so forth. Chronic unemployment of persons with disabilities, when it is frequently not necessary or warranted, casts an unfair light on the capabilities of these persons.

CHRONIC UNEMPLOYMENT
OF PERSONS WITH DISABILITIES AND THE ADA

The ADA itself cannot provide a job for every person with a disability. The ADA can, however, provide a framework for improved employer attitudes, reduced discriminatory practices, and overall increased awareness and communication among employers concerning the vocational capabilities of people with disabilities. Listed below are some of the more obvious benefits that will accrue to individuals with disabilities who wish to work following the passage of the ADA:

1. It is against the law for businesses to discriminate in their hiring practices against an otherwise qualified person with a disability.
2. The concept of reasonable accommodation is introduced into federal law as a means by which the employer must try to overcome the limitations of the potential employee.
3. Workplace environments need to be made accessible so that people with physical and/or sensory disabilities can be integrated, increasing the likelihood of employment for many persons with disabilities.

The implications of the ADA for changing the high unemployment rate of persons with disabilities are still unknown. It remains to be seen how businesses will react and, even more pertinent, how the United States economy improves. A poor economy will not yield sufficient jobs for any persons who are unemployed, whether they have a disability or not. It also remains to be seen if people with disabilities who were previously denied entry into the work force will try again with the passage of the ADA.

VOCATIONAL ALTERNATIVES
FOR ADULTS WITH DEVELOPMENTAL DISABILITIES

The following section describes three traditional vocational alternatives currently available to individuals with disabilities. These alternatives are: 1) adult developmental programs, 2) vocational rehabilitation facilities, and 3) placement into competitive employment. The section describes the basic nature and the major strengths and weaknesses of each alternative, as well as the research findings underlying the alternatives.

Adult Developmental Programs

In most cities and towns, young adults with mental and physical disabilities attend programs at special centers after they finish high school. These centers are called adult activity centers, developmental achievement centers, stimulation centers, and so forth. Such day programs have grown enormously in number, with approximately 2,000 in the United States, despite many efforts to expand real work opportunities (Wehman & Moon, 1988; Wehman, Sale, & Parent, 1992). Many other young adults are accepted in work activity or sheltered workshop programs. These sheltered workshops number well over 5,000. Unfortunately, not all persons with disabilities have access to such centers or workshops; therefore, many young adults remain at home.

At special centers, the day programs allow participants the opportunity to recreate, learn activities of daily living, learn academics, and be involved in some work skill activity. The more advanced vocational rehabilitation facilities provide for contract benchwork under sheltered conditions with other persons who have mental or physical disabilities. Facility employees typically earn an average of $8–$10 per day. Most parents and young people with severe disabilities, as well as professionals, have come to expect these forms of services. With increasing numbers of students leaving school and needing adult service, a move to further expand segregated adult day programs has been made by some states. In most states, adult activity centers cost from $4,200 per client (Virginia) to $7,500 per client (Maryland) annually. Rehabilitation facilities usually cost less, ranging from $2,500 to $3,000 per client annually.

In order to lower costs, the special day programs that take place in segregated centers must come to an end. This arrangement directs too many fiscal resources into buildings, not staff. A more significant disadvantage results from the segregation of people with severe disabilities from the community. Furthermore, the emphasis of these programs is not on finding employment with decent pay in the community—in spite of the many successful programs that have shown the potential of people with disabilities. The emphasis is on providing some form of daily work activity even if it is not performed in competitive work environments. The underlying assumption has been that individuals with disabilities are not "ready" and need much more training.

In the period of time between 1955 and 1975, there were very limited data and published research to suggest that individuals with significant mental and physical disabilities could benefit from work opportunities that yielded unsubsidized pay. During this time period, the establishment of a special day center where individuals could go for continued special education and developmental activities was considered the best option, in fact, often the *only* option. Unfortunately, this alternative is still very much in practice nationally because the thinking of many adult service administrators reflects a center-based ideology.

Alternatively, the way to best convert these existing centers from day program activity to integrated employment and career development activity needs to be considered. The emerging initiative toward supported employment (i.e., supported competitive employment, enclaves, and workcrews) provides a basis for alternative day activity, which is much more productive. Adult service administrators must evaluate and review the following issues as they consider converting center-based day program activity to industry-based supported employment:

1. Staff training needs that are necessary to develop new skills and philosophies in service staff
2. Analysis of funding streams and determination of the best ways to utilize resources from different agencies
3. Ability to mobilize staff opinion, parental attitudes, and the business community to accept the employability of clients with no previous work histories

These vital issues must be addressed in order to begin the long-term conversion from day programs to industry-based supported employment.

Vocational Rehabilitation Facilities

The employment of people with disabilities cannot be studied without looking carefully at vocational rehabilitation facilities. The U.S. Department of Labor (1977) reviewed a large sample of facilities (600) and reported a significant increase in the client population, from 39,254 in 1968 to 156,475 in 1977, an increase of 300%. This increase shows that many people/agencies have chosen the rehabilitation facility as a source of employment for persons with disabilities. Since such facilities have traditionally been a major source of employment for many people with disabilities, this selection is less an option than it is a predestined tract. Fortunately, the evaluation of programs designed to serve persons with disabilities is also receiving increased attention. Several studies of sheltered programs indicate that dependence upon the workshops to meet the needs of all persons with disabilities, especially those with severe disabilities, causes significant problems.

For example, in the U.S. Department of Labor study (1977), only 12% of regular program workshop clients were placed into competitive employment (this study did not discuss retention rate past the initial employment period). The hourly wages increased only 9% in 5 years, and the average hourly wage for all clients with mental retardation was $.58 per hour. These data support the contention that individuals with disabilities are underemployed, underutilized, and underpaid. Furthermore, research shows that the longer a person with a disability is placed in a day program with other persons with disabilities, the lower the probability that person has for success in a regular job (Buckley & Bellamy, 1986).

In general, vocational rehabilitation facilities have not been successful in moving people with disabilities into competitive employment and maintaining this employment. There are, however, significant disincentives that facilities have had to face. Some of these are listed below:

1. Financial support has not typically been provided for competitive job placements.
2. Financial support has not typically been provided for client training at job sites in the community.
3. Monetary support is not provided for follow-along services; that is, funds have not been provided for maintenance services designed to help difficult-to-train clients.
4. State and federal funding patterns have not typically encouraged workshops to allocate more of their time and resources to competitive employment.

There continues to be an expanding controversy between people who feel rehabilitation facilities and other adult day programs are not consistent with the best employment needs of most persons with disabilities and people who feel that these types of sheltered programs are a necessary vocational alternative. Two points related to this controversy are increasingly clear. These points are discussed throughout this chapter, but demand a brief description previous to any discussion.

Perhaps it would be more productive not to debate over which setting would be best to accomplish desired vocational outcomes, but to decide on which outcomes we want for persons with disabilities. For example, assume that competitive employment is a highly desirable outcome. What are the placement, training, and follow-along conditions that are necessary to effect that outcome regardless of the setting? What are the aspects of a workplace that enhance independence on the part of the client? This is not to say that a community-based vocational training site would not be more effective with client placement than a sheltered workshop benchwork activity or an adult activity center arts and crafts program. It is possible that that very same adult activity center can convert itself into an employment-oriented placement program with specific employment outcomes accomplished for clients.

The second point, which cannot be overlooked, is that there are 5,000 sheltered workshops (National Association of Rehabilitation Facilities, 1984) and over 2,000 adult day programs (Buckley & Bellamy, 1986) nationally. These programs continue to be a principal service delivery mode of vocational services for adults with severe disabilities. While they will be changed, modified, and improved, it is improbable that this will happen overnight. Therefore, it is more constructive to identify ways to facilitate their role in stimulating desired employment outcomes, which are characterized by decent pay and integrated employment.

Rehabilitation facilities have for a long time been considered the foundation of the United States's adult vocational service system for persons with disabilities. Over the past 2 decades the number of vocational facilities in the United States has grown tremendously, from 885 programs serving 47,000 clients in 1966 to 2,766 facilities serving 117,000 persons in 1975 (Victor, 1976). Even though the number of facilities in the United States has risen substantially, these programs have come under attack from a number of different government agencies, professionals, and advocates (U.S. Department of Labor, 1977; Whitehead, 1979). This public outcry over the limited outcomes obtained by sheltered workshop clients has left the movement in a state of confusion. Many facilities are facing increasingly greater financial constraints while, at the same time, struggling to find a role within newly emerging community-based employment programs for persons with disabilities.

While rehabilitation facilities vary considerably in terms of their size and the type of services they provide, all of these types of programs must meet the criteria of the Fair Labor Standards Act, which regulates the payment of subminimum wages to individuals with mental or physical impairments. The U.S. Department of Labor has authorized five different types of subminimum wage certificates to provide payment to persons with disabilities. They are as follows:

1. *Regular Workshop Program.* The regular workshop program provides a minimum wage floor of 50% of the current minimum wage for individuals or for an entire shop. This option is designed to provide long-term employment for individuals at a wage commensurate with their productivity.
2. *Training.* Training certificates (usually limited to 12 months) are designed to provide work adjustment or specific skill instruction to clients with disabilities in transitional employment programs. The purpose of

this option is not to maximize the amount of client earnings, but rather to "prepare" the worker for subsequent employment.

3. *Evaluation.* Evaluation certificates are issued for clients whose potential for subsequent employment is determined by their work performance. It must be noted that evaluation certificates allow workers to be paid at a rate far less than that which they might earn if paid on the basis of productivity. Evaluation certificates are generally provided on a 6-month basis, but may be extended for up to 18 months for a specific individual.

4. *Work Activity Program.* Work activity programs are designed for clients whose physical or mental disabilities are so severe as to make their productive capacity inconsequential. It is this type of program that has seen the greatest amount of growth during the 1980s. It should be clearly understood that these programs, for clients with supposedly "inconsequential" productive capacity, are the very programs from which clients are frequently placed directly into competitive employment using the individual placement model of supported employment (Wehman, 1981; Wehman, Hill, et al., 1985).

5. *Individual Rate.* Individual rate certificates allow two specific types of exceptions to the regulations described above. First, clients in regular workshop programs who do not produce at 50% of minimum wage may be paid at a rate of 25% of minimum wage with the prior approval of the state rehabilitation agency. Second, workers in work activity centers who produce 50% of minimum wage or above may remain in work activity centers if no other appropriate alternative is available for them.

Operational Problems in Vocational Rehabilitation Facilities   The major criticisms of the existing facility system have been described earlier. Clients in these programs generally earn insignificant wages. In addition, client earnings have not risen at a rate comparable to overall wages for workers in the United States. Facilities, by their very nature, are segregated with no particular intent to provide clients regular contact with individuals who do not have disabilities. These programs have come to be viewed as "dead end" facilities with little client movement into competitive employment (McLaughlin, Garner, & Callahan, 1987). In addition to these frequently cited concerns, rehabilitation facilities have traditionally been plagued by operational and organizational problems that have contributed to their shortcomings.

1. Facilities have generally been underfunded   Funding levels provided to these programs have often been inadequate to meet the actual costs. Workshops have too frequently been forced to rely on United Way contributions, fund raising activities, or other charitable contributions to support wages, staff salaries, and overhead costs. This situation has led many workshops to focus their efforts on "keeping their doors open;" that is, keeping the workshop operating, rather than focusing their efforts on facilitating the movement of clients into competitive employment.

2. *Facilities have failed to incorporate the most efficient business and industrial technologies* Rehabilitation facilities are generally labor intensive, nonautomated industries. Many times facilities fail to incorporate state of the art practices in marketing, production, and management. This failure to advance is frequently caused by a lack of available work. In order to provide work for the greatest number of individuals for the longest amount of time, workshops divide jobs into small units that provide "activity" for the largest number of clients. Workshops may fail to procure equipment or machinery that would make production more efficient, or rely too frequently on items for which they are the prime manufacturer, such as crafts or other low-profit merchandise.

3. *Facility staff are frequently not prepared to perform the marketing and production management activities necessary to maximize profits and client wages* In many instances, workshop and work activity center staff are human services professionals who do not possess the industrial management skills required in contract procurement and production activities. These staff members are frequently hired because they possess the skills and motivation to work in the required settings. While these individuals are highly dedicated and greatly skilled in working with individuals with disabilities, their lack of business knowledge coupled with the low salaries they generally receive, serve to limit the ultimate financial and employment outcomes for workshop clients.

The Future of Rehabilitation Facilities The preponderance of problems associated with the facilities in the United States have led many to advocate that these programs should be phased out or eliminated entirely; however, this argument should be viewed with caution. A more effective view may be to assist these facilities in making the transition to community-based employment programs, which would provide an array of support to business and industry. This approach would allow the programs to transfer their resources into options that hold the promise of greater client outcomes at equivalent or reduced public costs. Funds may be needed to assist workshops in making this transition. In addition, parent and consumer education programs should be initiated to assist clients and caregivers in accepting the risks and challenges associated with such a change. Finally, staff development programs must be designed to prepare existing workshop staff for the new roles and job responsibilities associated with the supported employment movement.

Clearly, the spirit and law of the ADA will continue the movement away from large, segregated work activity and toward real work in business and industry. Facility staff must ultimately decide for themselves how rapidly they will move toward an integrated approach, with consumer choice as the overriding factor in program design.

Placement into Competitive Employment

The majority of students with special needs who exit special education programs in public schools will be able to enter competitive employment with the assistance of a vocational rehabilitation counselor. This traditional approach to competitive employment placement involves providing individuals with a variety of "time-limited" services; that is, services that may be of an intensive nature, but are only provided for a specified, short period of time. Presently, traditional placement services have greatest applicability for individuals with mild disabilities; however, these services will be greatly enhanced by more openness and knowledgeability on the part of business and industry.

Vocational rehabilitation services can be divided, at a minimum, into the following four categories. First, *evaluation* services are those intended to identify a client's strengths and weaknesses, to identify potential job placement alternatives, and to provide the services required to secure these alternatives. Second, *preplacement* services are designed to allow the individual to maximize his or her employment potential. Third, *placement* services exist to assist individuals in securing a job that allows him or her to realize his or her vocational potential. Finally, *post-employment* services are provided in order to enable the client to maintain employment and to assist the client in future career enhancement. Vandergoot and Worrall (1979) describe this process as: 1) preparation for a job, 2) finding a job, and 3) keeping a job.

Time-limited placement services are most often initiated through a comprehensive vocational evaluation. While a tremendous amount of professional and financial resources continue to be expended in the evaluation process, in recent years, this vast expenditure has been questioned. Critics have charged that the outcomes derived from this process do not justify the large expenditures for vocational evaluation, and that financial resources should be channeled to other areas of the placement process. Wehman and McLaughlin (1980) have identified four types of vocational evaluation data. These include: 1) clinical assessment, which addresses formalized testing regarding medical conditions, educational skills, adaptive behavior, vocational interest and aptitudes, and other factors; 2) work samples, which are simulated activities that attempt to assess an individual's capacity for and interest in tasks associated with various job clusters; 3) situational assessment in which clients are placed in employment settings to assess their general work behaviors, skills, and attitudes; and 4) job try-out, which focuses on an individual's ability to adjust to a natural job setting.

Preplacement services refer to a variety of activities that vary in length and intensity. For example, clients may receive counseling services to aid in the development of appropriate work attitudes and to provide them with information about the types of available jobs. Some individuals may be placed into a transitional workshop to receive work adjustment training; that is, training designed to improve general work skills and attitudes. Other individuals may be placed into more formal types of training programs, including community colleges, vocational–technical centers, or college/university programs.

Placement services lie at the heart of the time-limited services approach. Generally, placement strategies fall into two categories—client-centered or selective placement. The client centered approach focuses on teaching the client general job-seeking skills. Rather than trying to obtain a job for the client, the rehabilitation professional tries to develop the client's job-seeking skills to the point where the client can locate and obtain his or her own job. In the selective placement approach, the rehabilitation professional takes a much more directive role by attempting to match the skills and needs of a particular client with the requirements and rewards of a specific job in the local community.

Post-employment service is an area that has typically been under-emphasized in the vocational rehabilitation process (Dunn, 1979). These services refer to follow-up activities often provided after an individual has successfully secured a job. These activities may include assessing client and employer satisfaction with job performance, initiating needed work adjustments, and preparing the client for future career enhancement and job mobility.

The key feature of these services is their time-limited nature. When an individual has successfully adjusted to the initial job, services are terminated after a short period of time. Many individuals with severe disabilities may be prevented from succeeding within this model because of the time factor, but for others it may be entirely adequate. Some individuals require assistance in determining the job for which they are best suited, need additional training to prepare for the job, require specific help in obtaining their first job, and need support to adjust to the performance and social demands of the job. For these individuals, the traditional approach to competitive placement continues to meet their needs.

Despite its successes, there are several shortcomings associated with this approach. For example, the typical vocational rehabilitation counselor may have an active caseload of well over 100, which makes it impossible for the counselor to be actively involved in all facets of the placement process for all individuals. This large caseload forces the counselor to purchase services from a variety of different providers for a given individual, a situation that too often results in disjointed and uncoordinated service programs. Another major shortcoming is the lack of post-employment follow-up services provided in the model. Services to many individuals are terminated after the client has completed just 2 months of successful employment. While the time-limited approach may be appropriate for many individuals with mild disabilities, it seems clear that other individuals require more intensive services to adjust to and maintain employment for extended periods of time.

CONCLUSION

This chapter describes the importance of real work and real pay for persons with disabilities, utilizing the ADA and its subsequent implementation as a backdrop. The different vocational alternatives that are available and some critiques of early alternatives are examined. An indepth look at rehabilitation facilities, which have been a major source of employment for people with disabilities, is also provided. Finally, information about time-limited job placement into competitive employment is presented.

One question that many people have is whether the ADA is primarily a law for persons with physical disabilities. People are asking this question because of the ADA's emphasis on physical accessibility issues. The author believes, however, that the ADA can and will provide the catalyst for social change in the employment prospectus of all people with disabilities. The spirit of the ADA calls for the inclusion of all people with disabilities into society and into the workplace—it is a law for the civil rights of persons with disabilities. As the ADA becomes better known throughout the United States, perhaps it will influence the development of positive attitudes toward this population. Education and public awareness will be very important, not just to the community, but also to persons with disabilities themselves. The ADA can help provide new hope and inspiration for many Americans.

The ADA also has the potential to make a wide-reaching impact on the attitudes and practices of employers regarding the hiring of persons with disabilities. It remains to be seen if employers will become involved in the development of job accommodations, if many lawsuits will be filed by people with disabilities, and, above all, if the rate of employment for people with disabilities will increase. Clearly, the state of the United States economy will have a major influence on the willingness of employers to hire new workers in general, not just those with disabilities.

REFERENCES

Brolin, D.E. (1985). Career education material for exceptional individuals. *Career Development for Exceptional Individuals, 8*(1), 62–64.
Buckley, J., & Bellamy, G. (1986). National survey of day and vocational programs for adults with severe disabilities: A 1984 profile. In P. Ferguson (Ed.), *Issues in transition research: Economics and social outcomes* (pp. 1–12). Eugene, OR: Specialized Training Program.
Dunn, K. (1979). What happens after placement? Career enhancement services in

vocational rehabilitation. In D. Vandergoot & J.D. Worrall (Eds.), *Placement in rehabilitation* (pp. 167–196). Baltimore: University Park Press.

Hasazi, S., Gordon, S., & Roe, R. (1985). Factors associated with the employment status of handicapped youth exiting high school from 1979–1983. *Exceptional Children, 51*(6), 455–469.

Hill, J., Seyfarth, J., Banks, P.D., Wehman, P., & Orelove, F. (1987). Parent attitudes about working conditions of their adult mentally retarded sons and daughters. *Exceptional Children, 54*(1), 9–23.

Louis Harris and Associates. (1986, February). *A survey of the unemployment of persons with disabilities.* Washington, DC: Author.

Louis Harris and Associates. (1991). *Attitudes toward people with disabilities* poll. Washington, DC.

McLaughlin, C.S., Garner, J.B., & Callahan, M. (1987). *Getting employed, staying employed: Job development and training for persons with severe handicaps.* Baltimore: Paul H. Brookes Publishing Company.

Mithaug, D., Horiuchi, C., & Fanning, P. (1985). A report on the Colorado statewide follow-up survey of special education students. *Exceptional Children, 51*(5), 397–404.

National Association of Rehabilitation Facilities. (1984). *A survey of supported employment needs from rehabilitation facilities.* Unpublished paper, National Association of Rehabilitation Facilities, Washington, DC.

Owens, P. (1991, March 29). ADA: What it will mean to business. *The Wall Street Journal,* p. 21.

Seyfarth, J., Hill, J., Orelove, F., McMillen, J., & Wehman, P. (1987). Factors influencing parents' aspirations for their mentally retarded children. *Mental Retardation, 23*(2), 16–18.

Smull, M., & Sachs, M. (1983). *Update. NRDD on persons with developmental disabilities.* Unpublished manuscript, University of Maryland, School of Medicine, Baltimore.

United States Commission on Civil Rights. (1983). *Attitudes toward the handicapped.* Washington, DC: U.S. Government Printing Office.

U.S. Department of Labor. (1977). *Sheltered work shop study, workshop survey, Volume 2.* Washington, DC: Author.

Vandergoot, D., & Worrall, J.D. (Eds.). (1979). *Placement in rehabilitation: A career development perspective.* Baltimore: University Park Press.

Venn, J., DuBose, R., & Merbler, J. (1977). Parent and teacher expectations for the adult lives of their severely and profoundly handicapped children. *AAESPH Review, 2,* 232–238.

Wehman, P. (1981). *Competitive employment: New horizons for severely disabled individuals.* Baltimore: Paul H. Brookes Publishing Co.

Wehman, P., Hill, M., Hill, J., Brooke, V., Pendleton, P., & Britt, C. (1985). Competitive employment for persons with mental retardation: A follow-up six years later. *Mental Retardation, 23*(6), 274–281.

Wehman, P., Kregel, J., & Seyfarth, J. (1985). A follow-up of mentally retarded graduates' vocational and independent living skills. *Virginia Rehabilitation Counseling Bulletin, 29*(2), 90–99.

Wehman, P., & McLaughlin, P. (Eds.). (1980). *Vocational curriculum for developmentally disabled persons.* Baltimore: University Park Press.

Wehman, P., & Moon, M.S. (Eds.). (1988). *Vocational rehabilitation and supported employment.* Baltimore: Paul H. Brookes Publishing Co.

Wehman, P., Sale, P., & Parent, W. (1992). *Supported employment: From research to practice*. Stoneham, MA: Andover Medical Publishers.

Whitehead, C. (1979). Sheltered workshops in the decade ahead: Work and wages or welfare. In G.T. Bellamy, G. O'Conner, & O.C. Karan (Eds.), *Vocational rehabilitation of severely handicapped persons*. Baltimore: University Park Press.

Wolfe, B. (1980, September). How the disabled fare in the labor market. *Monthly Labor Report: Research Summaries*, 48–52.

Chapter 4

Supported Employment and Opportunities for Integration

Paul Wehman

The preceding discussion focused on vocational alternatives for persons with disabilities and the effects that new legislation, such as the Americans with Disabilities Act (ADA), will have on employment practices. People with severe disabilities are one group who will need intensive, specialized, vocational support. The concept of supported employment has evolved in the 1980s as an alternative for these persons (Wehman & Moon, 1988; Wehman, Sale, & Parent, 1992). Supported employment will provide the opportunity for many people who are at substantial risk to gain and maintain employment. A host of different arrangements within or outside of industry (Lorenzini, 1992), in different occupations, and with different staffing patterns may be involved in supported employment.

The ADA does not specifically address the concept of supported employment in the law or its regulations; however, the underlying theme of the ADA, competitive work in a nondiscriminatory work environment, is highly consistent with supported employment. In fact, the recent trend toward greater consumer advocacy, choice-making, and empowerment of persons with disabilities is embedded in the philosophy of supported employment. This philosophy is reflected not only in the expansion of real work opportunities, but also in the career advancement and upward mobility of persons who have traditionally been confined to segregated work choices. The ADA does not focus on specific support mechanisms but instead requires a broader framework for business and societal change to develop reasonable accommodations.

SUPPORTED EMPLOYMENT: AN OVERVIEW

In the 1980s, individuals with developmental and other severe disabilities faced tremendous obstacles when attempting to access vocational rehabilitation services and obtain employment in their communities. Traditionally viewed as ineligible for vocational rehabilitation due to the severity of their disabilities, these persons were likely to earn token wages performing menial tasks in day programs. Now, many thousands of individuals with disabilities are able to earn significant wages in integrated community settings through participation in a new rehabilitation alternative termed supported employment.

Supported employment began as a philosophical commitment to improve the employment outcomes of individuals with severe disabilities. Supported employment is now a major national initiative (Wehman & Moon, 1988; Wehman et al., 1992) with its own technology, practical legislation, and funding system. In its simplest form, supported employment provides paid employment in integrated work settings to individuals previously excluded from work. The success of this approach lies in the provision of intense, individual training and support during the initial stages of employment, and of ongoing assistance, enabling an individual to maintain employment for extended periods of time.

Paid Employment

Supported employment is paid employment that cannot exist without a regular opportunity to work (*Federal Register,* June 24, 1992). The federal government has suggested that an individual should be considered to meet the paid employment aspect of supported employment if he or she engages in paid work for at least an average of 20 hours per week. This standard does not establish a minimum wage or productivity level for supported employment.

The amount of hours worked should not be viewed as the only criterion for supported employment, because some people (e.g., adolescents with severe disabilities) may choose to work only 15 hours per week. The stipulation that requires a certain number of hours to be worked per week, however, does convey the seriousness and impact that paid employment may have on young persons with disabilities.

Community Integration

Work is integrated when it provides frequent daily social interactions with people without disabilities who are not paid caregivers. The nature of vocational integration is a critical element of supported employment and requires careful attention by professionals who are looking for attractive job placements (Parent, Kregel, & Wehman, 1992). The federal government has suggested that integration in supported employment programs be defined in terms of a place where: 1) no more than eight people with disabilities work together and to which another program serving persons with disabilities is not adjacent, and 2) persons without disabilities who are not paid caregivers are present in the work setting or immediate vicinity.

For example, an individual with severe cerebral palsy who works in a local bank creating microfilm records of transactions clearly meets the integration criteria for supported employment (Sowers & Powers, 1991). These employment situations also meet the criteria: an enclave within a manufacturing plant that employs four individuals with severe emotional disorders who work together, a mobile janitorial crew that employs five persons with moderate mental retardation at community work sites, and a small bakery that employs persons with and without disabilities.

Ongoing Support

Supported employment exists only when ongoing support is provided. In contrast to time-limited support, which may only be provided for a few months, ongoing support continues as long as the client is employed. An individual should be considered to be receiving ongoing support when public funds are available on an ongoing basis to an individual or a service provider who is responsible for providing long-term employment support, and when these funds are used for specialized assistance directly related to sustaining employment. The new regulations provide a more flexible way of allowing the minimum twice-a-month ongoing support standard. For instance, phone calls and off-site meetings are acceptable examples.

The nature of ongoing support, which is ongoing through the entire span of the individual's employment, differs markedly from the time-limited nature of traditional rehabilitation services that were described in the previous chapter. This characteristic of ongoing support helps to diminish the concerns of parents and employers.

Severe Disability

Supported employment exists when the persons being served require ongoing support; it is inappropriate for persons who would be better served by time-limited preparation programs that lead to independent employment. The most appropriate way to determine who should receive supported employment is to assess the degree to which an individual is at-risk. Persons who are most likely to lose jobs shortly after placement because of their disability may be prime candidates for supported employment. This means that individuals with autism, severe mental retardation, and multiple disabilities would be the principal target groups for this approach. These individuals would not be able to hold jobs without permanent, long-term, follow-along support at the job site.

The ADA law and regulations will not ensure job placement and retention for any group of people with disabilities; however, people with disabilities who have been excluded from vocational services over the years, will need specialized ongoing assistance. This is true whether the disability involves mental retardation (Wehman & Moon, 1988), psychiatric problems (McDonald-Wilson, Revell, Nguyen, & Peterson, 1991), physical disability (Sowers & Powers, 1991; West, Callahan, Lewis, Mast, & Sleight, 1991), vision (Apter, 1992), or traumatic brain injury (Burke, Wesolowski, & Guth, 1988).

THE ADA AND SUPPORTED EMPLOYMENT

Are the ADA and supported employment compatible? Do consumer advocates and centers for independent living have issues with supported employment programs? In short, how does the trend toward consumer involvement relate to supported employment? To answer these questions, it may be beneficial to examine the beginnings of supported employment; that is, to look at how and why supported employment emerged as a service alternative for persons with disabilities. A new concept does not arise unless there is a need for it. Thus, supported employment emerged to serve the thousands of people with severe mental disabilities who were viewed as unemployable by most service providers and advocates. Persons with disabilities had the option to become involved in day programs, adult activity centers, or sheltered workshops, or to stay at home or to be placed in an institution. In the mid to late 1970s, a number of professionals began to experiment with different methods of service provision. The primary reason for this experimentation was to meet a need—the need for people to realize competitive employment, earn a decent wage, and have an opportunity to develop a real work history.

Supported employment was developed to enable consumers to make choices in the labor force. It focuses on consumer interest and provides an opportunity for individuals to identify a job, specify employment conditions, determine the wage level, select the job location, and decide the work hours. With 72,000 people currently employed through supported employment, it is clear that more and more individuals with severe disabilities are asserting their rights and working for the first time (Wehman, 1991).

Supported employment will not succeed without consumer involvement and consumer advocacy. The programs cannot be effective and will not flourish without consumer and family participation, support, and willingness to take the risks that are inherent in any competitive employment position. The early consumers that entered the work force in the late 1970s and early 1980s were pioneers. They took the risk of losing their placement in adult day programs so that they could take part in competitive employment programs. In most states, there were limited support systems to help place these individuals in other jobs if they failed.

Supported employment is deeply rooted in consumer interests and choice, as well as in the concept of inclusion. These roots are what has made supported employment one of the most popular and sustainable programs in the United States during the early 1990s, even in the face of a severe economic recession. Examples of several supported employment models that have been developed to facilitate employment for persons with severe disabilities are described in the text that follows.

THE INDIVIDUAL PLACEMENT MODEL OF SUPPORTED EMPLOYMENT

A supported work approach to competitive job placement requires specialized assistance to locate an appropriate job, intensive job site training for clients who are usually not "job ready," and permanent, ongoing follow-along (Wehman et al., 1992). A qualified staff person essentially establishes a one-on-one relationship with a client in need of individual employment services. Placement and ongoing training are provided at the job site, and the person is employed immediately with wages paid by the employer. Follow-along is differentiated from follow-up in that follow-along demands daily and weekly on-site evaluations of how the client is performing, while follow-up only requires periodic checking at established intervals of time. Competitive employment is defined as a real job, which provides the federal minimum wage, in a work area predominant with workers who do not have disabilities.

In the individual placement model of supported competitive employment described below, all workers are paid at or above minimum wage. A closely related model is supported employment or distributed work (Mank, Rhodes, & Bellamy, 1986). In this model, workers are employed in competitive settings, but work at subminimum wages. While the distributed work model is an appropriate alternative for certain individuals, employment at or above minimum wage should be the first priority of all supported employment programs.

Traditional placement into supported competitive employment is different from placement into competitive employment. The latter is time-limited; that is, once the client has been placed and trained at the job site to the satisfaction of the employer, the service is terminated. With supported employment there is a permanent commitment for follow-along services provided by professional staff. One approach, which has worked well in Virginia, has been for the Virginia Department of Rehabilitative Services to fund the initial job placement and intensive job site training costs through case service funds. The permanent follow-along support is paid for through local and state mental health/mental retardation funds. This shared responsibility is now being practiced in at least four areas of Virginia (Hill, Hill, Wehman, Revell, Noble, & Dickerson, 1987).

Staffing Issues Related to Supported Competitive Employment

Traditionally, neither rehabilitation counselors nor special education teachers, two professionals who might meet staffing needs, have been completely trained in the skills necessary for successful supported competitive employment. University field-based training programs will need to be developed in business settings. Close relationships must be established with business and industry and professionals working in supported competitive employment must understand the personnel practices of businesses. The success of the entire supported employment initiative, in fact, is highly dependent upon: 1) the willingness of business to hire persons with disabilities, and 2) the likelihood that business will allow professional staff to work at job sites. Experiences in Virginia, as well as in other areas around the country, seem to support a high level of business support.

It is probable that two types of job coaches are necessary—a senior coach, with either a bachelor's or master's degree, and a junior person. The senior person would provide job development and placement, initial intensive training, and employer relations work. Once the client becomes "stabilized" at the job site with greatly reduced staff assistance, then a less skilled job coach may be employed for follow-along (Harold Russell Associates, 1985). Much more emphasis must be placed on job development and placement skills, behavioral training, and work with parents, social security representatives, and other key agencies. In short, rehabilitation, special education, business, and social work skills are essential for effectiveness in this role.

There are, of course, a number of ways to meet staffing needs. For example, there is the intact unit approach that many rehabilitation facilities and other special center-based programs might find attractive. With this approach, approximately $20,000 (including fringe benefits) would be allotted for the senior staff person, $10,000 for the junior person, and $5,000 for travel and supplies for a total of $35,000. This group could expect to place approximately 12 persons with severe mental disabilities annually. Data from the Virginia group show that 66%–75% of placed individuals have retained their job for 6 months by the end of such a program (Wehman, 1981).

Another approach might be to deploy a small team of senior job coaches who, upon completion of placement and training of clients, turn over their cases to follow-along and retention specialists who have a much larger caseload of businesses in close geographical proximity. Undoubtedly, there is no shortage of ways to delegate the deployment of staff.

Facility Issues Related to Supported Competitive Employment

Supported competitive employment programs are labor intensive, not capital intensive. Therefore, a large facility to house persons with disabilities during the day is not needed since work with clients will take place directly in business and industry. From a cost standpoint, this factor is an attractive feature of this type of vocational option. Many supported employment programs (Rusch, 1986) are established on this basis. However, there is also no reason why effective placement and training programs cannot occur in community-based adult day programs, rehabilitation facilities, schools, and vocational technical centers. If, in fact, there already is an aggregate of professional personnel existing in a given setting, then it may be possible to redeploy some of these persons into supported competitive employment activities.

In Virginia, there are local rehabilitation facilities that receive rehabilitative case service funds to provide supported competitive employment for at-risk clients (Hill et al., 1987). As noted earlier in this chapter, facilities may become involved in transitional and supported employment services until clients become stabilized in their new job. This adjustment period may last from 4 to 12 weeks. At this point, the participating staff and business decide the level of involvement necessary by the supported employment specialist. Follow-along employment support services are then funded by the local mental health/mental retardation services. The resulting costs are typically much lower (Wehman & Hill, 1985). It appears that this approach has been one successful way to implement the program; however, it is probably too early to evaluate these efforts. Schools can also be logical settings for supported competitive employment efforts. With such high levels of national support for transition from school to work, many schools are experiencing greater amounts of pressure to provide placement for students with severe disabilities before graduation.

Although it has not been determined which settings are ideal, all of the settings described may be appropriate with the right staff attitudes, funding base, and local economy.

Needs and Concerns Related to Supported Competitive Employment and Severe Disabilities

It would not be appropriate to close without emphasizing that a supported work approach to competitive employment has definite potential to meet the needs of individuals with several types of severe disabilities. Nationally, the majority of the supported competitive employment programs have focused on persons with mild or severe retardation, individuals with autism, severe physical disabilities, head injuries, and significant psychiatric impairments. Each of these populations exhibits characteristics in travel, social skills, communication, and other adaptive behaviors that have reduced their likelihood for competitive employment. The amount of staff intervention that would be required and the amount that would be distributed over the duration of an individual's employment is unknown. Furthermore, the necessity for specific job coach competencies may vary according to the type of disability.

The overriding issue, however, is not about the type of disability, but whether or not the person will be able to gain and maintain employment. If not, then a supported competitive employment arrangement may be planned and undertaken by an appropriate service provider.

MOBILE WORK CREWS AND ENCLAVES

Mobile work crews and enclaves are two employment options for adults with disabilities that have existed for many years (McGee, 1975), but have not received attention within the supported employment initiative until recently (Mank et al., 1986). Both enclaves and work crews allow individuals, who were previously served in sheltered employment alternatives, an opportunity for meaningful employment in more integrated community-based settings. In both options, individuals with severe disabilities are provided continuous ongoing support by a human services professional. This support enables them to succeed in more challenging employment settings. Workers are paid based on performance, and wages are commensurate with those paid to workers without disabilities who are performing the same duties. While similarities exist between the two models, each model is discussed separately to differentiate the array of alternative approaches currently used to implement enclave and work crew options.

Mobile Work Crews

Mobile work crews or work force teams generally comprise four to six individuals with severe disabilities. These individuals spend their day away from a center-based rehabilitation facility or adult vocational program to perform service jobs in community settings. Mobile work crews may operate independently as private, nonprofit corporations, or may be a component of a large array of employment options operated by a rehabilitation or adult service agency. Whatever the organizational structure, the sponsoring agency contracts with community businesses or individuals to perform groundskeeping, janitorial, home maintenance, or similar tasks. Workers are generally paid by the sponsoring agency based upon productivity.

A training supervisor or manager who accompanies the crew on a full-time basis is responsible for training work crew members, providing ongoing supervision to maintain productivity and quality control, and guaranteeing that the contracted work is completed to required standards. The supervisor is

also responsible for all aspects of the operation, including securing and nego-
tiating contracts, training and supervising crew members, and maintaining
program records. While the small size of the crew allows for intense supervision and the inclusion of individuals with significant learning and production
problems, the reliance on a single staff member makes the operation of the
crew challenging. Since the crew functions away from the service agency or
rehabilitation facility, the manager is often isolated from other professionals.
Also, the need to provide continuous supervision to crew members often
makes it difficult for the supervisor to perform the required contract procurement and administrative activities. In larger communities, establishing a number of crews may be one way in which direct service and management functions may be shared to maximize total program effectiveness.

The flexibility of the work crew, both in terms of the type of work
performed and the make-up of the crew, allows the model to accommodate the
needs of individuals with a wide array of disabilities. The majority of work
performed is in the area of building and grounds maintenance, although
housecleaning in suburban areas, farm work in rural areas, and motel room
cleaning in areas with large tourist industries have also been identified as
successful alternatives (Mank, 1985). A crew may have contracts with a
number of different agencies and may perform work in a large number of
settings in the course of a week. While work crews have been successful in
areas with high unemployment rates, securing enough contracts to provide
work during all standard work hours is frequently a problem (Mank et al.,
1986).

Mobile work crews are an option that may have particular applicability in
small communities and rural areas. Service agencies in rural areas attempting
to provide supported employment alternatives to persons with severe disabilities face a unique set of challenges. Many rural areas often have a relatively
high unemployment rate. With little or no industrial base, service agencies
encounter serious problems obtaining an adequate amount of work. When
there is only a small number of resources within a large geographical area,
severe logistical problems are created for the agency. In addition, it is often
difficult for the areas to identify and recruit well trained staff who have the
skills necessary to implement supported employment alternatives. A major
strength of the mobile work crew model is its ability to provide stable employment in the types of work found in a local area for a small number of workers
with severe disabilities.

Enclaves

Enclaves are employment options in which small groups of workers with
disabilities (generally six to eight) are employed and supervised among workers without disabilities in a business or industry. Continuous long-term supervision is provided on-site by a trained human services professional or host

company employee. Workers may be employed directly by the business or industry, or remain employees of the nonprofit organization that provides support to the individuals (Rhodes & Valenta, 1985). Enclave members work alongside others performing the same work, although in some situations, workers with disabilities may be grouped together to facilitate training and supervision.

Enclaves provide an excellent alternative to both supported competitive employment and traditional sheltered employment. They also provide intensive on-site supervision designed to maximize worker productivity and prevent job termination. This will allow access to community-based employment settings for workers with substantial disabilities who might otherwise be unsuccessful when daily training and supervision is decreased during the follow-along stage of supported competitive employment. At the same time, enclaves provide extended employment in an integrated community setting for individuals who have traditionally been served in segregated workshops or work activity centers.

The model may also be contrasted with the mobile work crew approach. Crew workers will generally move to different work settings on a daily basis or may even work at several different sites in the course of a single day. Enclave employees are able to work in a single setting for a prolonged period of time. In addition, enclave employees, in some instances, will be paid wages and receive benefits directly from the company, whereas work crew members will remain employees of the sponsoring service agency indefinitely. In one case (Rhodes & Valenta, 1985) workers who had reached 65% of standard productivity were hired as employees of the host company at a competitive rate and with full fringe benefits.

The critical feature of the enclave model is the extended training and supervision provided to address low worker productivity and difficulties in adaptation to changing work demands. Systematic intervention is necessary to allow workers to acquire the needed skills and produce at an acceptable rate. This extra support may be provided by the host company but, in most instances, the support is the responsibility of the sponsoring service agency. The enclave supervisor is the person responsible for providing this extra support. It is a major commitment for the company to hire a group of workers with severe disabilities and allow the involvement of an outside service organization. The enclave supervisor must be highly skilled in effective instruction and supervision techniques, as well as sensitive to the production demands and concerns of the host company.

Major Outcomes Associated with Mobile Work Crews and Enclaves

Some positive outcomes associated with mobile work crews and sheltered enclaves are the physical and social integration of individuals with severe disabilities in natural work settings with the opportunity to earn significant

wages. Wages paid to work crew and enclave members are based upon productivity, with members earning a percentage of the standard hourly wage for
individuals performing similar work. Since the workers are usually clients of
a nonprofit service agency, fringe benefits are generally not provided; however, public costs are required to make up the excess costs incurred due to low
worker productivity and the need for intense, continuous supervision (Cho,
1983).

Mank et al. (1986) report data from two mobile work crew agencies in
which individuals earned from $130 to $185 per month. After 8 months of
employment, Rhodes and Valenta (1985) report earnings of $295 for an en-
clave of six individuals. While these figures may not seem particularly high,
they are quite significant when compared to earnings of clients in sheltered
employment alternatives (Noble, 1985). For example, in the enclave described above (Rhodes & Valenta, 1985) the individuals involved had aver-
aged wages of less than $40 per month prior to placement in the enclave.

The outcomes associated with the work crew and enclave options must
be evaluated in the context of the individuals served by these models. In most
cases, workers are not making maximum wage or only making a percentage
of the prevailing competitive wage, and public costs for the programs are not
significantly reduced from the costs of traditional workshop programs. Despite monetary concerns, the models are very justifiable on the grounds that
they provide employment in integrated settings for individuals who traditionally would have had no opportunity for such work. Individuals with medical conditions (e.g., seizure disorders or severe diabetes) or individuals who
exhibit significant maladaptive behaviors (e.g., stereotypic or inappropriate
behavior) may finally have an opportunity to secure and maintain employment
in a natural work setting.

SUPPORTED COMPETITIVE EMPLOYMENT:
ILLUSTRATIONS OF COMPETENCE

Michael is a 22-year-old student currently in his last year of school at a
segregated special education center, which he has attended since he was 6
years old. Testing psychologists have assessed him as having severe mental
retardation according to his scores on standardized intelligence tests. Michael's medical records report no significant sensory, perceptual, or motor
problems, but he has a history of epilepsy that has been successfully controlled for 3 years through daily medication. His school records indicate that
his speech is clear, although he interacts minimally with others using short,
incomplete sentences. Michael has acquired simple counting skills, basic
word recognition skills, some coin discrimination, and the ability to tell time
to the hour. He has a history of aggressive behavior. His family is very
supportive and encourages Michael to interact with peers and to use the public
bus system.

Michael has participated in a community-based vocational training program through his school for 3 years. Three days a week, Michael and four other students practice janitorial skills at a local business under the supervision of their special education teacher. Michael's major responsibilities include buffing, mopping, dusting, vacuuming, and emptying trash. His teacher describes Michael as a slow, steady worker who can complete up to three tasks independently with minimal supervision and reinforcement.

At the age of 21, Michael was referred to the vocational rehabilitation agency for employment services by the special education teacher at his school. The rehabilitation counselor made arrangements to provide Michael with transitional supported work services. A job coach met with Michael, his special education and vocational teachers, his rehabilitation counselor, and his family to discuss specific vocational goals and employment options. The transition term decided that a part-time job utilizing Michael's janitorial skills would be an appropriate and desired employment outcome.

After a thorough job/client match was completed by his job coach, Michael was hired as a maintenance worker in a local department store for 20 hours a week at a starting salary of $4.25 per hour. His job provided all employee benefits, including medical and dental insurance, paid vacation, sick leave, and an employee discount. As a maintenance worker, his major job responsibilities were to vacuum the carpet in nine departments of the store 4 days a week and to move the clothing fixtures and vacuum underneath them once a week. Prior to Michael's placement on the job, the job coach spent several days learning the job and developing a task analysis for use in training Michael. The job coach also determined the coworkers' production rates, and planned strategies for training Michael's job skills and increasing his production rate. School and transportation arrangements were made so that Michael could walk to work in the morning and ride the bus back to school in the afternoon.

A job coach accompanied Michael to work every day to provide training and support services and to model appropriate interactions with coworkers and customers. Training and production data were recorded daily to monitor his progress. Michael had acquired basic vacuuming skills in his vocational training program, but had difficulty generalizing these skills to a new environment and needed assistance with learning new patterns. Because Michael was easily distracted and failed to look at the clock, he was often unable to complete the job or take his break at the appropriate time. The job coach developed a work schedule based on the average time needed by Michael, the job coach, and his coworkers to complete the job. The schedule helped Michael to take his break on time and to leave work after he had completed designated sections of work. If production rates were maintained, Michael could finish in time to take a break with his coworkers and be able to stop at a fast food restaurant for lunch before catching the bus back to school.

By the end of 4 weeks, Michael was completing the job with 95%–100% accuracy and maintaining the established competitive performance rates. The job coach gradually began to decrease the amount of time spent training Michael directly, but remained on the job site to provide reinforcement, collect data, and provide supervision as needed. Over the next few weeks, the job coach continued to reduce intervention time with Michael. Eventually, he only had to make monthly follow-up visits to the job site. After 3 months of employment, Michael's salary was raised to $4.50 per hour and his supervisor reported that his work was "better than required."

Michael's teacher and family describe him as being more social and more mature since he began working. Additionally, they report that he is interacting with his peers more frequently, participating in more community activities, and independently initiating grooming skills. Michael has learned to cash his paycheck at a local bank each payday. He purchases clothing, records, food, and contributes to household expenses with his salary. His teachers report that he is admired by his peers at school, whom he frequently advises about the role of a working adult. His job coach, rehabilitation counselor, special education teacher, and family continue to work cooperatively with Michael to provide ongoing support services and to plan for independent living goals as he prepares to leave school.

Kathy, a 21-year-old student with Down syndrome, is currently finishing her final year of public school in a self-contained class for students with moderate mental retardation that is situated in an elementary school. She spends most of her day learning pre-academic and prevocational skills. She has minimal interaction with her peers and with her local community. Kathy speaks in short sentences, but her speech is difficult to understand for people who do not know her well. Kathy's records report no significant medical, academic, or psychological problems, other than obesity. Her teacher and family report that she is independent in many self-care skills, but that she often needs verbal prompting to initiate and complete routines. Her teacher describes her as "stubborn, and often flirtatious."

During her last year of school, Kathy was referred for supported employment services offered by her school system. At a transitional IEP meeting, Kathy, her special education teacher, vocational rehabilitation counselor, parents, and job coach targeted a part-time position in a fast food restaurant near Kathy's home. Because Kathy had no previous vocational training, the job coach spent a great deal of time assessing her work skills and her related vocational skills to ensure an appropriate job match. Kathy's family was hesitant and required reassurance by the job coach that Kathy would not lose her social security benefits and would receive continued support while employed.

Kathy's job coach secured a crew member position for her at a fast food restaurant that was located near her home and school. The job coach spent several days analyzing the position and developing a strategy for training Kathy before she was actually employed. The job coach also targeted city bus training for Kathy so that she could eventually ride to and from work independently. Kathy was hired to work 5 days a week for a total of 30 hours. Her salary was set at $4.50 per hour without benefits since she is only a part-time worker.

During the first month of Kathy's employment, her job coach accompanied her to work every day and assisted Kathy in completing nearly 90% of the job. Kathy's job duties included busing tables when customers were through eating, washing and drying food trays, and emptying the trash from the kitchen and dining area. The job coach used verbal cues, modeling, and, in some instances, physical prompting to train Kathy to compete her job sequence. The job coach designed a series of picture cue cards to help Kathy to follow her schedule, to complete her work, and to take a break at the appropriate time. Kathy's special education teacher and job coach, in cooperation with her family, taught Kathy about independent grooming skills (e.g., applying make-up, hair styling, and selecting the right clothes) to improve her appearance on the job. With the assistance of her job coach, Kathy is learning to interact appropriately with her coworkers during her break and they, in turn, are learning how to interact with her. In addition, Kathy's job coach is modeling appropriate social skills so that she learns to respond politely and interact with the restaurant's customers.

Gradually, over the next 2 months, Kathy's job coach reduced the intervention time spent directly with Kathy. Kathy is now able to complete almost 60% of her job and is able to ride the bus to and from work with minimal assistance from her job coach. The job coach still accompanies Kathy daily at work, but now spends more time observing Kathy and collecting production data than actually assisting Kathy with completing the job.

Kathy has received a favorable evaluation from her work supervisor who was at first reluctant to hire an individual with a severe disability. Through the use of the supported competitive employment model, Kathy is quickly becoming a productive employee. Her parents, teacher, vocational rehabilitation counselor, and job coach anticipate that she will be successfully employed with minimal support services from the job coach by the time she leaves school at the end of the year.

PARALLELISM BETWEEN CONSUMER ADVOCACY AND SUPPORTED EMPLOYMENT

While these case studies exemplify supported employment in action, they are also a good illustration of how supported employment is consumer-oriented. Both clients attained a higher level of vocational performance and a greater amount of dignity by working in the mainstream of society. There are numerous overlaps in philosophies as well as a significant number of parallels between the recent emphasis on consumerism and the supported employment programs that have rapidly emerged across the United States. All persons who are working in the field of disability, especially those who are service providers, should be aware of the following philosophies and parallels:

1. *The focal point of consumer advocacy and supported employment is persons with disabilities.* Traditionally, programs that provide services to people with disabilities have done so in large groups and in an aggregate format (i.e., sheltered workshops, large institutional settings). Supported employment does just the opposite. Effective supported employment programs, for the most part, provide individualized services and support to the individual worker based on his or her wants and needs. For example, if a consumer has a brain injury and, therefore, does not want or need frequent visits to the work site from an employment specialist, then the employment specialist will try to respect that wish. In contrast, if a person with a long-term mental illness is extremely nervous and anxious about employment, as is a family member, then the employment specialist will make him- or herself available on a more frequent basis.

2. *Real work is the desired outcome of consumer advocates and supported employment programs.* In many of the programs that serve individuals with disabilities, the outcomes and goals are unclear. The bureaucracy of service delivery seems to suffocate the whole intent of the program. The individual with a disability is classically lost "in the shuffle." A major strength of both the consumer advocacy movement and the supported employment movement is that the goals and outcomes are very clear in terms of desired outcomes. A competitive job, which provides the opportunity to earn a decent wage and work in good conditions, is paramount. This type of singular focus becomes very empowering to the professionals, advocates, and consumers who work in this environment. Each person knows their purpose and how their success or lack of progress will be measured.

3. *Consumers participating in consumer advocacy and/or supported employment programs have had their potential grossly underutilized.* The human potential of many persons with disabilities has been "wasted." Professionals, as well as members of the business and industry community, have considered these people as having little to offer, as being too expensive to work with, and, overall, as being poor investments for vocational rehabilitation. To be written off in this manner could be devastating to a person's self-esteem. Yet, that is exactly what has happened, resulting in perhaps the most striking parallel between the two movements. The same motivations that encouraged people to write the ADA were shared by the advocates who promoted supported employment opportunities for people with mental disabilities.

4. *Supported employment and consumer advocacy programs have proven themselves to be sustainable.* Weak programs, weak concepts, and "flash-in-the-pan" innovations will not last. Agency heads will not fund such programs, and the type of outcome data that warrants funding in tight times will not be generated. Supported employment began approximately twelve years ago and has endured two recessions. Supported employment has stood the test of 37 out of 50 states running deficits within the last year; it has withstood the frequent detractors who are only satisfied with the status quo of human services delivery programs. Consumer advocacy programs and other advocates of the ADA have fought for over 5 years, in some cases even longer, to acquire the type of federal legislation that can begin to change society's attitudes toward people with disabilities.

Consumer advocacy has staying power. The best concepts are not only those that work, but those that make sense to people on a moral and common sense basis. It is wise to seek input from the people who are being served in disability programs. These individuals could help run and take leadership roles in the programs, as well as provide feedback on ways to change the programs. It is only a matter of time before this type of consumer advocacy and involvement will thrive.

CHALLENGES OF CONSUMER ADVOCACY AND SUPPORTED EMPLOYMENT

There are a number of issues which must be taken into account and resolved as we consider the parallelism of consumer advocacy and supported employment concepts. The first issue regards the different constituencies that comprise each of these concepts. For example, in recent years, the consumer advocacy movement is more closely identified to by people with physical disabilities and by other groups of people with disabilities who are able to articulate for themselves. These persons are able to express their needs, wishes, and hopes in terms of society's responsiveness.

In contrast, supported employment has been and continues to be more closely aligned with persons who have mental retardation or are labelled as having a mental illness. These are people who are often unable to clearly articulate for themselves, or who seldom receive the respect necessary to make their wishes and needs known. Subsequently, the concept of an employment specialist or a job coach, who would assist these individuals in gaining entry into the labor force, was developed. In fact, in the late 1970s, when the author began his work in supported employment, the term used to identify the supported employment service provider was "trainer–advocate." This term was used so that the dual role of the employment specialist would be recognized. In order to resolve this issue of varying constituencies, these two major groups, made up of persons with physical and mental disabilities, must communicate more frequently and learn to understand the differing points of view that each group holds. Together, both groups can make the changes in the service provision system for persons with disabilities.

A second very powerful issue is that those who are identified most closely with consumer advocacy generally have a number of goals that they wish to achieve in systems change. These goals involve transportation, personal care attendants, and improvements in quality of residential choices, and have become paramount and overriding factors for thousands of people who are promoting greater consumer advocacy. Specifically, this means that as important as a positive vocational outcome is, there are other factors that are equally, if not more, important. Persons who are primarily identified as supporters of integrated and supported employment programs tend to have a somewhat more limited agenda. These persons want to see changes occur mainly in the vocational aspects of the system. In this sense, both groups have much to offer each other, since there are many people with physical disabilities who could greatly benefit from supported employment. Similarly, many supported employment participants and staff need to take an activist role in other important life areas (e.g., transportation or independence in community living).

A third issue that needs to be resolved between the two groups is very simple, but has a great deal of depth. Specifically, consumer advocacy proponents do not always understand the philosophies or practices that are associated with supported employment. At the same time, individuals who feel that supported employment is the only type of service issue do not recognize the consumer satisfaction, independence, and nonwork disability incentive issues that occur on a daily basis for people who are associated with consumer advocacy programs. It is essential that both groups begin to attend each other's conferences. There needs to be more professional communication and a greater integration of mutual goals. The power that both groups can have, if they work together as a cohesive lobbying force, is limitless. Together, they can have a tremendous impact on changing attitudes, values, and practices in society, as well as an influence on state and federal legislative action.

WHAT DOES THE FUTURE HOLD?

A very exciting vision of the future can be seen. This future merges the best of consumer advocacy, consumer involvement with sophisticated job matching technologies, and business and industry commitments. Assistive technology, electronics, robotics, and technological devices that have not yet been invented will enter the work place to help empower the worker with a disability, his or her coworker or supervisor, and, as needed, his or her employment specialist. In a sense, the employment specialist, other agents of supported employment programs, or centers for independent living will provide the impetus for these technologies to be implemented.

The future of consumer advocacy programs, supported employment programs, centers for independent living, technology transfer, and human behavioral interventions are limitless. The greatest opportunities ever available to integrate persons with disabilities into the labor force are now at hand. As the United States economy comes out of the recession, there will be jobs in all sectors, part-time and full-time, for persons with disabilities. The service delivery system and the community must work together to make this a reality.

CONCLUSION

The purpose of this chapter has been to provide information related to supported employment. In recent years there has been greater emphasis than ever before on helping individuals who have been unable to enter the labor force because of the severity of their disability. The statutory framework of the ADA and the emerging training technologies of supported employment have helped to fuel this movement.

One of the major advantages of supported employment programs is that all parties benefit; that is, business gains qualified labor with support of a job coach, the family's anxieties and concerns are reduced, the client receives individualized training, and the government's costs are reduced (Kregel, 1992). The community and the family play a critical role in helping unemployed workers with disabilities to obtain and maintain jobs.

The influence of the ADA on improved supported employment outcomes and opportunities is, as of yet, unknown; however, with the statutory regulations in place, it would certainly appear that greater work opportunity would occur for all persons with disabilities who want to work. The U.S. Senate Subcommittee on Employment of the Handicapped report (1986) revealed that 67% of all Americans with disabilities (ages 16–64) were not working. Of those who were working, 75% worked part-time. Is this the best that society can do for persons with disabilities? It is hoped that the ADA, along with supported employment programs and other innovative approaches, will lead to positive changes in the employment outlook for all persons with disabilities.

REFERENCES

Apter, D. (1992). A successful competitive/supported employment program for people with severe visual disabilities. *Journal of Vocational Rehabilitation, 2*(1), 21–27.
Burke, W., Wesolowski, M., & Guth, M. (1988). Comprehensive head injury rehabilitation: An outcome evaluation. *Brain Injury, 2,* 313–322.
Cho, D.W. (1983). An alternate employment model for handicapped persons. *Journal of Rehabilitation Administration, 8,* 55–63.
Federal Register. (June 24, 1992). State supported employment service program; find rules, pp. 28432–28442.

Harold Russell Associates. (1985) *Final Report: Consensus seminar, proceedings and recommendations.* Unpublished manuscript.

Hill, M., Hill, J., Wehman, P., Revell, G., Noble, J., & Dickerson, A. (1987). Supported employment: An interagency funding model for persons with severe disabilities. *Journal of Rehabilitation, July–September,* 13–20.

Kregel, J. (1992). The subtle and salient points of program evaluation: An illustration from supported employment. *Journal of Vocational Rehabilitation, 2*(2), 53–61.

Lorenzini, B. (1992, May 20). The accessible restaurant: Part II, employee accommodation. *Restaurants and Institutions,* 150–156.

Mank, D. (1985). *Work and quality of life: Personal description from the Specialized Training Program.* Unpublished manuscript.

Mank, D.M., Rhodes, L.E., & Bellamy, G.T. (1986). Four supported employment alternatives. In W.E. Kiernan & J.A. Stark (Eds.), *Pathways to employment for adults with developmental disabilities* (pp. 139–153). Baltimore: Paul H. Brookes Publishing Co.

McDonald-Wilson, K., Revell, G., Nguyen, S., & Peterson, M. (1991). Supported employment outcomes for people with psychiatric disability. *Journal of Vocational Rehabilitation, 1*(2), 30–44.

McGee, J. (1975). *Work stations in industry.* Omaha: University of Nebraska.

Noble, J. (1985, June 9). *Employment outcomes for people with developmental disabilities.* Unpublished paper, University Affiliated Program, Richmond, VA.

Parent, W., Kregel, J., & Wehman, P. (1992). *Vocational integration index.* Stoneham, MA: Andover Medical Publishers.

Rhodes, L., & Valenta, L. (1985). Industry based supported employment. *Journal of The Association for Persons with Severe Handicaps, 10,* 12–20.

Rusch, F.R. (Ed.). (1986). *Competitive employment issues and strategies.* Baltimore: Paul H. Brookes Publishing Co.

Sowers, J., & Powers, L. (1991). *Vocational preparation and employment of students with physical and multiple disabilities.* Baltimore: Paul H. Brookes Publishing Co.

U.S. Senate. Subcommittee on Disability. (1986). *Senate Subcommittee on Employment of the Handicapped report.* Washington, DC: U.S. Department of Education.

Wehman, P. (1981). *Competitive employment: New horizons for severely disabled individuals.* Baltimore: Paul H. Brookes Publishing Co.

Wehman, P. (1991, September). Paper presented on national supported employment outcomes to supported employment state directors, Washington, DC.

Wehman, P., & Hill, J. (1985). *Competitive employment for persons with mental retardation: From research to practice, Volume 1.* Richmond: Virginia Commonwealth University, Rehabilitation Research and Training Center.

Wehman, P., & Moon, M.S. (Eds.). (1988). *Vocational rehabilitation and supported employment.* Baltimore: Paul H. Brookes Publishing Co.

Wehman, P., Sale, P., & Parent, W. (1992). *Supported employment: From research to practice.* Stoneham, MA: Andover Medical Publishers.

West, M., Callahan, M., Lewis, M.B., Mast, M., & Sleight, L. (1991). Supported employment and assistive technology for individuals with physical impairments. *Journal of Vocational Rehabilitation, 1*(2), 29–39.

Chapter 5

Provisions of Reasonable Accommodation
What Do Employers Think?

Craig Michaels,
Paola Nappo,
Karen Barrett,
Donald A. Risucci,
and Charles Wm. Harles

Many professionals would argue that service delivery to persons with disabilities in the United States has changed dramatically since Wolfensberger (1970) first described the implications of the normalization principle as practiced in Scandinavian countries. Normalization dictates that "[all]

Preparation of this chapter was supported in part by the Rehabilitation Services Administration of the United States Department of Education through grant funds to the National Center for Disability Services to provide rehabilitation services to individuals with severe disabilities (Grant #H128A91055); however, the opinions herein do not necessarily reflect the position or policy of the Rehabilitation Services Administration or the United States Department of Education. We gratefully acknowledge the assistance of Lana Smart and Gary Kishanuk of the Industry-Labor Council of the National Center for Disability Services for making it possible to conduct the research presented in this chapter.

persons should be exposed to experiences that are likely to elicit or maintain normative (accepted) behavior" (Wolfensberger, 1970, p. 292). This principle also states that service provision by helping professionals should "enable a deviant person [Wolfensberger's use of the term deviant person is more appropriately replaced by 'person with a disability'] to function in ways considered to be within the acceptance norms of his society" (p. 291).

In recent years, the United States has witnessed the passage of the Rehabilitation Act of 1973 (PL 93-112) and its accompanying amendments; the passage of the Education for All Handicapped Children Act of 1975 (PL 94-142) (now known as the Individuals with Disabilities Education Act or IDEA) and its accompanying amendments; the passage of the Vocational Education Amendments of 1976; and, more recently, and perhaps most significantly, the passage of the Americans with Disabilities Act (ADA) (PL 101-336). Unfortunately, Wolfensberger's early warning that the principle of normalization is "deceptively simple" needs to be reiterated again today (Wolfensberger, 1970, p. 291). Rehabilitation professionals, parents, advocates, and consumers need to be cautioned that the tenets of the ADA may also be "deceptively simple." Now is not a time for complacency in relation to employment, community adjustment, or the full inclusion of individuals with severe disabilities.

People only need to carefully review the Bush administration's reform plan for the American public education system, *America 2000; An education strategy* (1991), to realize the real and immediate need for continued advocacy and lobbying to promote the dignity, value, and worth of all Americans. America 2000 (1991), which follows right on the heels of the ADA, speaks of setting up schools that will establish *new world-class standards in science and mathematics,* but fails to mention persons with disabilities in any of the reforms. The work of rehabilitation and special education professionals since the 1970s, that is, the identification and promotion of successful outcomes for youth with disabilities and the development of curricula and procedures to promote transition either to employment (Will, 1984) or to community (i.e., employment, adjustment to the residential environment, development of social/interpersonal networks) (Halpern, 1985) have been virtually ignored. Pawelski (1991) warns that:

the education goals as stated [in America 2000] are disappointing. The emphasis on content areas (i.e., reading, writing, and arithmetic!) and on striving as a nation to be number one in science and math by the year 2000 is shortsighted and demeaning; and it excludes the millions of Americans who will *never* [Pawelski's use of italics] achieve in those areas. America 2000 sets the stage for an elitist posture in education that could be dangerous to the very core of American values. (p. 283)

One lesson that society should have learned since the 1970s is that legislation alone does not, and will not, change attitudes. Furthermore, legislation will also not, in and of itself, bring us any closer to the realization of an America where all citizens are valued members of society.

DEFINING THE CONCEPT
OF REASONABLE ACCOMMODATION

The Section 503 regulations of the Rehabilitation Act of 1973 were the first laws to familiarize all employers who receive federal contracts or subcontracts with the basic notion of providing reasonable accommodations for qualified workers with disabilities. The Section 504 regulations require the same from all employers receiving federal monies and colleges and universities. Now, the passage of the ADA has further solidified the concept of reasonable accommodation, extending it to both smaller employers and employers who are not federal contractors or recipients of federal monies. As defined in the ADA, reasonable accommodation refers to a change in the work environment that will help a person with a disability function more productively. An accommodation is traditionally judged to be "reasonable" by the employer and/or supervisor based not only on the basis of cost, but also on its impact upon the actual job performance of the person with a disability. This concept of providing job accommodations for employees, or potential employees, with disabilities may seem "deceptively simple," especially when viewed in relation to the promotion and the sustainment of integrated competitive employment for individuals with severe disabilities.

The final regulations for the ADA further define reasonable accommodation as:

> modifications or adjustments to the work environment, or to the manner or circumstances under which the position held or desired is customarily performed, that enable a qualified individual with a disability to perform the essential functions of that position. (*Federal Register,* July 26, 1991, p. 35735)

These regulations describe accommodations as falling into three categories. This conceptual breakdown is based on the various aspects of employment and not on the type of accommodation or the investment of resources required to make the accommodation. The ADA describes the three categories of reasonable accommodations as follows:

(1) accommodations that are required to ensure equal opportunity in the application process;
(2) accommodations that enable the employer's employees with disabilities to perform the essential functions of the position held or desired; and
(3) accommodations that enable the employer's employees with disabilities to enjoy equal benefits and privileges of employment as are enjoyed by employees without disabilities. (*Federal Register,* July 26, 1991, p. 35744)

Michaels (1989a) and Young and Michaels (1986) have also conceptualized workplace accommodations as falling into three categories. Their conceptualization, however, focuses on the actual types of accommodations being provided and not on their position in the employment process. They describe the three categories of accommodations as: "(1) environmental modifications—

removal of architectural barriers; (2) equipment modifications—provision of assistive devices and special tools; and (3) procedural modifications— restructuring tasks, altering work methods, and changing work schedules" (Michaels, 1989a, p. 71).

The authors point out that while employers seem to be somewhat comfortable and familiar with providing environmental and equipment modifications, they continue to be reluctant to make procedural modifications. They also state that procedural modifications tend to be the most indefinite category of accommodations. This category almost always requires individual negotiation on a case-by-case basis because even persons with the same disability do not necessarily require the same type or form of accommodation.

Another potentially useful way of conceptualizing accommodations is through the investment of resources. This approach may, in fact, prove to be the most appropriate conceptualization for integrated competitive employment of persons with severe disabilities. The investment can be in terms of actual expense (e.g., purchase of adaptive computer equipment, installation of curb cuts) or in the allocation of staff time (e.g., the provision of extended one-to-one directions). In addition, the investment may need to be made only on a time-limited basis when an individual is initially hired. It may, however, require an ongoing investment of resources for the life of the given individual's employment.

Madeline Will's (1984) famous "Bridges" transition model can easily be adapted to this investment concept of providing accommodations. Will (1984) speaks of three transition bridges leading from school to work. She calls the first bridge "transition without special services." In the investment concept of accommodations, this first bridge does not represent any special investment of resources; in other words, there is not a need for special accommodations. This level might be appropriate for an individual with a disability who has developed appropriate compensatory strategies, which are both self-initiated and self-monitored. Will describes the second bridge as "transition with time-limited services." In the investment model, this level can be described as an initial investment. Accommodations will be provided for the hiring and training of an individual with a disability. The underlying assumption made at this second level is that the provisions are time-limited. Once the individual has been provided with the initial accommodations, he or she will no longer require them. The individual with a disability will eventually be as productive and socially appropriate as his or her coworkers. Will's final bridge is described as "transition with ongoing services" and has most often been the transitional "bridge of choice" for students with severe disabilities. In the investment model of accommodations, this third bridge describes the need for an ongoing investment of resources, as well as an ongoing commitment on the part of the employer, to accommodate an individual with a disability.

When conceptualizing the provision of reasonable accommodations for individuals with severe disabilities, it is useful to think of the modifications within all three categories mentioned in the ADA regulations (*Federal Register*, July 26, 1991). It is also useful to think in terms of the three categories mentioned by Michaels (1989a) and Young and Michaels (1986). Most important, it is probably critical to conceptualize the provision of these accommodations as requiring an ongoing investment of resources, as described in the third bridge in the Will analogy.

WHAT IS A SEVERE DISABILITY?

In reviewing definitions of severe disabilities that might be appropriate for the purposes of a study that would look at employers' perceptions of accommodations for workers with severe disabilities, emphasis was placed on identifying a definition that could potentially be operationalized in terms of concrete work behaviors. The Rehabilitation Services Administration's (RSA) definition for severity of disability determination for vocational rehabilitation services was selected. The RSA defines persons with severe disabilities (or, in the language of the RSA definition, "individuals with severe handicaps") as meaning an individual:

(1) who has a severe physical or mental disability that seriously limits one or more functional capacities (mobility, communication, self-care, self-direction, interpersonal skills, work tolerance, or work skills) in terms of employability; and

(2) whose vocational rehabilitation can be expected to require multiple vocational rehabilitation services over an extended period of time. (*Federal Register*, January 19, 1981, p. 5552)

In order to determine an individual's functional limitations within the areas mentioned in the RSA definition, the primary authors felt that it would be appropriate to develop a survey for employers that would focus on workplace behaviors. The survey describes the potential employee as an individual with traumatic brain injury (TBI). TBI was selected because:

1. TBI has been termed a "silent epidemic" that affects more than one million Americans each year.
2. The majority of these individuals are 30 years of age or younger and may have more than 40 years left in the work force.
3. Employers tend to have little to no information or experience with this population.
4. Individuals with TBI can manifest behaviors similar to individuals with other severe cognitive, physical, or emotional/psychiatric disabilities; therefore, this population can represent the broad spectrum of workplace behaviors demonstrated by individuals with severe disabilities.
5. There tends to be a lack of professional research data related to employment practices for this population, and more specifically, related to providing workplace accommodations for this population.
6. There is a lack of funds available for ongoing support for this population

(many individuals with TBI do not qualify for developmental disabilities support as they were injured subsequent to the age of 21); thus, the brunt of the responsibility for providing ongoing accommodations to promote and maintain integrated competitive employment of this population will be placed upon the employer.

Improved emergency medical care, advanced life support technology, sophisticated diagnostic equipment, and expanded patient management services have contributed to dramatic increased survival rates among persons with traumatic brain injury (TBI) (Lynch, 1983; Sale, West, Sherron, & Wehman, 1991). It has been estimated that 70% of all TBI survivors will be individuals 30 years of age or younger (Levin, Benton, & Grossman, 1982) and, of these, a majority will live 35–40 years postinjury. Society, however, has not kept pace to provide these individuals and their significant others with vocational and social support to make their lives meaningful and productive (DeJong & Batavia, 1989; Michaels, 1989b). Rates of return to work, although varied, are generally low and decline even more over time (Ben-Yishay, Silver, Piasetsky, & Rattok, 1987; Fraser, Dikmen, McLean, Miller, & Temkin, 1988; Kay, Ezrachi, & Cavallo, 1984; Kreutzer & Morton, 1988; Michaels, 1989b; Vander Kolk, 1991). Follow-up data indicate that "the neurological, psychological, and behavioral sequelae of brain injury are complex and obstruct long-term job retention" (Sale et al., 1991, p. 3). Controversy exists over what the optimal approach to job placement is for those with TBI (Fraser, 1988; Kundu, 1988; Sale et al., 1991; Vander Kolk, 1991). Unfortunately, literature concerning appropriate job accommodations and modification for persons with TBI is virtually nonexistent. Even a recent article (Vander Kolk, 1991), written specifically for job placement specialists on placement strategies for individuals with TBI, fails to mention any possible job accommodations. However, based upon the deficits of most individuals who have sustained brain injury, integrated competitive employment will be predicated upon the ability or willingness of the employer to provide accommodations that fall into the category of procedural modifications (Michaels, 1989a; Young & Michaels, 1986) and that will require an ongoing investment of resources. Parente, Stapleton, and Wheatley (1991), for example, indicate that an individual with TBI may "require considerable structure, cuing, and organization to perform the job effectively. Without this type of help, he or she may not be able to perform or may otherwise be unable to work at competitive speeds" (p. 37).

AN EMPLOYER PERSPECTIVE
ON REASONABLE ACCOMMODATION

The employer survey was conducted to gain a clearer understanding of employers' abilities and their willingness to make accommodations for potential employees with severe disabilities. This information may be very helpful to professionals in the fields of education and rehabilitation. It will help to promote an understanding of what types of accommodations can be considered "potentially reasonable" from the employers' perspectives. The study also sought to understand employers' unwillingness to make various accommodations for individuals with severe disabilities. "Undue hardship" is the most common reason offered for why an accommodation is potentially not reasonable. These reasons can be classified as follows:

1. The provision of the accommodation would not be fair to coworkers.
2. The provision of the accommodation would be too time-consuming for the manager, supervisor, or coworker involved.
3. The provision of the accommodation would be too costly either in terms of actual expenses, downtime, or lack of employee productivity (U.S. Department of Labor Employment Standards Administration, 1982).

Participating Employers

One hundred and thirty-two national companies, many of which are listed among the Fortune 1000, were surveyed in this study. All companies were members of the Industry-Labor Council (ILC) of the National Center for Disability Services. The ILC is a national membership organization of America's most influential companies and labor unions who are committed to improving employment opportunities and the quality of life for persons with disabilities. The ILC was established in 1977 as an outgrowth of the White House Conference on Handicapped Individuals. The organization is responsible for the following: 1) maintaining a telephone information hotline, 2) developing publications on current issues, 3) providing customized and generic training programs, 4) holding seminars and conferences, and 5) providing technical assistance to its members on employment-related issues.

Sixty-four percent, or 85, of the 132 members who were surveyed by mail responded. This response rate is above average, considering the survey was sent to the member representatives of such influential companies. Responding companies employed an average of 31,000 employees. Each person who completed the survey had direct responsibility for the supervision of approximately 325 employees. There was an equal representation of women and men, most had at least a 4-year college degree and had been with their employer for an average of 12 years. Approximately 12% of the respondents reported that they had a disability themselves and 82% of respondents reported that they had "contact" with people who had disabilities. Complete demographics for respondents are presented in Table 5.1 and demographic statistics for the companies are presented in Table 5.2.

Nature of the Survey

A survey instrument was developed that could directly gather information on potential accommodations for workers with severe disabilities who displayed

Table 5.1. Demographic statistics for survey respondents

Variable (N = 85)	Percentage (%)	M	SD
Sex			
Male	50.6		
Female	49.4		
Respondents with disabilities			
Yes	12.0		
No	88.0		
Highest education level			
Elementary	1.2		
High school	11.1		
Associate's degree	18.5		
Bachelor's degree	24.7		
Some graduate school	9.9		
Master's degree	29.6		
Ph.D.	1.2		
M.D.	3.7		
Contact with people with disabilities			
Yes	81.5		
No	18.5		
Age		42.20	9.98
Years of experience		14.84	10.61
Years with present employer		12.04	9.91
Number of employees responsible for		327.76	1,222.60

functional limitations within the seven critical employment areas mentioned by the RSA in their definition for determining severity of disability. To ensure the content validity of this instrument, a team of experts including a psychologist, a vocational rehabilitation counselor, and a training/placement specialist designed 14 scenarios featuring an employee, or a potential employee, with severe disabilities. Each scenario presents the individual demonstrating a functional limitation within one of the seven areas mentioned in the RSA definition. The same team of experts then brainstormed as many potentially reasonable accommodations as possible for the functional limitation demonstrated within each of the 14 scenarios. From the list of potential reasonable accommodations, the team of experts chose the three that seemed to be the most reasonable.

By embedding each functional limitation within a realistic scenario that might occur in the workplace, the 20 or so minutes each manager would take to complete the survey would, if nothing else, serve as a valuable orientation. It would present examples of creative solutions to accommodate the cognitive, physical, and emotional limitations presented within the scenarios, as well as familiarize the managers with individuals who have disabilities. Since

Table 5.2. Demographic statistics on participating companies

Variable	Percentage (%)	M	SD
Minimum educational requirement			
Yes	24.4		
No	13.4		
Depends on position	62.2		
Minimum physical standards			
Yes	18.5		
No	30.9		
Depends on position	50.6		
Requires pre-employment physical			
Yes	45.5		
No	45.4		
Depends on position	9.1		
Number of employees within company		31377.37	63431.80
Percentage of employees in management		29.07	30.14
Percentage of employees in direct supervision		23.22	22.43
Percentage of employees in clerical		22.44	17.09
Percentage of employees in sales		12.59	14.14
Percentage of employees in production		37.26	21.57
Percentage of employees involved in other		41.55	30.97
Company has employees with the following disabilities[a]			
Learning disability	52.9		
Physical disability	72.9		
Cerebral palsy	24.7		
Epilepsy	54.1		
Mental retardation	28.2		
Psychiatric disability	49.4		
Hearing impairment	64.7		
Visual impairment	50.6		
Traumatic brain injury	25.9		

[a]It should be noted that this question was answered based on the respondents' knowledge only, and not based upon review of personnel files, medical files, and so forth.

there would be little opportunity for the debriefing of employers following completion of the survey, it was critical that employers be left with *a sense of potential* (how a person with severe disabilities might be successfully integrated into the competitive work force) versus a *sense of doubt* (why a person with severe disabilities could never be successfully integrated into the competitive work force).

To further ensure the content validity of both the scenarios and potential accommodations, selected members of a professional advisory council made up of experts within the field of education and rehabilitation, consumers (persons with TBI), and family members reviewed and assisted in the refinement of the scenarios and accommodations. Table 5.3 presents the scenarios developed for each of the seven functional areas and the three potential accommodations developed for each scenario.

Following the refinement of the scenarios and accommodations, an additional column was added next to each accommodation. This column allowed respondents to indicate, for each accommodation, whether it was perceived as "too time-consuming," "not fair to coworkers," or "too costly." If an accommodation presented no potential obstacles, the respondent could check "not a problem."

Finally, to assure that both the survey and the survey instructions were clear and that a potential respondent would understand and be able to complete the survey, a small focus group made up of members of a local Projects With Industry (PWI) employer advisory council were selected to read and fill out the survey. This focus group provided input on the development of the final survey instrument.

Procedure for Collecting Survey Information from Employers The survey was mailed to the membership of the ILC along with a cover letter from the ILC manager. The cover letter gently urged each member to take the time to complete the survey and mail it back. This cover letter also suggested that the functional limitations presented by the hypothetical employee, while generally representative of severe disabilities, would not be representative of any one individual or of all individuals with severe disabilities. Anonymity was guaranteed to each company representative particularly in terms of the demographic information collected from their company. The cover letter assured them that the collected data would be used in aggregate form only, and that comparisons between individual companies would not be made. The letter requested each respondent to:

1. Read each scenario, consider the feasibility of the accommodation suggested, and rank them as a most feasible accommodation, a moderately feasible accommodation, or a least feasible accommodation.
2. Read the list of potential obstacles next to each accommodation. If a certain accommodation presented an obstacle, the representative was instructed to check off the obstacle.
3. Finally, after completing the survey, the representative was asked to rank the three scenarios he or she felt presented the greatest barriers to employment and the three that presented the least barriers to employment.

A second letter was mailed out 3 weeks after the initial letter, which again gently urged each member to return his or her survey. A telephone number was included in this second letter in case potential respondents needed another copy of the survey or had specific concerns or questions. All survey

Table 5.3. Survey instrument scenarios and potential accommodations for workers with severe disabilities

Scenarios	Accommodations
Interpersonal skills	
• Inappropriate during down time	• Structure work flow.
	• Provide additional responsibility.
	• Set strict rules of behavior.
Work tolerance	
• Difficulty learning new tasks	• Minimize distractions.
	• Break down instructions.
	• Allow for short breaks.
• Fatigues easily	• Allow flexible hours.
	• Schedule strenuous work early in the day.
	• Consider a part-time schedule.
• Inattentive during meetings	• Provide one-to-one instruction.
	• Use visual aids.
	• Provide more frequent breaks.
• Difficulty concentrating with background noise	• Place in minimal noise area.
	• Provide instruction in quiet area.
	• Give routine job with minimal concentration requirements.
Work skills	
• Difficulty remembering and organizing work	• Use work log to outline daily routine.
	• Have employee paraphrase instructions.
	• Give daily feedback.
• Unable to complete ancillary job duties	• Develop job sharing situation.
	• Restructure job duties.
	• Request an on-the-job evaluation by a specialist.
• Problems with productivity	• Provide one-to-one instruction.
	• Place in area where fast production is not crucial.
	• Organize work station with supplies readily available.
Self-direction	
• Difficulty initiating work	• Prompting by coworker.
	• Fifteen-minute check-ins with supervisor.
	• Spread out work.
• Difficulty with self-monitoring of actions	• Provide physical demonstration.
	• Provide immediate feedback.
	• Provide written directions.

(continued)

Table 5.3. (*continued*)

Scenarios	Accommodations
• Frequent lateness	• Counsel on procedures. • Restructure work hours. • Set up buddy system.
Communicaton	
• Difficulty expressing thoughts (speech)	• Encourage alternate forms of communication. • Encourage to gather thoughts first. • Ask employee to rephrase.
Self-care	
• Frequent poor appearance	• Provide counseling. • Reinforce on good days. • Review dress code in manual.
Mobility	
• Walks extremely slowly	• Give sedentary job. • Place near an accessible exit. • Set up work station to minimize walking.

results were entered into a database created in SPSS/PC DATA ENTRY II and later analyzed using SPSS/PC.

Results of Survey Information Collected from Employers Table 5.4 provides a summary of participants' responses concerning the feasibility of accommodations related to each of the scenarios described in the survey. For each accommodation, the percentage of respondents who perceived the accommodation as most, moderately, or least feasible is presented. The responses were also calculated for the percentage of respondents who felt that the accommodation was too time-consuming to implement, not fair to coworkers, not cost-effective, or not a problem to implement. The results will first be described within each of the following seven functional areas mentioned by the RSA, and second, in the 14 scenarios (see Table 5.3).

Interpersonal Skills When employees with severe disabilities engage in inappropriate behavior during down time, the majority of respondents indicated that providing additional responsibilities and structuring work flow were feasible accommodations for which there were generally no obstacles. Down time can be defined as the period of time when production drops and/or slows significantly. Both executive and social skills are required by the employee in that he or she may need to: 1) initiate other tasks, 2) "look" busy, and/or 3) slow down work speed in response to the work load. The option of setting strict rules of behavior was generally perceived as the least feasible accommodation, primarily because it is too time-consuming and not fair to coworkers.

Work Tolerance Respondents generally indicated that the following ac-

Table 5.4. Employer responses to survey regarding accommodations for workers with severe disabilities

Scenario	Accommodation	Feasibility			Obstacles			
		Most	Moderate	Least	Too time-consuming	Not fair to coworkers	Not cost-effective	No obstacles
Inappropriate during down time	• Structure work flow.	45.6	38.0	16.5	15.3	10.6	11.8	60.0
	• Provide additional responsibilities.	45.0	41.3	13.8	5.9	11.8	7.1	72.9
	• Set strict rules of behavior.	15.6	16.9	67.5	30.6	23.5	8.2	32.9
Difficulty concentrating learning new tasks	• Minimize distractions.	24.7	55.8	19.5	15.3	9.4	5.9	60.0
	• Break down instructions.	72.0	26.8	1.2	21.2	2.4	3.5	72.9
	• Allow short breaks.	3.9	15.6	80.5	17.6	42.4	25.9	22.4
Difficulty remembering and organizing work	• Use work log to outline routine.	84.1	7.3	8.5	12.9	0.0	3.5	80.0
	• Have employee paraphrase instructions.	14.3	41.6	44.2	28.2	2.4	9.4	54.1
	• Give daily feedback.	6.5	49.4	44.2	38.8	3.5	4.7	47.1
Unable to complete ancillary duties	• Develop job sharing situation.	18.2	42.9	39.0	18.8	27.1	32.9	27.2
	• Restructure job duties.	32.9	29.1	38.0	16.5	40.0	34.1	25.9

(continued)

Table 5.4. (continued)

Scenario	Accommodation	Feasibility			Obstacles			
		Most	Moderate	Least	Too time-consuming	Not fair to coworkers	Not cost-effective	No obstacles
Fatigues easily	• Request on-the-job evaluation.	54.5	24.7	20.8	18.8	4.7	18.8	52.9
	• Allow flexible hours.	12.2	62.2	25.7	1.2	34.1	18.8	40.0
	• Schedule strenuous work early in day.	12.3	23.3	64.4	12.9	5.9	21.2	40.5
	• Consider part-time schedule.	80.8	11.5	7.7	1.2	17.6	20.0	63.5
Difficulty initiating	• Prompting by coworker	5.2	54.5	40.3	21.2	64.7	17.6	9.4
	• 15-minute check-ins with supervisor	3.9	37.7	58.4	69.4	12.9	34.1	7.1
	• Spread out work.	93.7	2.5	3.8	12.9	0.0	9.4	70.6
Difficulty monitoring actions	• Provide physical demonstrations.	32.5	35.1	32.5	23.5	4.7	21.2	49.4
	• Provide immediate feedback.	32.9	36.7	30.4	27.1	1.2	8.2	58.8
	• Provide written instructions.	45.5	22.1	32.5	35.3	1.2	8.2	52.9

Category	Intervention							
Difficulty expressing thoughts (speech)	• Encourage other forms of communication.	27.3	35.1	37.7	30.6	3.5	12.9	57.6
	• Encourage to gather thoughts first.	74.4	21.8	3.8	8.2	1.2	0.0	82.4
	• Ask employee to rephrase.	13.3	37.3	49.3	15.3	1.2	1.2	71.8
Inattentive during meetings	• Provide one-to-one instruction.	56.3	30.0	13.8	37.6	10.6	15.3	43.5
	• Use visual aids.	38.7	48.0	13.3	24.7	1.2	20.0	48.2
	• Provide more frequent breaks.	9.3	16.0	74.7	52.9	18.8	38.8	9.4
Poor appearance	• Provide counseling.	70.9	22.8	6.3	4.7	0.0	3.5	83.5
	• Reinforce on good days.	37.2	44.9	17.9	2.4	0.0	2.4	84.7
	• Review dress code in manual.	10.5	22.4	67.1	4.7	0.0	4.7	72.9
Frequent lateness	• Counsel on procedures.	59.5	16.5	24.1	7.1	2.4	4.7	76.5
	• Restructure work hours.	31.2	35.1	33.8	4.7	37.6	25.9	40.0
	• Set up buddy system.	18.4	42.1	39.5	16.5	42.4	18.8	28.2
Productivity problems	• Provide one-to-one instruction.	45.0	36.3	18.8	34.1	9.4	16.5	45.9
	• Place in area							

(continued)

Table 5.4. (continued)

Scenario	Accommodation	Feasibility			Obstacles			
		Most	Moderate	Least	Too time-consuming	Not fair to coworkers	Not cost-effective	No obstacles
	where production is not crucial.	39.0	18.2	42.9	4.7	27.1	31.8	37.6
	• Organize work—make supplies available.	22.7	46.7	30.7	9.4	8.2	8.2	63.5
Difficulty concentrating with background noise	• Place in minimal noise area.	70.5	27.5	2.5	0.0	12.9	14.1	65.9
	• Provide instruction in quiet area.	26.7	54.7	18.7	10.6	7.1	16.5	58.8
	• Give routine job with minimal concentration requirements.	8.0	12.0	80.0	5.9	25.9	43.5	24.7
Walks very slow	• Give sedentary job.	28.6	35.1	36.4	1.2	25.9	20.0	44.7
	• Place near accessible exit.	13.0	39.0	48.1	0.0	4.7	17.6	62.4
	• Set work station to minimize walking.	70.9	20.3	8.9	2.4	9.4	7.1	72.9

commodations were moderately to highly feasible and that there were no obstacles to their implementation: 1) minimizing noise and distractions in the work area, 2) breaking down instructions for individual employees, 3) providing instruction in a quiet area, 4) providing flexible work hours, and 5) allowing a part-time schedule. The use of one-to-one instruction and visual aids were also considered quite feasible, but too time-consuming. In contrast, providing short breaks or allowing more breaks, scheduling strenuous work early in the day, and providing routine jobs with minimal concentration requirements were not perceived as being cost-effective and were potentially unfair to coworkers.

Work Skills The majority of respondents indicated that the use of work logs to outline daily routines, expert referrals for job evaluation, one-to-one instruction, and organization of work stations in which all supplies are available were all very feasible options and posed no major implementation problems. However, having employees paraphrase instructions and give daily feedback were perceived as too time-consuming to be feasible. Job sharing, restructuring of job duties, and placing employees in work areas where productivity is not crucial were generally perceived as unfair to coworkers and not cost-effective.

Self-Direction For problems related to an employee's ability to direct his or her own behavior, respondents generally thought it feasible to: 1) spread out work, 2) provide physical demonstrations, 3) give immediate feedback, 4) provide written instructions, and 5) offer counseling about procedures, despite the fact that these options were deemed to be somewhat time-consuming. Prompting by coworkers, 15-minute check-ins with supervisors, the development of a buddy system, and the restructuring of work hours, however, were perceived as not cost-effective, too time-consuming, and unfair to coworkers.

Communication The majority of participants responded that for employees with communication difficulties, it was very feasible to ask employees to gather their thoughts before speaking. They also felt that it was feasible to ask employees to rephrase statements and to encourage other forms of communication, but that these latter accommodations were somewhat time-consuming.

Self-Care The majority of respondents felt that it was generally feasible to accommodate an employee with poor personal appearance by providing counseling, offering reinforcement on days when appearance was good, and reviewing the dress code when necessary.

Mobility The majority of respondents felt it was feasible to set up a work station so that minimal walking would be required in order to accommodate an employee who has mobility problems. However, respondents felt it would be less feasible and not cost-effective or fair to coworkers to try to place an employee near an easily accessible exit or to give the employee a sedentary job.

When asked to rank the three scenarios that posed the least obstacles to accommodation, and thus to employment, the majority of respondents identified the scenarios relating to mobility, personal appearance, and concentration in noisy settings. In contrast, the scenarios related to self-direction, work skills, and work tolerance were viewed as presenting the greatest obstacles to accommodation and eventual competitive employment.

General Survey Comments in Relation to Integrated Competitive Employment Overall, survey respondents identified 51.8% of the suggested accommodations as presenting no obstacles. Respondents felt that 17.2% of the accommodations were too time-consuming to implement; 14.9% were not cost-effective; and 13.6% of the suggested accommodations were not fair to coworkers.

Employers were most willing to make the following accommodations: 1) minimizing or removing background noises to improve concentration, 2) counseling to improve poor appearance, and 3) modifying the environment to assist individuals who have mobility problems. Employers also appear to be willing to structure work flow, provide one-to-one instructions, encourage employees to use work logs, provide written instructions, and, when necessary, request an on-the-job evaluation by a rehabilitation specialist.

Employers appear to be reluctant to make accommodations that they perceive as too time-consuming, not cost-effective, or that will ultimately result in creating an employee who deviates from the existing "corporate culture." Employers are least willing to make accommodations related to the performance of ancillary job duties, fatigue, and chronic lateness. Employers also appear hesitant to allow employees to paraphrase instructions, use visual aids when giving instructions, give daily feedback on performance, allow job sharing, and use coworkers to provide instruction or prompting. In general, all accommodations involving coworkers were rated as unreasonable. Respondents tended to prefer to have a supervisor, rather than a coworker, involved in the provision and/or monitoring of any potential accommodation.

While rehabilitation and corporate professionals appear able to collaborate in the initial phases of placement and job training, their views tend to diverge in the employment/job maintenance process. For instance, employers appear willing to provide extended one-on-one instruction, similar to what might be provided by a job coach, while the various aspects of the job are learned. However, individuals with severe disabilities may require several forms of intervention (accommodations) provided simultaneously in order to maintain employment at acceptable levels of productivity (Sale et al., 1991). These accommodations will probably require an ongoing investment of resources and span the three categories of accommodations mentioned by Michaels (1989a) and Young and Michaels (1986): 1) environmental modifications, 2) equipment modifications, and 3) procedural modifications. The interventions will probably also need to be driven by a combination of players, for example, the employee, the job coach or placement specialist, the coworkers, and the employer/supervisor. Although rehabilitation professionals view this as supplying natural supports in the workplace, according to survey results, employers are hesitant to allow coworkers to provide this type of assistance. In addition, employers appear unwilling to allow involvement from ongoing supports. They feel that this may result in a worker who cannot assimilate to the existing corporate culture. At this point, neither employers nor rehabilitation specialists appear able to build in long-term supports (e.g., make the ongoing investment of resources in accommodations) necessary to maintain quality job performance. Initially, these accommodations may not be perceived as cost-effective or fair to coworkers; however, they will eventually help assure job retention of persons with severe disabilities.

Vocational rehabilitation specialists must begin to develop business partnerships that promote opportunities for job internships for persons with severe disabilities prior to actual job placement. These internships, within corporate settings, should be utilized as a method of increasing work tolerance and production, bridging the gap between vocational rehabilitation and employment, and most importantly, providing the potential employee an in-vivo opportunity to become mainstreamed into the corporate culture prior to gaining actual employment. In this way, the likelihood of a better job match, job retention, and the satisfaction of both the individual with the disability and the employer is maximized.

When developing placement opportunities for individuals with severe disabilities, placement specialists must request more detailed job descriptions. A thorough task analysis of all functions described in the job description should then be completed prior to the acceptance of a potential job. In addition to this, placement specialists should consider job shadowing another employee in the desired position for several days to gain insight into the types of direct and indirect ancillary duties that may be required. This will allow the prospective employee, the employer, and the placement specialist to negotiate for the necessary accommodations to ensure a successful job match.

THE ADA AND FULL INCLUSION OF PERSONS WITH SEVERE DISABILITIES

How much impact will the ADA have on employment of persons with disabilities, especially those with severe disabilities? It must first be understood that the ADA is not an affirmative action law, it is an equal opportunity law. The law requires that no covered employer shall:

> discriminate against a qualified individual with a disability because of the disability of such individual in regard to job application procedures, the hiring, advancement, or discharge of employees, employee compensation, job training, and other terms, conditions, and privileges of employment. (42 U.S.C. 12112, Section 102[a])

The ADA does not require preferential treatment, quotas, or affirmative action plans.

The ADA does differ from other civil rights and equal opportunity laws in that it requires individual characteristics to be taken into consideration when determining whether or not equal opportunity has been provided. Indeed it is a violation of the law "not to make a reasonable accommodation to the known physical or mental limitations of an otherwise qualified individual with a disability who is an applicant or employee" (42 U.S.C. 12112, Section 102[a]).

As noted at the beginning of this chapter, the provision of reasonable accommodations would be "deceptively simple" if it was the extent of the law. However, many employers feel that they are now being required, or will be required in the future, to spend large sums of money on accommodations. They hear lawyers telling them of the lawsuits they will face. Yet, persons with disabilities look at the same provision and see jobs being made available to them. In fact, they are being told that they now have the *right* to demand jobs. The question that seems to plague most people is what is the truth?

REASONABLE ACCOMMODATION UNDER THE ADA

The right to "reasonable" accommodation is not without limits. Terms such as "reasonable accommodation," "undue hardship," "qualified individual," and "essential functions" can cause both persons with disabilities and employers to have problems with the employment provisions of the ADA. The person with a disability must be a "qualified individual with a disability" in order to be protected under the law; that is, the person must be able to perform the essential functions of the job with or without reasonable accommodation. The persons with a disability must also have the same education or experience that would be required of any other person (42 U.S.C. 12111, Section 101[8]). Specifically, in the area of personal assistance, many persons with severe disabilities and their advocates feel that the ADA falls particularly short. While the provision of an aide or assistant (e.g., a job coach) to help in the completion of work-related tasks might be deemed a reasonable accommodation, in almost all instances, the provision of a personal assistant in the workplace for non–work-related tasks would *not* be considered reasonable. Obvious questions that must be answered, or at least asked, are: What is "reasonable"? What is "essential"? What really constitutes "undue hardship"?

With regard to whether or not an accommodation has to be made, Congress stated that the duty is usually triggered by a request from a person with a disability. In fact, in the absence of a request, it would be inappropriate to provide an accommodation. To facilitate the implementation of accommodations, Congress has suggested a four step process as follows:

1. Identify barrier(s) to equal opportunity
2. Identify possible accommodations
3. Assess the reasonableness of each in terms of effectiveness and equal opportunity
4. Implement the most appropriate accommodation that does not impose an undue hardship on the employer's operation, or permit the employee to provide his or her own accommodation. (Senate Report 101-116, 1989)

The report also states that the express choice of the employee or applicant shall be given primary consideration unless another effective accommodation exists that would provide a meaningful equal employment opportunity, or that the accommodation requested would pose an undue hardship (Senate Report 101-116, 1989).

The concept of reasonable accommodation applies to all employment decisions, not just those concerning hiring and promotion. As noted earlier in the chapter, reasonable accommodations may include a wide variety of options such as:

1. *Job restructuring, part-time or modified work schedules, or reassignment to a vacant position* This includes eliminating barriers to performance by eliminating nonessential job elements, redelegating assignments, exchanging assignments with another employee, and/or redesigning procedures for task accomplishment.
2. *Modification or adaptation of training practices and procedures in on-the-job training* This includes training at accessible sites and providing materials that are available in accessible formats (i.e., examinations in braille or on tapes, oral exams).
3. *Acquisition or modification of equipment or devices* This includes adaptive hardware or software, talking calculators, telephone handset amplifiers, mechanical page turners, and raised or lowered furniture.
4. *Modification or adaptation of existing facilities as to be accessible to and usable by employees with disabilities* Such accommodations require relocating furniture, building ramps, making restrooms accessible, and installing visible alarms.
5. *Provision of qualified readers for persons with vision impairments or of interpreters for persons with hearing impairments* (42 U.S.C. 12111, Section 101[9])

In addition to these examples listed in the regulations, the Equal Employment Opportunity Commission (EEOC) states that the list is not exhaustive and may also include such things as use of accrued leave or unpaid leave for necessary medical treatment, making employer transportation accessible, or providing personal assistants for page turning or to accompany a person on a business trip (Equal Employment Opportunity Commission and the U.S. Department of Justice, 1991).

An important question for persons with severe disabilities is whether or not "supported employment," or in a more generic sense, the ongoing investment of resources in providing accommodations (as described earlier in this chapter), constitutes a form of "reasonable accommodation." This question is important for all persons who will need long-term support services in order to be able to work in an integrated competitive work environment. The EEOC has noted in its Interpretive Guidance (*Federal Register,* July 26, 1991) that "supported employment" is not necessarily a reasonable accommodation. The EEOC states that:

> whether a particular form of assistance would be required as a reasonable accommodation must be determined on an individualized, case by case basis without regard to whether that assistance is referred to as "supported employment." For example, an employer, under certain circumstances, may be required to provide modified training materials or a temporary "job coach" to assist in the training of a qualified individual with a disability as a reasonable accommodation. However, an employer would not be required to restructure the essential functions of a position to fit the skills of an individual with a disability who is not otherwise qualified to perform the position, as is done in certain supported employment programs. (Equal Employment Opportunity Commission and the U.S. Department of Justice, 1991, p. I-59)

It is acceptable, however, for an employer to make such accommodations or modifications even though they are not required as reasonable accommodations under the ADA (Equal Employment Opportunity Commission and the U.S. Department of Justice, 1991).

It is important to remember that accommodations are made on a case-by-case basis. An employer does not need to be concerned with providing any accommodation unless and until a person with a disability, either an applicant or current employee, requests such an accommodation. Then, and only then, would the process begin of determining whether or not an accommodation is "reasonable."

Employers do not always have to "accommodate" persons with disabilities. If the accommodation would constitute an undue hardship it does not have to be provided. To determine whether or not an accommodation would impose an "undue hardship," the ADA and its regulations establish specific factors. For example, potential cost considerations for undue hardship include:

1. The nature and cost of the accommodation
2. The overall financial resources of the facility(ies) involved, the number of persons employed, and the effect on expenses and resources
3. The number, type, and location of the facility(ies) involved

4. The type of operations, including the composition, structure, and functions of the work force including the geographic separateness
5. The administrative and fiscal relationship between the facility and the overall entity. (*Federal Register*, July 26, 1991)

Employers must take alternatives into consideration when cost constitutes an undue hardship. If the person with a disability can provide or pay for the accommodation on his or her own, or if there is a third party, such as the state vocational rehabilitation agency or the state office of mental retardation/ developmental disabilities, that can pay part (or all) of the cost, these factors must also be taken into consideration. The availability of tax credits to the employer should also be taken into consideration (Equal Employment Opportunity Commission and the U.S. Department of Justice, 1991).

Financial considerations are not the only potential form of undue hardship. If the provision of accommodations would be unduly disruptive to the employer's other employees or to the functioning of the business, then the accommodations do not have to be made. The EEOC notes, however, that if the disruptions are based on the fears or prejudices of the employees and not the actual provision of the accommodation(s), the employer cannot claim hardship (Equal Employment Opportunity Commission and the U.S. Department of Justice, 1991). This would also apply if providing the accommodation(s) affected the morale of employees without compromising their ability to do their job. Thus, the survey finding that 13.6% of the accommodations were considered not fair to coworkers might not be used as a reason for citing undue hardship unless the provision of these accommodations also affected coworker job performance.

Rights of Persons with Disabilities

The ADA gives persons with disabilities rights that only a limited number of individuals have previously enjoyed under Sections 503 and 504 of the Rehabilitation Act of 1973. Persons with disabilities now have the right to equal opportunity in employment and to the reasonable accommodations necessary to make them qualified for a job. They have the right not to be discriminated against in the areas of hiring, advancement, compensation, training, and all other terms, conditions, and privileges of employment. Persons with disabilities have the right to be integrated, which it is hoped will ultimately translate into integrated competitive employment even for persons with severe disabilities. Persons with disabilities also are entitled to having their rights enforced by the EEOC on the same basis as other protected classes.

Rights of Employers

Employers have rights under the ADA as well. This is too often forgotten or not even considered in general discussions of the ADA. Employers have the right to determine the essential functions of a given job. Employers cannot be forced to change or eliminate essential job functions, and they can also insist that employment be limited to persons who are best qualified for the job. Employers can set reasonable qualification standards, including standards that can potentially disqualify persons who pose a threat to themselves or others. If a person with a disability needs an accommodation, the employer need not disrupt their business or spend an excess amount of money on the provision of that accommodation. In addition, small employers (those with less than 15 employees) are not even covered by the employment provisions of the ADA and, thus, are not required to provide any accommodations to employees or potential employees with disabilities.

Are the Rights of Persons
with Disabilities and Employers in Conflict?

Just as businesses must recognize the rights of persons with disabilities, persons with disabilities must also recognize that businesses have rights as well. While there are legally enforceable rights for both persons with disabilities and businesses under the ADA, the real implementation (and, thus, the eventual successful integration of persons with severe disabilities into the work force) will depend more on the level of understanding and cooperation that can be established between persons with disabilities and the business community. Rather than resting on our laurels with the passage of the ADA, professionals and organizations of and for persons with disabilities should be working now to help businesses comply, or get ready to comply, with the ADA. This outreach to the business community, however, must be done in a nonthreatening way. The idea should be to avoid litigation or even its threat. As stated earlier in the chapter, legislation does not in and of itself change attitudes. Society should realize that attitudes are the real barrier that persons with disabilities, especially those with severe disabilities, still face in relation to full inclusion and integration into the work force. There will still, of course, be cases where it will be necessary to resolve legal interpretations, but these cases should be the exceptions, not the rule, and they should be used solely for that purpose. It must be remembered that businesses are not overly familiar with persons who have disabilities and their special needs. In cases where there is a dispute between a person with a disability and a business over the issue of reasonable accommodation, the law encourages the use of alternative methods of resolution such as settlement negotiations, conciliation, facilitation, mediation, fact finding, minitrials, and arbitration (42 U.S.C. 12212, Section 513). Persons with disabilities and related advocacy organizations can help establish and staff some of these alternative dispute resolutions. A consortium of organizations that can act as a facilitator in identifying alternative means of providing accommodations when there is a dispute might be one example.

The concept of "reasonable accommodation" is just coming into the vocabulary of many businesses, especially those who were not previously covered under Sections 503 and 504 of the Rehabilitation Act. Small businesses, in particular, do not have access to information about the requirements of the law or how and where to get help. It will be up to advocacy organizations, rehabilitation facilities, Projects With Industry (PWI), independent living centers, supported employment programs and, most important, to persons with disabilities themselves, to provide the business community with information about the provision of accommodations and to assist in ultimately lowering the anxiety level of the business community in relation to the ADA.

CONCLUSION

This chapter presents the results of a survey designed to assess employer attitudes toward providing accommodations to facilitate the integration of persons with severe disabilities into the work force. The chapter also reviews the implications of the survey results within the guidelines provided in the ADA for determining "reasonable accommodation," "undue hardship," "qualified individual," and "essential functions." As stated earlier in the chapter, Wolfensberger's early warning that the principle of normalization is "deceptively simple" (1970, p. 291) applies equally to the ADA.

A historic look at the impact of other civil rights legislation provides a framework in which to evaluate the future implications of the ADA in terms of the full inclusion of persons with severe disabilities. History demonstrates that legislation can, and may, change overt behavior but, in the long run, legislation does little to change attitudes. Only real and meaningful contact can evoke such a change.

Although many people would argue that the "melting-pot concept" upon which America was established made this country great, it seems as if it has been carried too far. This concept has evolved into a national ideology that manifests in a desire for "sameness" and an intolerance of difference. America was established as a philosophical experiment to demonstrate how differences could be brought together. The beauty of this experiment was that all differences were to be honored so that each person was to be allowed and encouraged to follow his or her own set of beliefs and practices.

What does this mean in terms of the ADA or, more specifically, in terms of the full inclusion of persons with severe disabilities into the work force? At this time, employers seem willing to accommodate and accept persons with severe disabilities into the work force as long as that employee, ultimately, is no different than their other employees. Specifically, three trends emerge from the data presented in this chapter: 1) the provision of accommodations by employers must be provided on a time-limited basis, 2) the provision of accommodations must not result in creating an employee who differs from other employees, and 3) the provision of accommodations must not result in the differential treatment of the employee with disabilities.

In the national quest for sameness, words and phrases such as fair, appropriate, reasonable, and on an individual or case-by-case basis, have been replaced by one word, "equal." Employers currently tend to be more concerned with all employees being treated equally rather than appropriately (based upon the employee's individual needs).

ADA training programs for employers on hiring, accommodating, supervising, maintaining, and promoting persons with severe disabilities should assist employers to understand that "fair" should not be used as a synonym for "equal." Employers can be empowered so that they can successfully integrate potential workers with severe disabilities into the work force, if they could start to equate "fair" (on a case-by-case basis) with concepts like "appropriate" and "reasonable" instead. This revised interpretation of "fair" seems to be more consistent with the ADA guidelines that state, "whether a particular form of assistance would be required as a reasonable accommodation must be determined on an individualized, case by case basis" (Equal Employment Opportunity Commission and the U.S. Department of Justice, 1991, p. I-59).

The ADA is not now, and will not be in the near future, a panacea for the employment needs of persons with disabilities. It is, however, a valuable tool that people must learn to implement effectively. Used properly, the ADA can not only help open doors that were once closed for persons with severe disabilities, but it can also help to serve as a catalyst for the development of jobs and job opportunities for all persons with disabilities. Used improperly, it will produce seemingly endless litigation and further the gap between persons with disabilities and the business community.

REFERENCES

America 2000: An education strategy. (1991). (Source book: A long-range plan released by President Bush on April 18, 1991, # 1991-298-479/40655). Washington, DC: U.S. Government Printing Office.

Americans with Disabilities Act, PL 101-336. (July 26, 1990). 42 U.S.C. 12101, et seq. *Federal Register, 56*(144), 00000-35756.

Ben-Yishay, Y., Silver, S.M., Piasetsky, E., & Rattok, J. (1987). Relationship between employability and vocational outcome after intensive holistic cognitive rehabilitation. *Journal of Head Trauma Rehabilitation, 2*(1), 35–48.

DeJong, G., & Batavia, A. (1989). Societal duty and resources allocation for persons with severe traumatic brain injury. *Journal of Head Trauma Rehabilitation, 4*(1), 1–12.

Equal Employment Opportunity Commission and the U.S. Department of Justice. (1991). *Americans with Disabilities Act handbook.* Washington, DC: Author.

Federal Register. (January 19, 1981). *46*(12), 5552.

Federal Register. (July 26, 1991). *56*(144), 35735, et seq.

Fraser, R. (1988). Refinement of a decision tree in traumatic brain injury job placement. *Rehabilitation Education, 2,* 179–184.

Fraser, R., Dikmen, S., McLean, A., Miller, B., & Temkin, N. (1988). Employability of head injured survivors: First year post-injury. *Rehabilitation Counseling Bulletin, 31,* 276–288.

Halpern, A. (1985). Transition: A look at the foundations. *Exceptional Children, 51,* 479–486.

Kay, T., Ezrachi, O., & Cavallo, M. (1984). *Annotated bibliography of research on vocational outcome* (Publication No. 185-1). New York: New York University Medical Center, Research and Training Center on Head Trauma and Stroke.

Kreutzer, J.S., & Morton, M.V. (1988). Traumatic brain injury: Supported employment and compensatory strategies for enhancing vocational outcomes. In P. Wehman & M.S. Moon (Eds.), *Vocational rehabilitation and supported employment* (pp. 291–311). Baltimore: Paul H. Brookes Publishing Co.

Kundu, M. (1988). Guest editor's introduction. *Rehabilitation Education, 2,* 159–164.

Levin, H.S., Benton, A.L., & Grossman, R.G. (1982). *Neurobehavioral consequences of closed head injury.* New York: Macmillan.

Lynch, R.T. (1983). Traumatic head injury: Implications for rehabilitation counseling. *Journal of Applied Rehabilitation Counseling, 14,* 32–45.

Michaels, C.A. (1989a). Employment: The final frontier—Issues and practices for persons with learning disabilities. *Rehabilitation Counseling Bulletin, 33,* 67–73.

Michaels, C.A. (1989b). *Vocational rehabilitation programming for persons with traumatic head injury* (Grant Proposal 84.128A). Albertson, NY: Human Resources Center.

Parente, R., Stapleton, M.C., & Wheatley, C.J. (1991). Practical strategies for vocational reentry after traumatic brain injury. *Journal of Head Trauma Rehabilitation, 6*(3), 35–45.

Pawelski, C.E. (1991). America 2000: A brave new world of educational reform. *Journal of Visual Impairment and Blindness, 85*(7), 283.

Sale, P., West, M., Sherron, P., & Wehman, P.H. (1991). Exploratory analysis of job separations from supported employment for persons with traumatic brain injury. *Journal of Head Trauma Rehabilitation, 6*(3), 1–11.

Senate Report 101-116. (1989, August 30). *Americans With Disabilities Act.* Washington, DC: Committee on Labor and Human Resources.

U.S. Department of Labor Employment Standards Administration. (1982). *A study of accommodations provided to handicapped employees by federal contractors* (Final Report, Contract No. J-9-E-1-0009). Berkeley, CA: Berkeley Planning Associates.

Vander Kolk, C.J. (1991). Persons with traumatic head injury and job placement. *Journal of Job Placement, 7*(2), 15–18.

Will, M. (1984). *OSERS programming for the transition of youth with disabilities: Bridges from school to working life.* Washington, DC: Office of Special Education and Rehabilitative Services.

Wolfensberger, W. (1970). The principle of normalization and its implications to psychiatric services. *American Journal of Psychiatry, 127*(3), 291–297.

Young, J., & Michaels, C.A. (1986). *The hidden resource: Tapping the potential of workers with learning disabilities.* Albertson, NY: Human Resources Center.

Chapter 6

Provisions of Assistive Technology
Bridging the Gap to Accessibility

Shirley K. Chandler,
Thomas Czerlinsky, and Paul Wehman

Similar to the way that advances in behavioral technology influenced the development of supported employment programs in the 1980s (Wehman, Sale, & Parent, 1992), the emergence of a replicative, demonstrable assistive technology has allowed the spirit and law of the ADA to become viable. Assistive technology involves the use of new or modified devices, materials, or equipment, which enable people with disabilities to be more effective and competent in daily life activities. While the ADA does not involve specific discussions of assistive technology, the Technology-Related Assistance for Individuals with Disabilities Act (PL 100-407), passed by Congress in 1988, does include such discussions. This law, along with others, has directly influenced the availability and utilization of specially designed devices and accommodations meant to empower persons with disabilities.

As the focus now returns to work, medical rehabilitation, and community integration initiatives that were pursued during the 1980s, the doors to employment for an increasing number of individuals with severe disabilities have opened. With greater numbers of workers entering the community and the work force, many unique and individual problems have begun to evolve.

Some of these problems require job modifications, the use of adaptive or assistive technology, and the development of compensatory strategies. Rubin and Roessler (1987) suggest that technology designed to restore critical daily living functions be used to promote the integration of individuals with disabilities into society. It is hoped that, as progress is made, society will realize a future in which individuals with disabilities will have the same access to society's opportunities that individuals without disabilities do.

OVERVIEW OF LEGISLATION

Before the concept of "assistive technology" was actually introduced, progressive rehabilitation personnel used some of the principles of assistive technology to enable their clients to function with maximum independence (Sowers & Powers, 1991; Wehman, Wood, Everson, Goodwyn, & Conley, 1987). For example, technological adaptations and modifications have long enabled persons with disabilities, who could not do so otherwise, to operate motor vehicles safely and effectively. Is not the electric wheelchair also an application of assistive technology? Despite their previous use, these activities were not under the rubric of an official term; therefore, in the past, these activities did not benefit from broad, official federal mandates.

More recently, assistive technology has officially been a part of rehabilitation and vocational placement, beginning with the Rehabilitation Act Amendments of 1986 (PL 99-506). These amendments define rehabilitation technology services as "the systematic application of technology, engineering methodologies, or scientific principles to meet needs of individuals with handicaps in areas which include education, rehabilitation, employment, transportation, independent living, and recreation" (p. 35592). To ensure implementation of this concept, funding for assistive technology has been included under the umbrellas of the Education for All Handicapped Children Act of 1975 (PL 94-142) and the Education of the Handicapped Act Amendments of 1986 (PL 99-457), the Developmental Disabilities Assistance Act Amendments of 1987 (PL 100-297), the Social Security Act (PL 99-509), the Technology-Related Assistance for Individuals with Disabilities Act (PL 100-407), Medicaid, and Medicare.

The movement toward the implementation of assistive technologies is consistent with the concept that persons with disabilities can and should be fully functioning, integrated members of society. After all, community and work integration are both integral goals of the rehabilitation process. Integration. is supported by the Rehabilitation Act Amendments and the newest legislation affecting individuals with disabilities, the ADA, both of which prohibit discrimination against persons with disabilities. The ADA states that every effort must be made to provide for reasonable accommodations (see Chapter 5), while suggesting that costs remain within an affordable range.

Often, such accommodations require the implementation of various types of assistive technologies. The ADA does not specify which types of technology, assistive devices, equipment, or materials should be used to make community and work settings accessible, because such specifications would be considered as beyond the purview of the law and its regulations. In order to implement the ADA when assistive devices are required, the Technology-Related Assistance Act may serve as a possible resource. Through this act, there are funds available to all 50 states by the U.S. Department of Education for developing assistive technology devices and also for paying for technical assistance and training.

REHABILITATION TECHNOLOGY AND ITS APPLICATION

People who utilize the principles of assistive technology can be found within the rehabilitation system and within the scope of service providers who are involved in supported employment. These people are often referred to as rehabilitation technologists, but anyone within the system can also practice the application of assistive technology. Rehabilitation technologists do not have to be engineers. They may be occupational, physical, or speech therapists, employment specialists, or simply "handy persons." To function most effectively in providing assistive technologies, the rehabilitation technologist should be skilled in:

1. Assessing an employee and/or the environment
2. Selecting and installing commercially available adaptations
3. Designing, fabricating, and installing adaptations
4. Instructing the employee and employment specialist to use the adaptations
5. Repairing and/or modifying the adaptations

The applicability of the above skills to a range of rehabilitation service professionals should be immediately evident. For example, the employment specialist, a critical person in the process of providing supported employment services to persons with severe disabilities, is commonly faced with issues related to assistive technology, such as: 1) assessment, 2) selection and/or fabrication, 3) funding, 4) training, 5) maintenance, and 6) client involvement. Clearly, the skills outlined above can play a vital role in all aspects of an employment specialist's activities.

Major Uses of Adaptations

Although assistive technology is relevant to all phases of the rehabilitation process, Garner and Campbell (1987) have pointed out that devices and adaptations resulting from the application of the principles of assistive technology are primarily used for two major purposes. The first purpose of such devices and adaptations is to correct or remediate one or more specific impairments. For example, hearing aids enhance auditory capabilities, glasses correct or compensate for some types of visual impairments, and adaptive positioning equipment often helps the individual to overcome a deficit or an inability to independently assume and maintain a specific posture. Thus a specific adaptation of assistive technology can directly focus upon deficits that would otherwise hinder the individual from being involved in successful employment or community integration.

The second purpose of devices and adaptations resulting from the application of assistive technology is aimed at assisting the individual to learn specific materials and/or to perform specific tasks rather than upon the remediation of specific deficits. Therefore, individuals are able to practice, learn, or relearn those skills and abilities that will enable them to function satisfactorily at work or within the community. Increased skills and abilities empower the individual, allowing him or her to become more self-sufficient. Clearly, there can be quite a bit of overlap between these two purposes; adaptations and devices can focus upon the remediation of specific deficits, as well as upon modifying the environment so that individuals can more fully partake of their environment.

An important bit of information that seems to be critical for the rehabilitation professional who wants to be successful in the utilization of such devices and adaptations is that the entire concept is rooted in technology. American society is highly technological, and changes in technology often occur rapidly and seemingly without fanfare or warning. Rapid, sudden technological changes occur in both "high technology" concepts (e.g., advances in computerization, communication technology, medical spinoffs) or "low technology" concepts (e.g., tool modifications, the development of new materials to be used in the devices). In either case, the rapid emergence of new and advanced technological devices requires that personnel involved in the field remain constantly alert. Advances may apply not only to the typical channels of information transmission within the human services channels, but also to information sources outside the typical realm.

Implementation of Rehabilitation Technology

Vocational analyses are major factors in ensuring the successful hiring and retention of employees with disabilities. Information about the job, its purpose, its actual tasks, and the requirements for successful performance are provided by the job analysis. It also identifies a range of skill areas that can be enhanced by the use of assistive technology. Assistive devices can help with job performance by enhancing the mobility, environmental control, and communication of persons with disabilities. As employment specialists perform vocational analyses of the work site and identify the tasks necessary to perform the job satisfactorily, they should keep in mind that incorporating assistive devices would allow an individual with severe disabilities to be able to perform a job for the first time or improve performance on an existing job. Previously, such a job might have been extremely difficult for the individual or even beyond his or her physical or cognitive capabilities. Although initially created to make a job site more accessible, assistive devices can also be used in many aspects of an individual's life. The Office of Special Education and Rehabilitative Services (OSERS) Task Force on Rehabilitation Engineering (1988) classified rehabilitation engineering services into the following areas: 1) personal vehicles and driving aids, 2) prosthetics and orthotics, 3) home modifications, 4) work sites and vocational equipment modifications, 5) communications and controls, 6) computer applications, and 7) quantification and diagnosis of human performance. Various devices and adaptations related to these areas are listed in Table 6.1.

Adaptive devices, however, are not necessarily the panacea for all work

Table 6.1. Areas of use for assistive devices

Mobility
Driving Aids
Biofeedback Techniques
Robotics
Sonicguide
Pathsounder
Ultrasonic Spectacles
Laser Cane

Communication
Computers
TDD
Talk-Tone
Viewscan
Electrowriter
Automated typewriter
Kurzweil Reading Machine
Speech Plus Calculator
Canon Communicator

Health Maintenance
Implantable Medication Systems
Prosthetic Urinary Sphincter

Cognitive/Intellectual Functioning
Computers with voice synthesizers
Computers

Visual Functioning

Social and Recreational Activities
Microcomputers

Daily Living

site and other environmental problems. They must be carefully evaluated lest they turn into frustrating barriers for the individual. It is critical to assess the consumer's unique needs and requirements. First, the individual with the disability and the assistive device that might be instituted or developed must be evaluated, then the functioning needs of the individual must be integrated with the functioning characteristics of the assistive device (Taber, 1986). The idea is for rehabilitation clients to benefit from the technology, but not become a "slave" to, or suffer from, that technology.

Evaluation of the individual should include consideration of muscle control, behavioral patterns, mobility, and communication skills. The operational manual for commercially produced assistive devices should be easy to understand and include step-by-step instructions for installation and operation, as well as information concerning the availability of replacement parts. Additional areas of concern involve the availability of service contracts and, in the case of device failure, "loaner" devices. If the employment specialist or any other member of the rehabilitation team develops an assistive device, he or she should take into consideration the following factors: 1) ease of operation, 2) safety of the device, and 3) impact upon the work site or environment in which it is used.

Work Site Modifications Work site modification has been defined as the analysis of the individual with the disability and the potential job tasks with the ultimate outcome of designing an effective and appropriate assistive device. This process may include the fabrication, installation, and verification of the usability of such a device, as well as determination of whether or not the device will meet the productivity and safety standards necessary for the work site. Many of the devices are custom designed for specific individuals or job tasks and come in "groups of one" with no generalization to other applications or work sites (Leslie, 1986).

Actual work site modifications depend heavily upon a functional evaluation of the individual's capability and the tasks of the job. In many cases, it is an easy matter to develop an assistive device that allows the individual with the disability to return to work at his or her previous job. This is often the case where traumatic injuries have occurred, and the individual has the capacity, social, and/or educational background to seek employment or return to former employment with minimal support. However, the individual with severe congenital disabilities may face a different problem. Although it is likely that the individual with the traumatic injury will generally have had some vocational experience (Greenwood, 1985), it is possible that the individual with congenital disabilities may have lived in a sheltered environment, may have a limited educational background, or may, in fact, have no vocational experience.

The goal of work site modifications should be to maximize the individual's functional capability and independence. This goal should be accomplished in a safe and cost-efficient manner and without extensive modifications, unless such modifications are absolutely necessary (Puckett, 1989). Evaluations should include a task analysis of the job and of all tasks required to perform the job. Environmental factors should also be taken into consideration. Table 6.2 lists questions that should be addressed (Puckett, 1989).

High technology solutions are not always the answer to work site productivity. Such solutions present a variety of problems if used with individuals who have severe cognitive disabilities. Often, these individuals do not have the educational or intellectual sophistication to utilize the devices and, thus, such devices may not aid the individual in retaining his or her job. In some cases, the devices may cause more frustration than benefits. A study by the Berkeley Planning Associates (1982) showed that the majority of work site modifications could be done for under $200. However, even this small expenditure can be a concern for supported employment personnel if no funding source is available. Funding is a very real consideration when planning a work site modification.

An additional consideration that must be addressed is whether or not the individual can be expected to operate at the same level of productivity as that of his or her coworkers. Consideration must also be given to the work environment. It should remain hazard-free for both the individual and his or her coworkers. If the assistive device has not resulted in a productivity level that is consistent with the employer's needs or has resulted in an unsafe environment, the employer may feel that he or she has made an unreasonable accommodation. However, there are several other questions, such as those listed in Table 6.3, that must be answered prior to the actual selection, design, or development of a specific assistive device.

Design and Construction of Assistive Devices In the job development and analysis stage, the following steps are helpful when placing an individual who may need an assistive device. The first step, the actual selection of the job, necessitates that the employment specialist ensure the worker's successful

Table 6.2. Work site modification questions

How will the individual get to work?

How will the individual enter the work site?

What are the specific tasks required for the job?

Which tasks can be performed without modification?

Do modifications consider job sharing with coworkers, job redesign, level of technology required, and cost factors?

What access will the individual have to food service and rest room areas?

Is there more than one accessible entrance/exit?

Are there any special medical needs?

What safeguards are needed for the individual or coworkers if equipment is modified?

Table 6.3. Preselection concerns for assistive devices

How expensive or complicated is the device?

Is another solution simpler?

Is there another less expensive device that gives the same results?

Does the system increase the individual's dependence on a technical device without a back-up in case of equipment failure?

Does the system work in both the home and the work environment?

Can an off-the-shelf, or commercially available piece of equipment be used instead of a custom design?

Will the device last long enough to justify its cost?

performance after the assistive device has been installed. The second step, the task analysis, assesses both the individual's abilities and the job requirements. This analysis will help the employment specialist ascertain how much the job must be redesigned in order to accommodate the individual selected for placement on the job. At the same time, the specialist should remain aware of the potential for promotions and future jobs for the individual, and the part that the selected assistive devices will play in those future plans.

Not only will the individual worker need to be trained to learn the necessary job tasks, but he or she will also need to be trained to use the assistive device. The individual will have a continued need for the employment specialist's support when using the assistive device, especially if the assistive device is relatively complex (i.e., a device that needs daily set up or intervention). When purchasing expensive assistive devices, a trial placement may give the employment specialist an opportunity to determine whether or not the device will meet the needs of the worker and the employer prior to purchase. This would avoid disappointment should the device not live up to prior expectations.

Nisbet et al. (1983) listed 11 dimensions to consider when constructing and designing assistive devices. They are as follows:

1. The number of environments in which the device can be utilized;
2. The number of activities for which the device can be utilized;
3. The cost-benefit ratio (the amount of money required vs the effects that will accrue);
4. The time required to use the device;
5. The number of integrated interactions that will occur through the use of the device;
6. The safety of the device;
7. The enjoyment and comfort that will be realized by the individual from the use of the device;
8. The maintenance requirements of the device;
9. The amount of training needed to teach the individual to use the device effectively;
10. The age appropriateness of the device; and,

11. The social significance of the device (the effect it has on the acceptance, respect, pride, etc. of the individual by others). (p. 7–8)

These dimensions outline the areas that need to be considered by the employment specialist or the rehabilitation professional before a work site or job is redesigned. In design, construction, or selection, the assistive device should perform at an acceptable rate and quality of performance.

Illustrations of the ways in which assistive technology can be applied are presented in Table 6.4. Although the ADA provides a statutory framework for assistive technology to be applied, it does not provide for specific devices, funds, materials, and so forth. It is, after all, a civil rights framework.

Cognitive Compensatory Strategies

Cognitive rehabilitation strategies have been developed to improve independent living, intellectual, and vocational skills of persons with brain dysfunction (Kreutzer & Wehman, 1991). Most recently, cognitive rehabilitation has been identified with specially written computer software. The computer software and hardware are viewed as tools that allow the patient to practice a series of tasks. The therapist assumes that practicing selected tasks will enhance the cognitive skills underlying the tasks and generalization will result in improved concomitant skills that are required for daily living. Examination of the few research investigations reported in current literature suggests that computer cognitive rehabilitation results in cognitive improvements that are primarily evident in improved neuropsychological test scores. For example, Ruff and Camenzulli (1991) conducted a study that compared changes in test scores for patients who had undergone computer cognitive rehabilitation and for subjects in a control group. Preliminary findings suggested that improvements in intellectual and attentional skills were a result of the computer-based rehabilitation program.

Despite preliminary research, which suggests that computer cognitive rehabilitation can yield improvements in standardized test scores, fundamental questions remain regarding the transfer of cognitive skills to functional community skills. There is little evidence that computer cognitive rehabilitation generalizes from the treatment setting and results in improved daily living skills. For example, a recent review of the cognitive rehabilitation literature (Gouvier, Webster, & Blanton, 1986) revealed that cognitive rehabilitation for visuoperceptual impairments can yield improvements in driving ability. The author's conclusion was based on examination of only a single study. The investigators failed to report similar findings for other types of cognitive and psychomotor impairment. Gouvier and colleagues (1986) commented that questions regarding the durability of treatment effects produced in the laboratory must be resolved prior to addressing real-life generalizability issues.

One purpose of this section is to describe an alternative assistive strategy

Table 6.4. Adaptive devices and task modifications

Nature of device	Name of adaptation	Application	Description	Cost	Expertise needed for development or use
Alternative input method for computer	Headpointers	For typists who cannot use their hands to type; allows input by typing on computer keyboard with a rod extending from the headpiece. Only one key can be typed at a time. Typist would need a device to hold down shift or control keys. Control of head movement is necessary; must be able to move head forward/back, side-to-side, and up/down.	A slender rod extending from top of headpiece that is adjustable in length. Headpiece consists of a rigid headband or helmet with chin strap. A variation is in chin pointer that has the rod extending at chin height allowing for less visual interference.	$20–$125 for commercial pointers	Slight to moderate
	Expanded keyboard	An alternative input method for computer users who lack the coordination to use the standard keyboard. Keys require only light touch. Person needs	A flat board (14″ × 21″ or larger) with a matrix of pressure-sensitive "keys," which respond to light touch. The keys are ³⁄₄″ or larger and recessed ¹⁄₈″ below	From $250 to $550 complete	Moderate

		good range of motion in the arm since the keys are far apart.	surface so typist's hand can rest on board without touching keys. The expanded keyboard plugs into the computer by cable and does not interfere with normal keyboard input. The expanded keyboard requires a controller firmware card installed in the computer. It may also require controlling software.		
Computer postioning	Computer work stations	To incline the keyboard of the computer toward the user; especially helpful for those typing with headpointers. Also adjusts angle of computer and allows keyboard to be lowered for enhanced typing height. Organizes work stations, cords, and receptacles and	Work station mounts onto table. Provides an adjustable inclined surface for each computer so keyboard can be lowered and keys can be angled toward typist. Monitor sits at eye-level on shelf above computer so it is not affected by incline. All parts of system are turned on	Moderate, plus time and equipment	Skilled

(continued)

Table 6.4. (*continued*)

Nature of device	Name of adaptation	Application	Description	Cost	Expertise needed for development or use
		provides access to printer by several computers.	by single switch mounted at front of station.		
	Positioning device for computer	To incline the keyboard of the computer toward the user; especially helpful for those typing with headpointers.	Adjusted plywood incline and base tilts computer to desired angle. Strap secures computer to incline; lip on front prevents computer from sliding forward. Monitor can be mounted above or beside computer rather than on top.	Minimal; plywood, bolts, time, and equipment	Moderate
Calculator	Calculator keyguard	A client who has difficulty touching the number pad of the calculator correctly	A paper pattern of the calculator keys is made and then transferred to a hard	$5 for materials	Moderate

		plastic (e.g., Plexiglas). Holes are drilled to correspond to the keys. Small pieces of plastic are glued to the sides to raise the keyguard slightly above the keys. The keyguard can be taped in place with plastic tape and easily removed.		
		due to incoordination or a client who inputs numbers via headpointer may do so more easily when using a keyguard over the calculator keys.		
Calculator positioning	Inclined board for calculator	Clients who use headpointers can access the calculator keys more easily if the calculator is angled at a more vertical than horizontal position.		
		The plywood incline has a base, a hinged front piece with a retaining lip to hold the calculator, and a back piece with adjustable height. By making the back taller, the calculator becomes more vertical.	$5–$10	Moderate

The rating scale for expertise needed is: NONE = purchase item ready-made; no installation experience needed; SLIGHT = purchase item ready-made, minor set up or modification required; MODERATE = some experience or skill needed either in using or fabricating the adaptation; SKILLED = expertise needed in designing and fabricating the adaptation.

that employs the personal computer, which may be implemented by the individual at home, school, or work. Consequently, assumptions regarding generalization are necessary and improvements in functional life skills can be directly observed. Durability of treatment can be assured if the patient maintains records and if collaboration with the clinician is ongoing. Rather than being used as a tool, the computer is used to prepare materials that can immediately help to compensate for the patient's intellectual impairments. Compensatory techniques may include personalized notebooks, checklists, and schedules that ensure routine and minimize the effects of memory and attention failures. Furthermore, the patient can also be taught to utilize software in the same manner as professionals and to organize information, which yields benefits in work efficiency.

Personal computers, along with word processing, data base, and spreadsheet software, can be used to expedite the preparation of compensatory materials. For example, word processing software can be utilized by the therapist to develop checklists and sets of instructions for patients during each therapy session. Persons with traumatic brain injuries often suffer from significant memory deficits. Written information, received by the patient at the treatment session, helps ensure that instructions will be followed. Word processing software and software that corrects spelling errors can be used by the patient to improve his or her writing ability, which will benefit academic and vocational performance. Spreadsheet software can be used as a tool to help patients budget and maintain financial records. Additionally, persons with brain injury can use data base software for record keeping by using the same strategies that help homemakers and businesspeople keep efficient records. The ideal situation is one in which both the therapist and patient have compatible computers. This would allow work from the therapy session to be continued at home.

The Appleworks software program developed by Apple Computer can be used to prepare compensatory materials for patients. Appleworks has proven to be extremely useful because it is user-friendly, fast, and flexible. It can perform a wide variety of tasks including word processing, spreadsheet analysis, and data management, and it can be used by the clinician for business and administrative tasks, as well as patient care activities. Appleworks is also compatible with the Apple II series of computers including the IIgs, IIc, and IIe.

Typically, the first step in developing compensatory strategies is to complete a thorough evaluation. The purpose of the evaluation is to determine the individual's strengths and weaknesses particularly in regard to areas that have direct implications for independent living and vocational potential. The patient and family are carefully interviewed and a series of tests, which measure intellectual, motor, and linguistic skills, are administered. The second step involves a task analysis—a thorough evaluation of the step-by-step process necessary for task completion. The final step involves development of a series of specific instructions and/or materials to be utilized by the patient. These techniques may be utilized in the home, workplace, or academic setting. Table 6.5 lists instructions that might be given to a client with a severe cognitive deficit.

When using compensatory strategies for persons with head injury, clinicians and family members will need to consider a variety of factors. Motivation, functional reading skills, and some degree of self-awareness are critical factors in the successful use of the interventions described. The authors encourage the dissemination of information pertaining to compensatory strategies. Persons with mental retardation and those with neurological disorders,

Table 6.5. Instructions for life activities

1. *Consistency and regularity* are important means of compensating for problems related to memory deficits. Completing tasks routinely (at the same time and in the same sequence each day) will enhance your memory and reduce overall stress levels.

2. *Reduce stresses in the morning* and ensure that you get to work on time. Try to organize yourself the previous evening. Activities for the evening are listed on your "Night Before Checklist;" activities to be carried out each morning before work are listed on your "Morning On-Time Checklist." Also, it might be helpful to buy a coffee maker with a timer that you can set the night before.

3. Decide which chores you will do and, if applicable, which chores your spouse will do. Be as consistent as possible in adhering to your chosen responsibilities.

4. Try to set *reasonable expectations* for yourself. Expect to make at least some mistakes.

5. Do not be concerned about leaving a mess at home before you leave for work. You can always clean up when you return home after work.

6. If you must choose between eating breakfast or getting to work on time, choose the latter and skip breakfast. Keep healthy snacks (e.g., fruit, granola bars) in your desk drawer at work in case you are running late in the morning.

7. Try to work things out, as we discussed, so that *you are responsible for* making coffee and, if applicable, *your spouse is responsible for* making breakfast. Ask him or her to help you by: 1) having breakfast ready at the same time each morning, 2) warming up your car each morning, and 3) feeding any pets. Note that including breakfast in your routine will help your memory and reduce overall stress levels.

8. *Organize your keys, wallet, briefcase, and sunglasses* each night before bed. Keep them in the same place and near each other in order to avoid looking for them in the morning.

9. If you are running late for work, don't rush by driving too fast and/or not being cautious. It is *more important for you to get to work safely* than to get there on time.

such as multiple sclerosis, dementia, and strokes, are also likely to benefit from these techniques. Additional research is needed to identify more clearly the types of techniques that will work best for each unique set of problems.

CONCLUSION

A thorough examination of current literature indicates that there are many areas in which work site modifications and assistive devices would enable persons with disabilities to function more productively as employees (Leslie, 1986). Legislation such as the ADA has only addressed several of these areas. Many programs still need to implement work site modifications and assistive technology.

The individualized transition plan (ITP) for students who receive special education services in preparation for transition from school to work is one example. In the ITP, students need to learn about modifications and assistive technology for the workplace so they can plan for their careers and utilize the information when they are placed in vocational/occupational training classes. Continued emphasis must also be placed on advancements in computer and related technology, as well as on inexpensive robotics to be used at the work site. Technology must be viewed as a means to provide increased experience, opportunity, and independence for persons with severe disabilities.

With the passage of the ADA and the increasing demand for workers in the job market, individuals with disabilities who had not previously been considered for employment are now being considered for even greater vocational opportunities. Assessment procedures must include not only the capabilities of the individual with the disability, but must also describe the limitations of the environment and plan alternative strategies for enhancement of performance (Puckett, 1989). The goals of supported employment and rehabilitation should be to return individuals to society in an independent and integrated manner. In order to promote this integration, employment specialists and rehabilitation professionals must remain alert to information on assistive devices both within the commercial avenues and "outside the typical realm of human services" (Garner & Campbell, 1987), such as hardware, computer, and other technology stores.

The use of assistive devices and rehabilitation technology can provide the means to overcome many of the physical and psychological barriers faced by an individual with a disability, and thus will provide for increased productivity not only at the work site but in all areas of the individual's life. It cannot be emphasized enough that research in assistive technology and the widespread dissemination of these results should be a priority for rehabilitative and federal initiatives.

REFERENCES

Berkeley Planning Associates. (1982). *Study of accommodations provided by federal contractors: Final report, Volume 1: Study findings.* Washington DC: U.S. Government Printing Office.

Garner, J.B., & Campbell, P.H. (1987). Technology for persons with severe disabilities: Practical and ethical considerations. *The Journal of Special Education, 21*(3), 24–32.

Gouvier, W., Webster, J., & Blanton, P. (1986). Cognitive retraining with brain-damaged patients. In D. Wedding, A. Horton, & J. Webster (Eds.), *The neuropsychology handbook.* New York: Springer.

Greenwood, R. (1985). *Designing jobs for handicapped workers.* Chicago, IL: Conference proceedings

Kreutzer, J.R., & Wehman, P. (Eds.). (1991). *Cognitive rehabilitation for persons with traumatic brain injury.* Baltimore: Paul H. Brookes Publishing Co.

Leslie, J.H. (1986). *Worksite modification: A pragmatic perspective.* Washington, DC: The Catholic University of America, DATA Institute.

Nisbet, J., Sweet, M., Ford, A., Shiraga, B., Udvari, A., York, J., Messina, R., & Schroeder, J. (1983). *Utilizing adaptive devices with severely handicapped students.* Madison: Wisconsin University–Madison.

Office of Special Education and Rehabilitation Services Task Force on Rehabilitation Engineering. (1988, May). *Rehabilitation Engineering Services in the State–Federal Vocation Rehabilitation System.* Washington, DC: Author.

Puckett, F.D. (1989). Worksite modifications. In P.N. Hale (Ed.), *Rehabilitation technology services: A Guide for the rehabilitation counselor.* Rustin: Louisiana Tech University, Center for Rehabilitation Science and Biomedical Engineering.

Rehabilitation Act Amendments, PL 99-506. (1986). *Federal Register,* Vol. 51, 35392.

Rubin, S.E., & Roessler, R.T. (1987). *Foundations of the vocational rehabilitation process.* (3rd ed.). Austin, TX: PRO-ED.

Ruff, R.M., & Camenzulli, L.F. (1991). Research challenges for behavioral rehabilitation: Searching for solutions. In J. Kreutzer & P. Wehman (Eds.), *Cognitive rehabilitation for persons with traumatic brain injury* (pp. 23–34). Baltimore: Paul H. Brookes Publishing Co.

Sowers, J., & Powers, L. (1991). *Vocational preparation and employment of students with physical and multiple disabilities.* Baltimore: Paul H. Brookes Publishing Co.

Taber, F.M. (1986). Adaptive devices and the computer. *The Exceptional Parent, 16*(6), 29–30.

Wehman, P., Sale, P., & Parent, W. (1992). *Supported employment: From research to practice.* Stoneham, MA: Andover Medical Publishers.

Wehman, P., Wood, W., Everson, J., Goodwyn, R., & Conley, S. (1987). *Vocational education for multihandicapped youth with cerebral palsy.* Baltimore: Paul H. Brookes Publishing Co.

Chapter 7

The Challenge of Public Transportation and Mobility

Paul Wehman

A ccording to the ADA there are several very substantive requirements that public and private transportation systems must meet to be in compliance with the laws. Title III of the ADA is fully devoted to the issues of transportation accessibility and mobility. As the creators of the ADA and its advocates realized, the ability of an individual to participate independently or semi-independently in work and community life is heavily dependent upon community mobility. *Community mobility* refers to movement from one place to another within a particular setting, as well as the ability to travel between two community locations. This concept was originally developed in program practice and in the literature related to working with individuals who have visual impairments. In this context, community mobility is referred to as orientation and mobility training. Orientation refers to a person's awareness of the environment in relation to space, objects, and other persons. According to La Grow, Wiener, and La Duke (1990) and Laus (1974), awareness of one's surroundings and one's relationship to those surroundings as they relate to everyday living is essential to independent mobility. If orientation training can be conceptualized as the cognitive component of community travel, mobility training can be conceptualized as the actual physical behavior involved in movement from one place to another. Together, these concepts refer to the complex set of behaviors that are required to ensure access to community activities.

Lack of mobility skills can be detrimental to a person's ability to acquire and hold a job, and participate in the community. According to Saenger (1972), the majority of 520 adults with severe mental retardation surveyed in New York City had few or no independent travel skills. Consequently, these individuals were dependent on an expensive chartered bus system to take them to and from work. As stated by Tobias and Cortazzo (1963), "when people with mental retardation are dependent on adult assistance for locomotion beyond the immediate environs of their home, the range of possible activities becomes very restricted and isolation becomes the rule" (p. 26). A major leader in the disability rights movement, Frank Bowe (1979), adds that "without means of transportation to educational, vocational, cultural, recreational, and commercial facilities in the community, it is virtually impossible for most severely disabled people to live outside of an institutional environment" (p. 484). Taylor and Taylor (1989) explored the issue of public transportation in social casework practice with long-stay psychiatric clients who participate in community mental health practice. The authors emphasize the importance of helping these clients to understand how to cognitively map out the community environment.

Given the integral relationship between community mobility and community functioning, a great deal of attention needs to be focused on preparing individuals with disabilities to become able to travel more independently. What type of control over life and how much self-empowerment can be realized for a person with serious travel restriction? Program initiatives in the area must be concerned with increasing the opportunity for community travel and also with teaching specific mobility skills. The ADA only addresses accessibility; however, instruction and support are also needed in order to aid in the mobility of persons with disabilities in the community. Travel training programs, such as the Millet Learning Center Curriculum (1989) developed in Saginaw, Michigan, help students with physical impairments to receive extensive community travel training. This training is accomplished by frequent trips into the community and direct instruction by school personnel.

FACTORS AFFECTING MOBILITY

The ability of a person to be independently mobile depends on several factors, specifically physical and attitudinal barriers. Of these factors, the one that most influences the degree of mobility attained by individuals with disabilities is the opportunity to travel from one place to another. Removing physical and attitudinal barriers to independent or semi-independent community mobility can allow for increased travel. Mobility can be greatly restricted by both of these barriers.

Physical Barriers

As noted at the beginning of the chapter, physical barriers limit accessibility and consequently reduce a person's chances for full community participation. The ADA has taken a major step in addressing those issues and concerns. In addition, there have been several developments in the past few years that have increased the accessibility of various forms of transportation, public buildings, and community housing; however, many physical barriers still exist that are not recognized by most people. Such barriers include: 1) inaccessible transportation, 2) lack of convenient parking, 3) steep inclines, 4) curbs and stairs, 5) small doorway openings, and 6) inadequate restroom facilities.

Addressing the issue of transportation, Bowe (1979) states that "accessible transportation serves both as a practical necessity and philosophical basis for independent living" (p. 474). Without accessible transportation, an individual with a physical disability has fewer opportunities for independent functioning. In response to this problem, the Urban Mass Transportation Act (PL 88-365) was passed. This law was specifically designed to encourage "special efforts" to develop transportation systems that could be used by citizens with physical disabilities (e.g., elevators, vouchers to be exchanged for private transport).

The federal commitment to increasing accessibility for citizens with physical disabilities extends beyond the transportation issue. As early as 1968, the Architectural Barriers Act (PL 90-480) was passed by Congress to ensure access to federally financed buildings and facilities. Since its passage, several additional pieces of legislation have strengthened the movement toward improving the physical accessibility of community services and housing. These include the Rehabilitation Act of 1973 (PL 93-112) and its amendments in 1974 (PL 93-516). These acts were the first federal efforts to encourage uniform guidelines for physical accessibility. Unfortunately, the Rehabilitation Act carried with it severe penalties; for example, the loss of federal funds for agencies who did not comply and who were not the recipients of federal monies.

The impact of barrier-free design and the movement to increase the accessibility of transportation and other community services has been felt in many cities throughout the United States. In many communities, extensive physical modifications have been made, such as the construction of ramps, widening of doorways, installation of elevators, cutting out of curbs, and purchase of lift buses. Although these modifications have removed many barriers to independent mobility, obstacles still exist. Realistically, many of these obstacles are not going to be eliminated since some of these obstacles are beyond the control of engineers and educators (e.g., weather conditions, natural terrain). Because it is likely that mobility obstacles will remain in every community, efforts must be directed toward teaching individuals to overcome these problems. For example, people with disabilities should, if possible, be taught how to:

1. Walk up and down stairs with and without using handrails.
2. Step up and down curbs.
3. Climb in and out of vehicles.
4. Use restroom facilities with narrow doorways and no railings.
5. Walk on uneven terrain and different textured surfaces.
6. Walk from place to place under inclement weather conditions.
7. Enter and exit buildings with a variety of doorway sizes and types.

This training will be undertaken by teachers, counselors, and other professionals who work with individuals who have disabilities in various centers for independent living, schools, and training programs.

By combining environmental changes with specific instruction programs, people with physical disabilities are provided easier access and gain more skills for independent travel within their communities. Community mobility programs should reflect this dual concern for improving physical accessibility and training skills. This combination of emphases should result in maximal community mobility for all people. The Pedestrian Safety Training Curriculum (1990), developed in Illinois, provides a useful training curriculum to aid in the mobility and independence of persons with disabilities. The training manual provides material to help individuals to cross sidewalks, alleys, and driveways safely and to overcome such obstacles as swinging or revolving doors.

Attitudinal Barriers

A person's ability to travel independently within the community is not restricted only by physical obstacles. Attitudinal barriers can also severely restrict a person's opportunity to learn mobility skills. Much too often, parents and professionals contribute to these barriers, which result from a combination of overprotectiveness and lowered expectations. According to Perske (1972), "such overprotection endangers the client's human dignity, and tends to keep him from experiencing the risk taking of ordinary life which is necessary for normal growth and development" (p. 29).

To overcome problems related to overprotectiveness, the importance of community mobility needs to be articulated to parents and other caregivers. Detailed programs for improving mobility skills need to be developed in a way that shows the relationship between supervised instructional activities and long-term goals of independent travel. If mobility programs are formulated in this manner, it may be possible to eliminate overprotectiveness barriers and raise expectations for independent community mobility. Such an approach demonstrates respect for each person's dignity by providing mobility opportunity with concurrent training activities. As individuals acquire independence in various mobility skills, supervision should be faded and the person's "dignity of risk" should be respected.

When independent community travel for young adults with severe mental retardation was first discussed with one group of parents, the most common concerns were identified as fears regarding: 1) sexual molestation, 2) kidnapping, 3) injuries or accidents, 4) getting lost, 5) ridicule by others, 6) failure to learn due to mental retardation, 7) helplessness in emergencies, 8) physical stress, 9) danger in traveling in inclement weather, 10) failure to recognize impending dangers or hazardous situations, and 11) detriment to parents' health because of worry (Cortazzo & Sansone, 1976). In all probability, these parents had encountered many professionals who minimized the benefits that independent or semi-independent living could have for their sons and daughters. The professional community has only recently begun to emphasize the concept of independent living and related skills instruction. In the past, curriculum sequences for individuals with severe disabilities did not typically include community mobility training. Recent evidence shows that curriculum emphases are now changing to reflect a greater concern for independent living and the skills required for that lifestyle. As a result, independent travel is becoming a higher priority to both parents and professionals.

To enlist the support of parents and professionals for travel training programs, Vogelsburg and Rusch (1980) suggest the use of a signed consent that includes: 1) an explanation of the purpose and procedures of the program, 2) a description of potential discomforts or risks, 3) a description of benefits, 4) an offer to answer any program-related questions, and 5) a provision that the trainee can withdraw from the program. Following the initial training period, many fears are alleviated and much support can be generated for the continued use of mobility skills. If parental fears persist, individual counseling can be used to reduce these concerns and generate program support.

In communities where such programs have been conducted, the acquisition of independent travel skills by individuals with disabilities has resulted in increased support from parents. According to Laus (1974), the public bus training program, which involved students with mental retardation (IQ 36–51) who attended school in Pittsburgh, resulted in parents viewing their offspring as young adults rather than as dependent children. For the parents, the success of this program was an excellent demonstration of the overall purpose of the public school program, which is aimed at reducing dependency and promoting independence in all aspects of community life.

Overprotectiveness and lowered expectations can combine to present attitudinal barriers that severely limit the person's ability to acquire independent living skills. However, the development of responsible and effective community mobility training programs can alleviate parents' fears concerning the safety of their son or daughter and, consequently, raise the expectations that both parents and professionals have for independent living. The development of such programs will significantly increase an individual's opportunity to acquire independent travel skills.

MOBILITY MODES

The removal of physical and attitudinal barriers will increase community mobility opportunities for many individuals, enabling these persons to go shopping, to go to movie theaters, or to go to the library. In order for a person to take full advantage of these community resources, a variety of mobility skills are necessary. Movement from one place to another in the community can be accomplished in several different ways and with varying degrees of independence. In Figure 7.1, a matrix of mobility modes and a range of potential destinations are presented. The mobility modes identified in this matrix are ambulation without assistance, ambulation with assistance, independent use of conveyance, dependent use of conveyance, and public transportation. Each of these modes is discussed below and specific examples within each mode are also presented.

Ambulation without Assistance

Walking is the typical way in which people move from one place to another within a particular setting. Walking between two locations in the community is usually referred to as pedestrian travel, which has been referred to as primarily the behavior of crossing streets and intersections. In a study by Horner, Jones, and Williams (1985), the effects of general case instruction for teaching street crossing to three persons with severe mental retardation are examined. Each of these persons was taught how to cross the street independently across a group of 20 "nontrained" streets. The method of training used in this study is suitable for replication. Mobility skills, such as walking, are often taken for granted. Yet, without accessibility, outlined by the provisions of the ADA, millions of people with physical disabilities would not be able to travel independently.

Ambulation with Assistance

Due to sensory or physical disabilities, many individuals require assistance in order to ambulate independently. This assistance may be in the form of a cane, crutches, a seeing eye dog, or a sighted guide. For the most part, professional discussions in the literature regarding these ambulation aides have been restricted to individuals with normal intelligence who have visual or physical disabilities. However, because many persons with mental retardation have concomitant sensory and physical disabilities, these discussions need to be expanded to include persons with severe disabilities so that they can learn how to use ambulation aides to travel in their home communities.

Mobility modes	Home	Neighborhood	School	Community	Extracommunity
Ambulation without assistance (walking)					
Ambulation with assistance (use of a prosthetic device such as a cane or seeing eye dog)					
Independent use of conveyance (use of wheelchair, bicycle, or car)					
Dependent use of conveyance (passenger in wheelchair, car, van, or bus)					
Public transportation (use of elevator, car pool, taxi, bus, or train)					

Figure 7.1. Community mobility matrix

Independent Use of Conveyance

A *conveyance* is a means or way by which a person or object is carried from one place to another. Conveyances that can be used independently by persons with disabilities who are not ambulatory include manual wheelchairs, electric wheelchairs, tricycles and bicycles, mopeds and motorcycles, cars, and vans. The skills required to use these conveyances vary considerably in difficulty, from the relatively simple skills required to operate an electric wheelchair to the complex skills needed to drive a van.

On the whole, very little programmatic research has been conducted to determine the practicality of training persons with severe disabilities to use various conveyance means independently. As a result, there is uncertainty in the field as to whether or not it is realistic to teach specific means of mobility. As Gold (1976) has stated:

> the decision to teach or not to teach any task to people who have severe and profound handicaps must be based on whether or not that task can be analyzed into teachable components rather than some general feelings about the difficulty of the task. (p. 81)

Centered on the ideas of the above statement, Zider and Gold (1981) conducted a behind-the-wheel training program for two adults with mental retardation. As a result of this program, both subjects met criterion on the following skills that were taught in a simulator and driver training vehicle: 1) correct positioning of self and equipment, 2) starting engine and engaging vehicle in drive, 3) maintaining speed and braking, and 4) turning and passing. Although the results of this study are encouraging, this area of instruction will undoubtedly remain controversial for persons with mental retardation due to the potential risks involved. It remains to be seen if persons such as those trained in this study can make the necessary discriminations that will enable them to maintain a reasonably safe driving record.

Although controversy will persist regarding the feasibility of teaching certain individuals with disabilities to operate automobiles, the task analysis approach used in the Zider and Gold (1981) study could easily be applied to other conveyances. Innovative programs may evolve and the independent mobility of persons with disabilities may be significantly advanced. Failure to conduct such analyses and related program development results in many individuals being unnecessarily dependent on attendant services for mobility within community settings.

Dependent Use of Conveyance

Many individuals with disabilities are transported from one place to another with the assistance of attendant staff. Various conveyances that are frequently used are wheelchairs, cars, vans, and buses. Although many individuals need assistance to travel, a large range of skills comprise the continuum of dependence to independence in the use of various conveyances. Unfortunately, little attention has been focused on this range of skills; however, the "principle of partial participation," as described by Brown et al. (1979), provides a rationale for showing dignity and respect toward all skills on the continuum.

The principle of partial participation contends that even if a person cannot perform an entire skill independently, he or she should be encouraged to participate as independently as possible; therefore, if a person must be pushed from place to place in a wheelchair, he or she should be taught to assist in the process. With certain individuals, this assistance might be as minimal as cooperating in a transfer from the chair to another location. This approach was used with two adults with mental retardation who were nonvocal and quadriplegic (Zanier, McPhail, & Voelker, 1989). The adults were taught to operate a power wheelchair using a device controlled by head movement. A four-phase microcomputer-aided training model developed in this study was designed to gradually shape the skills necessary for wheelchair operation.

Furthermore, there are several skills that may be required of individuals who are passengers in different vehicles. These include getting in and out, locking and unlocking doors, fastening and unfastening seat belts, remaining seated, keeping doors closed, and being socially appropriate during the trip. Failure to perform some of these basic skills may result in a person being denied the opportunity to participate in community activities.

Public Transportation

In addition to pedestrian travel, public transportation is the community mobility mode that has received the most research attention. In many communities, the public bus is the most prevalent means of transportation. Consequently, several training programs for persons with disabilities have been directed at this transportation mode. These programs are timely since there seems to be an increase in the dependence upon and the use of public transportation, especially the bus systems. For example, due to an increased awareness regarding energy conservation in the late 1980s and early 1990s, public transportation has been given a boost. Furthermore, in most communities with a population of over 30,000, some form of public bus transportation exists. Therefore, it can be expected that present public transportation systems will be maintained or expanded and that new systems will be initiated. These developments ensure that public transportation opportunities will become available to individuals with disabilities if they are not already. Unfortunately, this increase in opportunity has not necessarily been matched by increased ridership by citizens with disabilities. This is due to accessibility problems and the lack of independent mobility skills. In this section, the results of several training programs developed to improve the independent use of public transportation are summarized. These studies have collectively demonstrated that under the appropriate instructional conditions most persons with disabilities can learn to use the public bus as a means of transportation in their communities.

As early as 1963, Tobias and Cortazzo expressed the opinion that the commercial bus system was a disproportionately expensive mode of transportation for transporting adults with mental retardation to and from community-based programs. When a day services program for these adults was being planned, only 9 of 72 accepted applicants could reach the program without assistance. After 6 months of individualized tutoring and practice sessions, 31 clients were traveling independently. This eliminated the need for one chartered bus and resulted in a savings of $3,100. Additional data regarding the effectiveness of public transportation training for adults with mental retardation were provided by Cortazzo and Sansone (1976). These authors summarized the results of travel training programs involving 378 adults. Of the 378 trainees, 199 learned to travel independently between their homes and the day program, with an average training time of 1 1/2 months per trainee. Based on the success of this travel training effort, one program was able to reduce its annual budget for travel from $21,000 to $10,000 in only 3 years.

The early demonstrations, which showed that persons with mental retardation could learn to use public transportation systems, have been followed by more specific investigations regarding the effectiveness of various training procedures. For example, Kubat (1973) used experimental and control groups of 13 subjects to evaluate a training program consisting of: 1) discussion of appropriate bus riding behavior, 2) demonstration of the route by escorting the client in a private vehicle, 3) simulation of the bus ride in a private vehicle, and 4) opportunity for the trainee to ride the city bus with direct instruction from the trainer. For all experimental subjects, this training sequence resulted in acquisition of independent bus riding behaviors in approximately 12 hours of training.

Neef, Iwata, and Page (1978) conducted a comparative study of classroom instruction versus in vivo training of public bus transportation skills. This study consisted of classroom training for five young adults with mental retardation and in vivo instruction for two other individuals. With both groups of subjects, a multiple baseline across subjects was used to demonstrate the effectiveness of the training procedures. Classroom instruction included: 1) manipulation of a doll through the steps of appropriate bus riding, 2) presentation of photographic stimuli (slides) so that subjects could identify relevant and irrelevant cues for particular bus riding responses, and 3) training on a simulated bus with slides projected to show sequenced locations along a bus route. In vivo training involved a subject and trainer actually riding the bus on its daily route. The trainer contingently praised correct responses, provided explicit feedback for errors, and modeled correct responses. The bus riding behaviors targeted in this study were: 1) locating, 2) signaling, 3) boarding, 4) riding, and 5) exiting.

According to Neef et al. (1978), the results of this study strongly support the classroom training approach since the bus riding skills could be generalized to the natural environment. Average training time was 8.85 hours per subject in classroom training as compared to 33.25 hours for those subjects trained in vivo. The effectiveness of classroom travel training was maximized by using realistic simulations, minimizing distracting stimuli, and providing opportunity for repeated practice of difficult behaviors. Although classroom training was demonstrated to be extremely effective in this study, the subject was labeled as being mildly retarded (mean IQ = 56). More recently, Welch (1985) showed how students could generalize public transportation skills through simulated training in the classroom. These students had an average intelligence of 40–55. Generalization from classroom experience to community performance may be more of a problem with a population that has a greater amount of severe intellectual disabilities.

Although numerous bus riding programs are discussed in the literature, there were few reports involving the instruction of persons with disabilities on the use of other means of public transportation. Other means include the use of escalators and elevators, participation in car pools, the use of taxi services and the subway, and travel by train or airline. The lack of published program initiatives involving these mobility means probably reflects the fact that these means have been largely unavailable or unused by individuals with severe disabilities. As independent or semi-independent living and gainful employment become a reality for more individuals, the need to explore training techniques to maximize use of various public transportation alternatives is imperative.

MOBILITY DESTINATIONS

A person's mobility training needs are determined by the settings he or she must travel within and between, which can be referred to as potential mobility destinations. In developing individualized mobility training programs, a detailed analysis of these destinations and the skills that are required to move within and between them should be conducted. Several mobility destinations are identified in Figure 7.1, including home, neighborhood, school, community, and extracommunity settings. Based on the mobility requirements identified through the detailed analysis of mobility destinations, individuals should be able to be assessed to determine specific training priorities. These specific training priorities may highlight environmental modifications needed to increase accessibility and to develop alternative mobility modes.

As indicated in Figure 7.1, each person's mobility plan should reflect a dual concern for mobility mode and destination. This dual emphasis provides a concrete idea of the functional value of community mobility; that is, community mobility should provide people with skills that enable them to participate more fully in community life. Independent mobility skills are essential to the goal of maximal community participation.

RECOMMENDATIONS FOR AN
INCLUSIVE TRANSPORTATION SYSTEM

As the previous discussion centered on learning and modes and types of travel training instruction for persons with developmental disabilities, it may be helpful to take a look at how one state, Virginia, is planning for improved transportation accessibility. This system includes *all* persons with disabilities, as well as those who are elderly and cannot leave their homes without specialized transportation assistance. The appendix following this chapter is part of a report conducted by Virginia Lt. Governor Donald Beyer's Commission on Disability (1992) for the Transportation Subcommittee. These recommendations for improved transportation accessibility are currently being studied by the Virginia General Assembly.

CONCLUSION

The ADA will aid in the improvement of community mobility opportunities for persons with disabilities. As noted earlier in the book, there are very stringent transportation regulations to which communities will need to adhere. The attention to public and private transportation accessibility is probably one of the strongest aspects of the ADA.

With this said, it would be naive to assume that there will not be controversy, even backlash, over the implementation of some of the ADA's regulations, particularly in the transportation area. For example, in an especially biting editorial, the *Richmond Times-Dispatch* notes:

> one area shopping mall discovered that it must add dozens of handicapped spaces to its lot, even though the spaces it currently provides seldom are full. So dictatorial is the ADA that businesses cannot, for example, reserve a next-to-the-front door parking space for an "employee of the week," such spaces have to go to the "disabled" . . . these are matters best resolved by local governments, not Washington, DC. (May 7, 1992, p. 20)

Editorials like these will make implementing the ADA's regulations even more of a challenge. Yet, as persons with disabilities are empowered by the attainment of greater accessibility within their communities, they will be more able to offset such negative reactions. It is important for the strong transportation aspect of the ADA to be considered a positive force on increased mobility and, consequently, on independent living for persons with disabilities.

REFERENCES

Beyer Commission on Disability. (1992, January). *A report to the Virginia General Assembly*. Richmond, VA.
Bowe, F. (1979). Transportation: A key to independent living. *Archives of Physical Medicine and Rehabilitation, 60*, 473–486.

Brown, L., Branston-McClean, M.B., Baumgart, D., Vincent, L., Falvey, M., & Schroeder, J. (1979). Using the characteristics of current and subsequent least restrictive environment in the development of curricular content for severely handicapped students. *AAESPH Review, 4*(4), 407–424.

Community travel for physically impaired students: The Millet curriculum. (1989). Saginaw, Michigan: Millet Learning Center.

Cortazzo, S., & Sansone, R. (1976). Travel training. *Teaching Exceptional Children, 43*, 74–78.

Gold, M.W. (1976). Task analysis of a complex assembly task by the retarded blind. *Exceptional Children, 43*, 78–84.

Horner, R., Jones, D., & Williams, S. (1985). A functional approach to generalized street crossing. *TASH, 10*(2), 71–78.

Kubat, A. (1973). Unique experiment in independent travel. *Journal of Rehabilitation, 2*, 36–39.

LaGrow, S., Wiener, S., & LaDuke, R. (1990). Independent travel for developmentally disabled persons. *Research in Developmental Disabilities, 11*(3), 289–301.

Laus, M.D. (1974). Orientation and mobility instruction for the sighted mentally retarded. *Education and Training of the Mentally Retarded, 9*, 70–73.

Neef, N.A., Iwata, B.A., & Page, T.J. (1978). Public transportation training: In vivo versus classroom instruction. *Journal of Applied Behavior Analysis, 11*, 331–344.

Pedestrian Safety Training Curriculum. (1990). Illinois State Office of Secretary of State. Springfield, Illinois.

Perske, R. (1972). The dignity of risk. In W. Wolfensberger (Ed.), *The principle of normalization in human services.* Toronto: National Institute on Mental Retardation.

Richmond Times-Dispatch. (1992, May 7). Disabling law editorial. Richmond, VA, p. 20.

Saenger, G. (1972). The adjustment of severely retarded adults in the community. In H.B. Robinson & N.M. Robinson (Eds.), *The mentally retarded child.* New York: McGraw Hill.

Taylor, B., & Taylor, A. (1989). Social casework and environmental cognition. *Social Work, 34*(5), 463–467.

Tobias, J., & Cortazzo, A.D. (1963). Training severely retarded adults for greater independence in community living. *Training School Bulletin, 60*, 23–37.

Vogelsburg, R.T., & Rusch, F.R. (1980). Community mobility training. In F. Rusch & D. Mithaug (Eds.), *Vocational training for mentally retarded adults* (pp. 111–128). Champagne, IL: Research Press.

Welch, J. (1985). Teaching public transportation problem solving skills to young adults with moderate handicaps. *Education and Training in Mental Retardation, 20*(4), 287–295.

Zanier, D., McPhail, P., & Voelker, S. (1989). A microcomputer-aided mobility training program for the multiply handicapped. *Mental Retardation and Learning Disability Bulletin, 17*(1), 51–62.

Zider, S., & Gold, N.W. (1981). Behind the wheel training for individuals labeled moderately retarded. *Exceptional Children, 47*, 632–639.

Appendix

Virginia's Recommendation for Statewide Accessible Transportation

STATEWIDE POLICY AND REGIONAL COORDINATION OF SPECIALIZED TRANSPORTATION

ISSUE: Transportation for the elderly and persons with disabilities is fragmented throughout the state. In some areas there is little transportation available; in others, there are duplicate systems operating below capacity. There is no statewide policy and little local coordination of transportation services.

Previous state efforts to coordinate have been conducted at the middle-management level and lacked authority to determine state policy. Local governments have not been significantly involved.

Local and regional coordination of existing resources with a consistent statewide policy offers the opportunity to stretch existing resources and improve the effectiveness and accessibility of transportation for persons who are dependent.

RECOMMENDATION: Establish a Specialized Transportation Council, appointed by the Governor, to develop and implement a comprehensive policy of coordination for specialized transportation services to the elderly, persons with disabilities, and other transportation disadvantaged Virginians. Membership should include the Secretary of Health and Human Resources and the Secretary of Transportation. The council should be adequately staffed and have the assistance of all state agencies involved in specialized transportation. The Council should assist local governments in developing regional coordinated transportation plans and set standards for safe and efficient provision of services by the providers designated in the regional plans.

The language proposed to establish the Council is as follows:

Policy of the Commonwealth The General Assembly declares that it is the policy of the Commonwealth to support the development of safe, cost-effective, coordinated specialized transportation services for transportation disadvantaged Virginians.

Nature of Specialized Transportation Specialized transportation is provided to the transportation disadvantaged for activities including but not limited to employment, medical services, legal and financial services, human service agencies' programs and services, and shopping.

The "transportation disadvantaged" are persons who are unable to use fixed route public transportation and are unable to independently operate a motor vehicle because of a physical or mental disability or economic circumstance.

Creation of the Specialized Transportation Council To this end, the Governor shall establish a Specialized Transportation Council. The membership of the Council shall be:

The Secretary of Health and Human Resources
The Secretary of Transportation
Five persons including an urban transportation provider, a rural transportation provider, and two consumers.

The Chairman shall be appointed by the Governor. Members shall serve a term of 4 years and may be reappointed for a second 4-year term.

The Council will direct the work of its staff and of an interagency staff committee composed of representatives from the following agencies: Aging, Deaf and Hard of Hearing, Education, Medical Assistance Services, MHMRSAS, Board for Rights of Virginians with Disabilities, Rehabilitative Services, Social Services, Transportation and Visually Handicapped.

Duties of the Council The Council shall recommend strategies, standards, policies, and guidelines for the development and implementation of statewide transportation services for the transportation disadvantaged:

1. Developing a comprehensive statewide specialized transportation plan based upon regional and local coordination of public transportation systems, private for-profit and not-for-profit transportation providers, human services transportation providers, and local volunteer resources
2. Developing criteria for and administering the Specialized Transportation Incentive Fund and other funds under its authority to fund innovative and cooperative specialized transportation demonstration projects
3. Identifying barriers to coordinated delivery of transportation services and initiating corrective actions
4. Developing incentives for public–private partnerships
5. Developing initiatives for eliminating constraints upon volunteers who provide transportation and creating incentives for these volunteers
6. Developing certification standards for human services transportation providers
7. Hiring staff necessary to carry out its other duties

Coordination of Local Specialized Transportation   Each Planning District Commission, through its Metropolitan Planning Organization (MPO) where it exists, shall establish an advisory transportation coordination committee to guide the coordination and administration of specialized transportation with human services agencies, public transportation systems and, where appropriate, with private for-profit and not-for-profit transportation providers.

The membership of the Transportation coordination committee shall be composed of, but not limited to, transportation disadvantaged consumers, providers of specialized transportation, local governments, local public transportation systems, and local private for-profit and not-for-profit transportation providers.

By July 1, 1993, each Planning District Commission, shall submit to the Specialized Transportation Council a plan for cost-effective coordination of specialized transportation services in the planning district of localities. An approved plan shall be implemented by July 1, 1994.

Each provider of specialized transportation services supported by state funds or state-administered federal funds shall meet the certification standard established by the Specialized Transportation Council.

PUBLIC TRANSPORTATION RESOURCES

ISSUE: The implementation of the Americans with Disabilities Act (ADA) may be the impetus for some human services agencies to reduce their transportation expenditures by shifting clients into public transportation systems.
RECOMMENDATION: State human services agencies should require maintenance of effort in transportation by their local agencies by insisting that local agencies work with public transportation systems, where present, to maximize levels of service.

ISSUE: There is a need for expansion of public transportation throughout the state, but many local governments are unable or unwilling to provide public transportation.
RECOMMENDATION: Where appropriate, expand local human services transportation programs to offer public transportation. Require coordination with human services transportation as a prerequisite to public transportation funding.

ISSUE: In some urban areas, there is little coordination of human services transportation.
RECOMMENDATION: Require all local human services agencies to participate in the coordination plans submitted by Planning District Commissions.

PRIVATE FOR-PROFIT AND NOT-FOR-PROFIT TRANSPORTATION PROVIDERS

ISSUE: Providers complain that the reimbursement rate and the administrative paperwork make Medicaid transportation unprofitable.

RECOMMENDATION: Increase reimbursement rate for DMAS clients, streamline documentation and pre-authorization process.

ISSUE: Private for-profit providers lack access to adequate and affordable training for staff, including administrators and drivers.

RECOMMENDATION: Include private for-profit and not-for-profit providers in VDOT training for administrators and drivers and offer other opportunities to coordinate training with human services and public transportation providers.

ISSUE: Some private for profit providers are not aware of programs they are eligible to participate in through DMAS.

RECOMMENDATION: DMAS should target private for-profit providers and publicize program eligibility.

HUMAN SERVICES TRANSPORTATION PROVIDERS

ISSUE: Most federally funded human services transportation programs are restricted to serving only a narrow group of clients (e.g., elderly, JTPA clients, Head Start children). This makes it difficult to operate vehicles at full capacity and increases the operating cost per unit. Some apparent restrictions may be based on inadequate information.

RECOMMENDATION: State human services agencies should review and identify regulatory restrictions on their transportation programs, and seek waivers or changes in operations that will allow greater coordination and sharing of resources among their local agencies.

ISSUE: Agencies need to generate additional revenue to meet funding cuts and support vehicle replacement and increasing operating costs. Some programs are prohibited from charging fees for services; others can charge but do not have adequate cost data to set realistic fees.

RECOMMENDATION: State human services agencies should:

1. Review and identify regulatory restrictions on charging fees, provide training in determining actual operating costs, and assist local agencies in developing flexible fee structures that enable programs to cover appropriate cost but do not impose undue hardship on consumers.
2. Evaluate how Medicaid can be better used to pay for client transportation, using fees collected and local funding to maximize federal share.

ISSUE: Local agencies need to coordinate with local government resources to reduce operating costs and seek the most cost-effective methods of operation.

RECOMMENDATION: With the encouragement and assistance of state agencies, all local agencies should realistically evaluate subcontracting for transportation with public transportation providers, private for-profit operators, or other local agencies.

VOLUNTEER RESOURCES

ISSUE: Volunteers are a potential source of committed, sensitive personnel for transportation. A statewide corps of trained volunteer drivers, assigned and coordinated locally, can reduce operating costs, add flexibility and responsiveness, and develop public/private partnerships.

RECOMMENDATION: Establish a statewide "Volunteer Transportation Service Corps" with the following components:

- Co-sponsored by major Virginia corporations and state advocacy groups for the elderly and persons with disabilities
- Recruit particularly among sponsoring corporations' retirees, as well as general public
- Establish quality control by certifying volunteers who have completed required professional training in safety, defensive driving, sensitivity to disabilities
- Establish local or regional chapters corresponding to regional specialized transportation plans
- Place particular emphasis on evening and weekend service when transportation is not available

ISSUE: Liability issues discourage the use of volunteers and private automobiles.

RECOMMENDATION: Exempt or limit the liability for certified volunteer drivers while performing approved transportation.

ISSUE: Incentives are needed to encourage use of volunteers' personal vehicles for transporting clients who do not need lift-equipped vans. For taxpayers who itemize deductions, Federal income tax regulations allow a deduction on Schedule A of $0.12 per mile for volunteer travel. Virginia allows eighteen cents for taxpayers who itemize deductions.

RECOMMENDATION: On the Virginia income tax form, allow a deduction at the federal rate for business mileage (currently $0.26) for all certified volunteer drivers, including those who do not itemize deductions, for approved transportation mileage.

ISSUE: The value of approved transportation provided by certified volunteers represents a tangible contribution to the agency and supplements other local funds.

RECOMMENDATION: Allow the value of approved services provided by certified volunteers to count toward local match for human services transportation programs.

The above proposals provide many creative solutions and alternatives for the improvement of transportation options for persons with disabilities. These issues and recommendations reflect a great deal of intensive labor on the part of many concerned citizens. Although these proposals have been in the process of development for years, the passage of the ADA has helped to stimulate their visibility.

Part III

The ADA as a Catalyst for Social Change

As a consequence of the ADA's existence and impact, many related reform programs and progressive activities are expected to be implemented in the 1990s and beyond. The authors certainly hope that the ADA will serve as a catalyst to help eliminate the substandard practices in housing for persons with disabilities, as well as increase the number of therapeutic recreation programs and facilities that are available; therefore, these issues are addressed in this section. In addition, the authors will explore some of the effects that the ADA will have on the education of persons with disabilities.

It is impossible to predict the extent to which the ADA will influence other programs and activities, especially those involving issues that are not specifically addressed in the law; however, there is every reason to believe that the spirit and the intent of the ADA will have positive, influential effects on a wide range of disability issues. Again, the ADA will only be a successful catalyst for social change if the regulations are implemented without negative feedback from society toward what some may consider to be an obtrusive law.

Clearly, people who are receiving services, as well as those who are working in the disability field, are being given a wonderful opportunity to communicate with their peers who do not have disabilities. Accounts extolling the virtues of the ADA have appeared in newspapers and magazines throughout the United States. For example, the *New York Times* writes:

a law to ban job discrimination against disabled people takes effect in a week and is widely expected to force changes in employment practices as far-reaching as those that followed the laws that opened jobs to women and blacks. (Kilborn, 1992, p. 1)

The extensive amount of publicity concerning the ADA as a catalyst for social change offers an opportunity for professionals to make long-lasting inroads to the bias against accepting persons with disabilities into society. This section will help detail how this bias can be overcome.

REFERENCE

Kilborn, P. (1992, July 19). Big change likely as law bans bias toward disabled: 14 million to be covered. *New York Times,* Vol. CLXI, p. 1.

Chapter 8

Family Empowerment

*H. Rutherford Turnbull, III,
David F. Bateman, and
Ann P. Turnbull*

Many families across the United States fear that although their children are involved in special education programs, their future dreams will be denied as a result of discrimination within the community. At a 1990 Senate Subcommittee on Disability Policy meeting concerning the Americans with Disabilities Act (ADA), Danny Piper, a 19-year-old boy with Down syndrome from Ankeny, Iowa, was the center of attention. His mother, Sylvia, gave testimony to which many families who have children with disabilities could relate. She expressed her fears that community discrimination will deny Danny his dreams (Harkin, July 13, 1990).

Influenced by Sylvia's testimony, Senator Tom Harkin (D-Iowa), the sponsor of the ADA, later dedicated the law to "the next generation of children (with disabilities) and their parents" (Harkin, July 13, 1990). He stated that:

> with the passage of the ADA, we as a society make a pledge that every child with a disability will have the opportunity to maximize his or her potential to live proud, productive, and prosperous lives in the mainstream of our society. (Harkin, July 13, 1990, p. 9687)

Why is the Piper testimony and the testimony of the many organizations that represent families of persons with disabilities so important? The answer is that the testimony proves that the ADA is not just a law for persons with disabilities, but a law for their families as well. There is, after all, a clear and direct link between family members. This link has been established anecdotally (Turnbull & Turnbull, 1985b). Moreover, federal law recognizes this link, providing for a significant amount of parent participation in the education of their children who have disabilities (Turnbull, 1993). Federal law also establishes programs that attempt to preserve the integrity and unity of families by providing various forms of support (Turnbull & Barber, 1986).

The ADA is the latest Congressional recognition of the family systems theory; that is, if an action discriminates against a person with a disability, it also affects that person's family. Physical and attitudinal barriers, as well as other discriminatory practices, cause segregation and relegation of persons with disabilities to lesser services. Accordingly, the ADA's empowerment is double-barreled, it affects persons with disabilities and their families. Obviously, the less dependent a person with a disability is upon his or her family, the more independent the family. For example, when Danny Piper is able to earn money, he will be less financially dependent upon his family. When transportation systems are accessible to him, his family's driving responsibility will lessen. When he is able to use a telephone relay system, his family will be able to communicate with him wherever he lives or works. When public accommodations, in general, are more accessible, his family will have fewer advocacy responsibilities. These positive aspects are only a few of those that the ADA has to offer.

Unfortunately, the ADA is not entirely positive for families. The individual's struggle for the opportunity to participate in the mainstream of society, to live "a proud and independent life" (Harkin, July 13, 1990, p. 9689), to enjoy the values of equality, independence, and freedom, and not to be "deprived of the[ir] basic guarantees of life, liberty, and the pursuit of happiness" (Bush, July 26, 1990) is not simply erased by one law. Families still face formidable tasks that are addressed later in this chapter.

Despite some of its pitfalls, the ADA clearly promises more for families than almost any other federal disability law. The ADA provides persons with disabilities and their families with a new set of principles to follow; it fundamentally affects children's education rights under the Individuals with Disabilities Education Act of 1990 (IDEA) (previously titled the Education of the Handicapped Act); and it affects the norms of society in significant ways. This chapter describes the ADA's effects with respect to principles, the IDEA, and societal norms.

PRINCIPLES FOR FAMILIES AND THE ADA

The ADA sets the "Nations's proper goals" for individuals with disabilities and their families (through the family systems theory). The law adopts the position that, with the proper support, individuals are capable of attaining these goals, and it provides support by prohibiting discrimination. The ADA strives for "equality of opportunity, full participation, independent living, and economic self-sufficiency" for persons with disabilities. Although some people are satisfied with "second-class citizenship" for themselves and others with disabilities, families have every right to great expectations. Families do themselves a disservice, and professionals do families a disservice, by learning to be "realistic" and to accept the world, the person with the disability, and themselves "as is."

Congress has found that "persons with disabilities, as a group, occupy an inferior status in our society, and are severely disadvantaged socially, vocationally, economically, and educationally" (42 U.S.C. 12101, et seq., Sec. 2[a][6]). They are a "discrete and insular minority who have been faced with restrictions and limitations, subjected to a history of purposeful unequal treatment, and relegated to a position of political powerlessness in our society" (42 U.S.C. 12101, et seq., Sec. 2[a][7]). Under these conditions, it was not unreasonable for families to entertain less than high hopes, for professionals to counsel them to be "realistic," and for both to endorse a status quo that afforded cold comfort—but still some comfort. Yet the ADA seeks to achieve "equality of opportunity, full participation, independent living, and economic self-sufficiency" (Sec. 2[a][8]) for individuals (and inferentially their families); it counsels them, their families, professionals, and society to have "great expectations" for the future.

Some families are satisfied to allow professionals or others to make choices on their behalf. Many institutions, segregated schools and classrooms, sheltered workshops, and limited residential choices have been created by families operating under a now outdated ideology. Families still defend these institutions, experiencing jet lag in coping with deinstitutionalization (Avis, 1985) and the current trend toward defacilitation.

Families are, however, competent decision makers, often regarding their limited choices as more the consequence of social limitations (the social construct theory) than of any type of inherent limitations. This perspective on choice is consistent with the ADA's perspective, which seeks "equality of opportunity" (including the opportunity to make a choice) for individuals with disabilities (42 U.S.C. 12101, et seq., Sec. 2[a][8] and [9]) and which bars discrimination in a wide sector of public and private life (42 U.S.C. 12101, et seq., Sec. 2[a][3]).

It sometimes is said that some families, like some individuals with and without disabilities, do not contribute much to society. Indeed, a prevailing societal, professional, and legal view has been that individuals with disabilities are "takers" and not "makers," dependent and not independent, in other words, a drain on society. That is not the view of the ADA. No sufficient justification exists for the ADA unless it is that individuals with disabilities (and by inference, their families) have been prevented from making the contributions of which they are capable. These individuals and their families have not been held back because of their inherent limitations, but because of the ways that society and its laws, customs, practices, and prejudices have discriminated against them and prevented them from making those contributions. Indeed, Congress recites the many ways and the sectors of society in which discrimination has occurred that causes them to be limited in their opportunities. It has claimed that discrimination is a "serious and pervasive social problem" (42 U.S.C. 12101, et seq., Sec. 2[a][2]), that individuals with disablilties "occupy an inferior status in our society (42 U.S.C. 12101, et seq., Sec. 2[a][b]), and that individuals with disabilities are a "discrete and insular minority" that have been subjected to discrimination based on "stereotypic assumptions not truly indicative of the individual ability of such individuals to participate in, and contribute to, society" (42 U.S.C. 12101, et seq., Sec. 2[a][7]).

Relationships, the sinews that bind families and people to each other and create "community," deserve constitutional protection under the First Amendment. Positive relationships are not just by-products but explicit goals of the doctrine of the least restrictive alternative (Turnbull, 1993; Turnbull, Biklen, Brookes, Boggs, & Ellis, 1981). Not only are they the expected results of the ADA's ban on discrimination, but they are the most certain social security system, the greatest safety net, that most families and individuals have. Relations are definitely stronger, longer-lasting, and more certain than any governmental benefits. Yet, the existence of practices and laws that "isolate and segregate" individuals with disabilities and bar them from "full participation" in most, if not all, of the public and private sectors have been the barriers that have kept people with disabilities and their families from establishing needed relationships, as the ADA explicitly acknowledges.

Finally, although it is true that some families and individuals with disabilities do not object to second-class citizenship, many families have strived and succeeded against great odds to achieve full citizenship. In doing so, these families took the path that the ADA now makes more accessible. It is no accident that in reversing the Supreme Court's *Cleburne* decision (*City of Cleburne, Texas v. Cleburne Living Center, et al.,* 1985), which denied special protection under the Fourteenth Amendment to individuals with disabilities, Congress found that these individuals have been barred from even the most elementary rights of citizenship, the right to vote, and the right to have access to state–local and public accommodations (42 U.S.C. 12101, et seq., Sec. 2[a][3]).

What are the new views of persons with disabilities and their families? The ADA uses its own terms, a language that is appropriate for statutes. The authors suggest, however, that the ADA reflects these principles, which are based on the Beach Center on Families and Disability (1990) Statement of Principles:

1. *Inherent strengths* Families have many natural capacities. Nevertheless, they may need support to affirm positive contributions, achieve great

expectations, obtain full citizenship, act on their choices, and enjoy relationships.

2. *Great expectations*   Visions can become realities. Families need new perspectives of what life can be, as well as support for fulfilling these dreams.
3. *Choices*   Families can direct their own lives. Enabling families to act on their preferences allows them to build on their strengths.
4. *Positive contributions*   Persons with disabilities can contribute positively to their families. People with disabilites enrich not only their families, but also their communities and society.
5. *Relationships*   Connections are crucial to family unity. Family members need to be connected to each other and to friends in the community.
6. *Full citizenship*   Less able does not mean less worthy. People with disabilities and their families are entitled to full participation in American life.

It is now appropriate to demonstrate how, under the IDEA and the ADA, families and individuals with disabilities can put these new principles into effect, ensuring that they will be more than just hollow hopes.

THE IDEA, THE ADA, AND FAMILY ACTION

For many families, the IDEA is one installment of a contract between themselves, their family members with disabilities, and the government for a lifetime of services and accessibility. The ADA is simply another installment on the same contract.

The IDEA contract is that the individual with a disability will receive free appropriate early intervention (Part H) and special education (Part B). In short, the school system is required to provide an education that will ensure the development of skills that the individual will use during and after school. The ADA guarantees that the government will prohibit discrimination against an individual with a disability who is otherwise qualified to participate in employment, transportation, telecommunications, state–local government, and public accommodation services, programs, and facilities. Together, the IDEA and the ADA constitute a contract for services (IDEA) and for nondiscrimination (ADA) so that the person who acquires skills from the special education services can put them to use during and after the school years.

These laws ensure that special education will address transition to society and focus on specific outcomes. They also ensure that most of American society will not discriminate against any individual who is "otherwise qualified" (i.e., the person has acquired the needed skills through special education). To see how these results are obtained, it will be helpful to describe the IDEA's six major principles and their relevance to the ADA, and to indicate the ways in which families are or can be involved in the implementation of the IDEA and the ADA.

Zero Reject

The IDEA assures a free appropriate public education for all children with disabilities and, to carry out that assurance, establishes a rule of "zero reject" (Turnbull, 1993). This rule prohibits the exclusion of any child from the benefits of the law and promotes the inclusion of all children into a system of special education, regardless of the severity of a child's disability (*Timothy W. v. Rochester School District,* 1989). The IDEA and the ADA clarify and restate this rule of zero reject in several ways:

- IDEA (Sec. 1401[a][1]) makes it clear that students with autism and traumatic brain injury are included as "children with disabilities." This is not a change in the law so much as it is a clarification. These students were covered by the law previously, but now the law identifies them as a separate and distinct class entitled to the law's benefits.
- IDEA (Sec. 1401[a][24]) makes it clear that students in Bureau of Indian Affairs schools are entitled to the Act's benefits if they are qualified students with disabilities. This merely clarifies the Act and is not a major substantive amendment.
- IDEA (Sec. 1401[a][27]) adds a new definition of persons who are "underrepresented," including "minorities, the poor, the limited English proficient, and individuals with disabilities." This emphasis on outreach to underrepresented groups is consistent with the Act's "service priorities" (those not served get the first use of the federal funds and those with the most severe disabilities get the second).
- IDEA (Sec. 1422) clarifies that students who are deaf-blind are to be provided with an education that includes a transition plan and curriculum that prepares them for independent living and competitive employment. This amendment is also consistent with the "service priorities" provisions of the act.
- IDEA (Sec. 1423[a][1][I]) makes it clear that early education programs should include students prenatally exposed to drugs and/or alcohol whose parents are substance-abusers. These children are covered by the Act if they need special education and should not be excluded from its benefits simply because of the cause of their disabilities.
- ADA (Sec. 3[2] and Sec. 104[d][2]) confirm the United States Supreme Court's ruling (*School Board of Nassau County, Florida v. Arline,* 1987) that people with contagious diseases are "disabled." The ADA also confirms that students with AIDS are entitled to the benefits of the IDEA only if they need special education due to the effects of AIDS (Turnbull, 1993).

- ADA (Sec. 512[a]) also confirms the United States Supreme Court's ruling (*Honig v. Doe*, 1988) that concluded that the zero reject rule exists but has an exception. In this case, the Court ruled that a student may not be removed from his or her present placement and program (the "stay-put" rule) during the time when disciplinary proceedings are underway; however, a "safety valve," was created, which allowed the schools to seek the student's removal in "appropriate cases." The ADA states that in disciplining children with disabilities who are using illegal drugs or alcohol, education agencies may use their regular disciplinary procedures and are not required to use the due process procedures of the IDEA.

Just as the IDEA's zero reject rule is for inclusion and against exclusion, so too is the ADA. The ADA prohibits the physical and attitudinal barriers that have kept people with disabilities out of the "mainstream" and, thus, makes it possible for these people to participate.

Nondiscriminatory Evaluation

The IDEA's second principle is one of "nondiscriminatory evaluation," a principle that requires the local education agency (LEA) to fairly evaluate the student's capacities and disabilities so that it may provide effective special education (Turnbull, 1993). The IDEA only addresses this principle indirectly. For example, as previously stated, Sec. 1401(27) of the IDEA defines certain "underrepresented" populations and requires state education agencies (SEAs) and local education agencies (LEAs) to make special efforts to provide services to these populations. Moreover, Sec. 1409 requires the Department of Education to conduct or fund special studies on the overrepresentation of minority students (principally, students of color) in special education. In these two provisions, the IDEA implicitly acknowledges that a bias based on socioeconomic, racial, or ethnic characteristics may have existed against these populations. The recognition of that bias in testing is the basis for the principle of nondiscriminatory evaluation (Turnbull, 1993). It should go without saying that the ADA does not distinguish between individuals on the basis of race, ethnicity, or socioeconomic status; it protects all people in an equal manner.

Appropriate Education

The greatest changes in the IDEA occur with respect to the principle of an "appropriate education." The greatest impact of the ADA on students and other individuals with disabilities also occurs in this context. There are two amendments of the IDEA that influence this result: 1) Sec. 1401(a)(20) adds a requirement to the IEP mandating "transition services" for certain students, and 2) Sec. 1401(a)(19) defines "transition services." Each of these amendments warrants separate discussion.

Sec. 1401(a)(20) now requires a "statement of the needed transition services for students." This statement is to be added to the student's IEP "no later than age 16 and annually thereafter (and, when determined appropriate for the individual, beginning at age 14 or younger)."

"Transition services" are defined by Sec. 1401(a)(19). This term has several components. First, it includes a "coordinated set of activities for the student," which must be "designed within an outcome-oriented process." This set of activities must "promote" various outcomes, such as "movement from school to post-school activities, including post-secondary education, vocational training, integrated employment (including supported employment), continuing and adult education, adult services, independent living, or community participation." The wording in this list of outcomes (particularly, the use of "or") suggests that they are not all mandatory; arguably, at least one must be in the individualized transition plan (ITP). In addition, this set of activities "shall include instruction, community experiences, the development of employment and other post-school adult living objectives, and, when appropriate, acquisition of daily living skills and functional vocational evaluation."

This particular amendment represents a significant change in the IDEA. Until now, the act was generally process-oriented; it told the LEAs and SEAs what process to follow in order to educate children with disabilities. Now, however, the Act makes it explicit that there shall be certain outcome-oriented education. Accordingly, a student's IEP should contain goals that are consistent with these outcomes. The student's progress, or lack of progress, toward these outcomes may be evidence that the student is not receiving an appropriate education. Furthermore, the student's curriculum should be community-based (in order to produce the targeted outcomes) and delivered in the most integrated setting (so that the skills will be learned in the natural setting and generalize to that setting).

Sec. 1401(a)(19) of the IDEA relates to the United States Supreme Court's decision in *Board of Education of the Henrick Hudson Central School District v. Rowley* (1982). In this case, the Court held that a student is entitled to the opportunity for "educational benefit," and that the student's progress toward educational goals is evidence that the "benefit" test is being met. Thus, if a student's transition goals are not being met, it is likely that the student can successfully claim a violation of the "benefit" test and a denial of appropriate education under the Court's decision.

Furthermore, this amendment also requires the IEP/ITP process to take into account the student's choices with respect to his or her goals after school. This affirms that the student's participation in the IEP process is appropriate. It also is an implicit recognition that special education should require the student to develop decision-making skills as part of his or her progress toward "independence," a desired outcome of special education.

Congress also required that the ITP include a statement of the interagency responsibilities and/or linkages that the student needs before leaving school. In addition, the LEA must reconvene the student's IEP team in order to identify alternative strategies for meeting transition objectives when an agency that has agreed to provide transition services fails to do so.

Finally, with respect to "transition" issues in general, several provisions of the IDEA acknowledge that transition planning is a generic skill and that transitions are appropriate at various student and family life stages. For example, Sec. 1477 provides for an individualized family service plan and Sec. 1425 relates to transition planning for adolescents. Sec. 1409(c) relates to grants, contracts, and cooperative agreements awarded by the Department of Education, and allows the Secretary to require recipients to address transition issues.

Two new definitions are added by Sec. 1401(a)(25) and (26) of the IDEA, "assistive technology device" and "assistive technology service," respectively. These definitions are the same as those used in the Technology-Related Assistance for Individuals with Disabilities Act of 1988 (PL 100-407). This act leaves the decision up to the state as to how a system of technology-related assistance for individuals with disabilities will be developed, and who will benefit from it. Under the IDEA, if a student with a disability needs technology-related assistance and the student's IEP calls for such assistance, the student may obtain this assistance from his or her LEA or from the statewide system. Thus, assistive technology services or devices are part of the student's education program as appropriate. A student's IEP should demand these services and devices when appropriate in order to be regarded as legally sufficient. In a sense, the requirement concerning technology affirms the decision in *Timothy W. v. Rochester School District* (1989) that, at least for students who have profound disabilities, "state of art" special education includes the use of assistive technology and devices.

Sec. 1401(a)(16) of the IDEA affects "related services." These services include therapeutic recreation, social work services, and rehabilitation counseling. Again, this is not so much a change as a clarification. Before the amendments, recreation and counseling services were listed as related services; the amendments clarify that recreation now includes therapeutic recreation and that counseling services now include rehabilitation counseling (consistent with the Act's expectation for vocational outcomes as a result of special education).

Special provisions for the early education of students with disabilities are amended by Sec. 1423 of the IDEA. Early education programs should focus on the transition of infants and toddlers from early intervention into preschool special education (or regular education). The use of assistive technology devices and services should also be promoted in the programs.

Sec. 1401(a)(19) of the IDEA and the amendments to the Social Security

Act of 1988, which allow the state Medicaid fund to pay for certain related services, show that Congress does not want any gaps in services. In fact, Congress expects state and local education and healthcare agencies to work together to fill any gaps that do occur in service or funding for students with disabilities. This expectation, in effect, affirms the "appropriate education" rule by providing for services and allocating their costs across various agencies.

In summary, the ADA's purpose and goals are consistent with the IDEA's. The ADA's purpose is to provide clear, strong, consistent, and enforceable standards that prohibit discrimination against individuals with disabilities, regardless of their age, nature of disability, or extent of disability. The ADA recognizes that discrimination occurs in many ways, for many reasons, and in almost all sectors of society.

In carrying out the goals of equal opportunity, full participation, independent living, and economic self-sufficiency, and by prohibiting discrimination in so many private and public sectors of society, the ADA is consistent with the IDEA in terms of the expected outcomes for individuals with disabilities. The ADA assumes that these individuals will participate in society in a variety of ways. The IDEA now states that transition services must be geared toward that type of participation. When education furnishes the training that helps the student develop the skills to reach these goals, it is appropriate education. Once the student has these skills, nondiscriminatory practices will ensure that there will be no barriers to the student's use of them. Thus, the IDEA focuses on the individual and attempts to remediate the student's disabilities, while the ADA focuses on society and bans discrimination against the individual. Together, these laws fall under the principle of "dual accommodation" or "mutuality," emphasizing that both the student/individual and society must change and be changed so that they can accommodate each other.

It is notable that the principle of "dual accommodation" or "mutuality" is not unlimited under either the IDEA or the ADA. With respect to the IDEA, the courts have allowed LEAs to raise a "cost defense" if it is suggested that they are not furnishing an appropriate education. This defense essentially allows schools to escape providing certain services or facilities if the cost of doing so is unreasonably high (Turnbull, 1993). With respect to the ADA, Congress also allows costs to be a defense. When an accommodation to a person with a disability causes an "undue hardship" on an employer, public accommodation, state–local government, transportation service, or telecommunication service, the accommodation is not required.

Yet, even the cost defense and undue hardship defense reflect the fundamental approach of the IDEA and the ADA—individualization. The IDEA requires an individualized education with goals and strategies that are set out in a student's IEP/ITP or in an individualized family service plan (IFSP) for infants/toddlers and their families. Likewise, the ADA requires an individualized approach, since unreasonable accommodation is based on the burden as it occurs in the context of one or more individuals with disabilities.

Least Restrictive Education

The IDEA contains a presumption that favors the education of children with disabilities in the same sites and programs as those who do not have disabilities. However, this principle of "Least Restrictive Environment" (sometimes referred to as the "integration" principle) is a rebuttable presumption and need not be followed when inappropriate for the student (i.e., when the nature and extent of the student's disability makes education in integrated sites and programs inappropriate, even after auxiliary aids and services are provided) (Turnbull, 1993). The presumption is usually overcome when the student's disability is rather severe; the extent of the disability, not its nature, governs the courts (Turnbull, 1993). To carry out the principle of least restrictive education, many educators and families have advocated for community-based, community-referenced curricula that could be taught in regular education sites and programs. The IDEA addresses this principle in the following ways:

- Sec. 1401(a)(16)(A) restates the "continuum" of allowable settings for special education, from regular classrooms to personal residences, hospitals, and institutions.
- Sec. 1424(a)(3) provides special grants to state and local education agencies to help them with their integration efforts.
- Sec. 1424(b) requires extended school year programs to make special efforts to integrate children with and without disabilities.
- Sec. 1426(a)(3) and (4) place special emphasis on the integration of students with severe emotional disturbances.
- Sec. 1431(b) provides for special grants for inservice education of regular educators to train them to accommodate special education students in their programs.
- Sec. 1401(a)(17) clarifies that therapeutic recreation is a related service, emphasizing that students in special education will have opportunities to learn skills that will help them participate in community park/recreation programs.

Despite the IDEA's provisions, however, it seems that the ADA is far more dedicated to the integration principle than the IDEA. This is so because the ADA does not set up a rebuttable presumption of integration, but instead requires accommodations for people with disabilities so that they will have the opportunity to live in an integrated society.

Procedural Due Process

The IDEA gives students and their families two major ways to obtain the rights created under the first four principles. One of those is the principle of "procedural due process," which is a technique of accountability (Turnbull, 1993). This principle allows the family of a student participating in special education to litigate a grievance against the LEA or SEA by a "due process/administrative hearing" and, thereafter, by a trial in federal or state court. The principle also allows the family to recover attorney fees if it "prevails." The IDEA and the ADA significantly strengthen this technique of accountability.

The IDEA (Sec. 1403) reverses the Supreme Court's decision in *Dellmuth, Acting Secretary of Education of Pennsylvania v. Muth et al.* (1989). The Court had ruled that an SEA is immune from a lawsuit brought against it by a student with a disability. By passing this new amendment, Congress made it clear that a state is not immune from suit in a federal court for a violation of the EHA and that a court may award remedies in law and equity against a state that loses such a lawsuit.

The ADA (Sec. 2[a][7]) reverses another United States Supreme Court decision that had weakened the ability of individuals with disabilities to sue state or local governments. In *City of Cleburne, Texas v. Cleburne Living Center, et al.* (1985), the Court adopted the principle that stated that the courts may not give individuals with mental retardation any special protection from discrimination by state or local governments was adopted. The case involved a city zoning ordinance that allegedly discriminated against a group home for individuals with mental retardation. The issue was whether courts had to specially scrutinize the ordinance and other laws to determine if they were discriminatory under the Fourteenth Amendment Equal Protection Clause. Alternatively stated, the issue was whether or not individuals with mental retardation (and, by inference, other disabilities) are entitled to be treated like persons of color and women, to whom the courts give special protection from discriminatory state and local government laws. The Court held that individuals with mental retardation were not entitled to special protection under the Equal Protection Clause.

The result of the *Cleburne* decision was to make it far more difficult for courts to strike down, on equal protection grounds, any state or local government laws that discriminate against individuals with disabilities. The *Cleburne* decision adopted the proposition that a law will be upheld if there is any plausible reason for it, regardless of whether or not it has a discriminatory impact. Unlike other discriminatory laws that discriminate against women or persons of color, those that adversely affect individuals with disabilities do not require special justification and do not receive special scrutiny by the courts. Thus, the decision effectively prevented individuals with disabilities from using the Equal Protection Clause when they attacked discriminatory laws.

The ADA (Sec. 2[a][7]) has reversed this result by declaring that individuals with disabilities are a discrete and powerless minority. It is more likely that individuals with disabilities will now rely on the Equal Protection Clause when suing to overturn discriminatory laws. In addition, the courts will be hard pressed to overturn a Congressional finding of fact concerning individuals with disabilities. It will also be difficult for them to ignore Congress's resulting mandate that the courts must give special protection under the Equal

Protection Clause to individuals with disabilities and that they must closely scrutinize any state or local government laws that discriminate against such people.

Another consequence of the ADA's overturning of *Cleburne* is that individuals with disabilities will now sue under federal statutes (e.g., the ADA and the IDEA), as well as under the Equal Protection Clause. In order to win, an individual must prove two facts: 1) that he or she suffered a violation of the statute, and 2) that he or she suffered other damage or injury, over and above the damage suffered under the statute (Turnbull, 1990). If they can prove a double injury, their remedies will be under the statute and under other federal law (Civil Rights Act, Sec. 1983, 1964). In some cases, the remedies will be different depending on the statute. For example, under the ADA, certain remedies are given, but money damages are not allowed to be rewarded. Under the Equal Protection Clause and the Civil Rights Act, money damages are allowed to be rewarded. In sum, an individual with a disability is now in a much better position to enforce rights under the IDEA and the ADA than ever before. Not only are the statutory and constitutional remedies available, but the courts must also very closely scrutinize the action of state and local government.

Like the IDEA, the ADA (Sec. 502) makes it clear that a state is not immune from suit by an individual and cannot invoke a defense of "sovereign immunity." Under recent United States Supreme Court decisions, an individual may not sue a state for violating a federal statute unless the statute is explicit and crystal clear. The ADA satisfies the "explicitness" standard. Also like the IDEA, the ADA (Sec. 505) makes it possible for an individual who prevails in a lawsuit to recover attorney fees incurred in the lawsuit. The ADA also lays down the general rule that individuals with disabilities must have administrative hearings ("exhaust their administrative remedies") before they may file a lawsuit in federal or state court.

Finally, the ADA (Sec. 513) encourages alternative means of resolving disputes, including settlement negotiations, conciliation, facilitation, mediation, fact finding, mini-trial, and arbitration. Similarly, the IDEA encourages alternative dispute resolution in two respects: 1) it permits the states to use dispute resolution under Part B (Sec. 1415), which concerns special education; and 2) it encourages their use under Part H (Sec. 1480), which concerns early intervention. In short, the IDEA and the ADA adopt similar approaches to the principle of due process. Both support the right to administrative hearings, with appeals to the courts; the right to sue under a statute as well as under the Equal Protection Clause; and the right to recover attorney fees if the lawsuit is successful.

Parent Participation

The IDEA's final principle, "parent participation," is also a means for ensuring accountability (Turnbull, 1993). Although the IDEA does not change the

170 / Turnbull, Bateman, and Turnbull

principle significantly, it does expand its utility. The IDEA (Sec. 1415[1][17]) clarifies that related services include those services that benefit parents, for example, social work can include work with the student's family. Rehabilitation counseling can also include parents, especially when the student is receiving (at least by age 16) an IEP/ITP.

Finally, the early childhood education provisions of the IDEA (Sec. 1423) make it clear that parent education should be included as part of the student's early education and transition planning should involve the families of preschool children. In addition, it is suggested that adults with disabilities serve as role models in early childhood education programs. The programs should also address the needs of preschoolers exposed prenatally to maternal substance abuse (through programs of social work, school health, and training services for the mothers).

SIGNIFICANCE OF THE ADA AND THE IDEA FOR FAMILIES

It is far too early to predict clearly or confidently the significance of the ADA and the IDEA for families, but the glimmerings of significance are on the horizon. For example, on a macropolitical level, there are many more political and legal battles to fight. These battles will involve some families directly, although most will only be involved indirectly. They will often be waged by the families' advocacy organizations (i.e., The Arc, formerly the Association for Retarded Citizens, or United Cerebral Palsy). However, families and their organizations must still be involved in the regulation-making phases. They must also ensure effective advocacy to enforce the laws and create factual defenses to the undue burden defense of reasonable accommodations.

Politically, the exclusion of the insurance industry from the ADA's coverage is highly problematic. Insurance is a major fringe benefit of many jobs, ensuring access to affordable and appropriate healthcare. The political compromise, the exclusion of the insurance industry to avoid the loss of the votes necessary to pass the ADA, may be addressed on three levels: 1) in the state legislatures, 2) in Congress as part of an amendment of the ADA, or 3) as part of comprehensive healthcare legislation. The latter is clearly the optimal route. The insurance industry is too powerful to confront in a head-to-head legislative battle. For families, the goal has to be to complement the ADA with comprehensive healthcare legislation, enacted in Congress.

The power of public opinion is also problematic. For many years, it has been clear that incrementalism in law reform is the pattern. This pattern is not only effective (after all, the ADA is a product of the Civil Rights Act of 1964 and the Rehabilitation Act antidiscrimination provisions of 1975), but also politically adept (to lose the sympathetic imagination of the dominant majority of persons without disabilities would be politically disastrous). Therefore, families must learn to skillfully court public opinion.

On a more personal and immediate level, individual families face the future with optimism and more arrows in their quivers than ever before. The IDEA now creates a new equal access doctrine, stating that students with disabilities now have access to the same and different resources of the education system as children without disabilities and for the same and different outcomes. This is a major benefit, expressed in the ITP provisions and in the orientation of the IDEA from a process-oriented law to an outcome-oriented law. It is a benefit because it teaches families that appropriate education is assured by a community-based, community-referenced curriculum. This curriculum helps a student develop the skills needed to participate in those sectors of society now affected by the ADA. It also is a benefit because, even though Congress did not frontally amend the least restrictive education provisions of the IDEA, it did express that it intends the curriculum to be delivered in integrated settings.

The ADA expands the equal access doctrine from education to other domains of the person's and family's life. They now are entitled to the same resources as other individuals, for the same purposes. These resources include opportunities in employment, transportation, public accommodations, state–local government services, and telecommunications. The access is also for the same purposes: 1) to participate in the mainstream (Harkin, July 13, 1990; Bush, July 26, 1990); and 2) to have "equality of opportunity, full participation, independent living, and economic self-sufficiency" (42 U.S.C. 12101, et seq., Sec. 2[a] [8]).

This equal access concept is evident from the parallels between the IDEA and the ADA. The IDEA's zero reject principle, with its tenet of educability and purpose of inclusion, has become the ADA's zero reject principle for life, with a tenet of employability and ability, and thus of inclusion. The IDEA's appropriate education principle has become the ADA's reasonable accommodation rule. The IDEA's least restrictive environment principle has become the ADA's ban against physical and attitudinal barriers in adult life, with its promise of inclusion and full participation. The IDEA's due process principle has been incorporated into the ADA's enforcement provisions. And the IDEA's parent participation principle has become the ADA's participation rule, which states that the person with a disability (and, thus, the person's family) will participate in deciding if, how, and how much to exercise the new equality of opportunity that the ADA creates.

But more than mere legal parallelism is involved, more than a continuation of the promises of education. Both the IDEA and the ADA have shaped the views and values of families and students. The ADA, along with the IDEA, gives families reasons for having great expectations, for realizing the positive contributions their members can make, for being able to act on their choices, for playing upon their strengths, and for attaining full citizenship. Unarguably, the IDEA and the ADA, together, create a contract of lifetime support and access for individuals with disabilities and their families. The

IDEA's rights to a free appropriate public education are the basis for ADA's rights to nondiscrimination and participation in not just the public sectors but in the private sectors as well. The IDEA's Part H rights to early intervention become, in due course, Part B rights to early childhood education and then, also in due course, to appropriate education and transition services. Simultaneously, The ADA's rights to nondiscrimination and participation are available to the infant-toddler, preschooler, and student as well. The social contract envisioned by Rousseau and the Enlightenment philosophers has, at last, been realized (at least as a matter of formal law, if not yet fully as reality) for individuals with disabilities.

CONCLUSION

Accordingly, as rights to education and participation are enforced and as individuals with disabilities, their families, and the majority of persons without disabilities see each other in new ways (as educable, employable, able, and entitled to and benefiting from education and participation), it is likely that the norms of society will change. The norm in the schools now involves the inclusion of students with disabilities and their families; it is likely that the norm outside the school setting will mirror the norm in the schools as the ADA is implemented.

The consequence will be that the "forms" of society will change, as well. The physical, attitudinal, and economic barriers that once excluded students with disabilities from education have been steadily disappearing. It is not unreasonable to expect that they will also disappear in the other areas of American society. That certainly is the ADA's intent and, it is likely, based on the IDEA's imperfect results, that this intent will be realized.

In summary, it can be said that the ADA and the IDEA are two laws that:

1. Affect entire families, not just their members with disabilities.
2. Change the laws, slogans, and results by which families can live.
3. Extend the Supreme Court's decision in *Brown v. Board of Education of Topeka* (1954). (That decision, like these laws, had a singular, albeit vital, purpose—to ensure by law that the rights of citizenship apply to all people, not just to a few.)
4. Reflect the social construct or transactional nature of disability—a "disability" may be an unchangeable trait of the person, but a "handicap" is that which the world creates by failing to accommodate to that difference.

At last, the underlying motives of federal law have been confirmed and applied to all sectors of American life. These motives are altruism (a concern to help those with disabilities), rebalancing power (eliminating the disadvantage that individuals with disabilities have experienced), anti-institutionalization (ensuring participation in the mainstream and barring segregation in institutions), and equal opportunity (creating a level playing field on which all may participate) (Turnbull & Barber, 1986). Not since Congress enacted the Education for All Handicapped Children Act of 1975 (PL 94-142) and the antidiscrimination provisions of the Rehabilitation Act (Sec. 504) has there been such a confluence of opportunity. This opportunity allows persons with disabilities and their families to apply and benefit from laws that have complementary purposes and provisions, to adopt and live by new creeds and slogans, and to establish, through laws and creeds, new norms and forms for society.

REFERENCES

Americans with Disabilities Act, PL 101-336. (July 26, 1990). 42 U.S.C. 12101, et seq. *Federal Register, 56*(144), 35544–35756.
Avis, D.W. (1985). Deinstitutionalization jet lag. In A.P. Turnbull & H.R. Turnbull, III (Eds.), *Parents speak out: Then and now* (pp. 193–199). Columbus, OH: Charles E. Merrill.
Beach Center on Families and Disability. (1990). *An introduction to the Rehabilitation Research and Training Center on Families and Disability.* Lawrence: University of Kansas, Institute for Life Span Studies.
Board of Education of the Henrick Hudson Central School District v. Rowley, 458 U.S. 176, (1982).
Brown v. Board of Education of Topeka, 347 U.S. 483, (1954).
Bush, President George, message on signing the ADA. (1990, July 26). 26 Weekly Comp. Pres. Doc. 1165.
City of Cleburne, Texas v. Cleburne Living Center, et al., 473 U.S. 432, (1985).
Civil Rights Act, PL 88–352. (1964). 42 U.S.C.
Dellmuth, Acting Secretary of Education of Pennsylvania v. Muth et al., 491 U.S. 223, 109 S. Ct. 2397, (1989).
Harkin, statement of Senator. 136 Cong. Rec. S. 9684, 9687, (daily ed. July 13, 1990).
Honig v. Doe, 484 U.S. 305, (1988).
Individuals with Disabilities Education Act, PL 101-476. (1990). 20 U.S.C. 1400, et seq.
School Board of Nassau County, Florida v. Arline, 480 U.S. 273, (1987).
Timothy W. v. Rochester School District, 875 F. 2d 954, (1st cir. 1989), cert. den. 493 U.S. 983, (1989).
Turnbull, A.P., & Turnbull, H.R., III. (1985a). Developing independence. *Journal of Adolescent Health Care, 6*(2), 100–119.
Turnbull, A.P., & Turnbull, H.R., III. (Eds.). (1985b). *Parents speak out: Then and now* (2nd ed.). Columbus, OH: Charles E. Merrill.
Turnbull, H.R. (1993). *Free appropriate public education: The law and children with disabilities.* Denver, CO: Love Publishing Co.
Turnbull, H.R., III, & Barber, P.A. (1986). Federal laws and adults with developmental disabilities. In J.A. Summers (Ed.), *The right to grow up: An introduction to adults with developmental disabilities* (pp. 255–277). Baltimore: Paul H. Brookes Publishing Co.
Turnbull, H.R., Biklen, D., Brookes, P., Boggs, E.M., & Ellis, J. (1981). *The least restrictive alternative: Principles and practices.* Washington, DC: American Association on Mental Retardation.

Chapter 9

Education Reform

Debra Neubert and Sherril Moon

The passage of the Americans with Disabilities Act (ADA) has many implications for the public education of children and youth with disabilities in the United States. It particularly underscores the need to merge and improve the separate systems (regular, remedial, bilingual, and special) of education that now exist so that all students receive appropriate training in the least restrictive environment. Upon signing the ADA, President George Bush said, "Today, America welcomes into the mainstream of life all people with disabilities. Let the shameful wall of exclusion finally come tumbling down" ("Americans with Disabilities Act," 1990). Certainly, experts for several decades have asserted that the process of mainstreaming and inclusion must begin during the early childhood and school-age years. More recently, the need for educators to engage in careful transition planning to ensure that students with disabilities move to appropriate postsecondary environments has received increased attention. (Chapter 8 by Turnbull, Bateman, and Turnbull provides an incisive analysis of how the Individuals with Disabilities Education Act [IDEA] relates to special education, transition, and the ADA, and thus complements this chapter.) The purpose of this chapter is to delineate some of the critical issues that educators of young people with disabilities must address as the work of dismantling barriers to independence and productivity is renewed under the legal imperative provided by the ADA.

REFORMING THE EDUCATION SYSTEM

Throughout the 1980s, initiatives designed to reform the education system have been abundant. Reform initiatives in regular education resulted in expanded minimum competency testing programs, increased graduation requirements, and increased efforts to restructure schools (Carnegie Forum on Education and Economy, 1986; Holmes Group, 1986). Vocational education reform is most evident in the Carl D. Perkins Vocational and Applied Technology Education Act of 1990 (PL 101-392), which stresses increased integration of academic and vocational skills, provision of funds to those districts where the need for programmatic improvement is greatest, and increased emphasis on postsecondary training opportunities (Wirt, 1991). In the field of special education, calls for a merger between special and regular education, increased integration of students with severe disabilities, and service for the needs of "at-risk" children and youth have prompted considerable debate among professionals on how to best serve students and train professionals (Lilly, 1989; Pugach, 1988; Sailor et al., 1989). Also evident is the creation of new partnerships between education and the private sector (Hoyt, 1991).

Issues that have prompted education reform are numerous and generally center on public sector dissatisfaction with student performance and private sector dissatisfaction with worker competence. While educators across the United States struggle to design structures that will introduce meaningful change, they often face a public who does not have the patience necessary to allow an evolutionary process of change. In addition, Pipho (1991) points out that:

> while all the reforms are well-intentioned, individually they are built on the premise that a good prototype will gather followers and eventually turn the whole system around. In reality, these efforts sometimes produce the equivalent of a different gas station on each corner—all selling different brands of a product designed for the same purpose and each trying to gather a loyal following. (p. 422)

In the coming decade, it will be important for educators to not only be open to change but to understand the ways in which the various reform initiatives can be incorporated into a comprehensive strategy to improve education. Efforts to reform the education system need to be based on sound research that discerns effective practices from trends in public perception and federal policy.

Reforming the Current System of Special Education

As Lipsky and Gartner (1989) point out, the passage of the Education for All Handicapped Children Act (PL 94-142) may have been one of the most important accomplishments in American public education. There is no longer a question of how to receive entitlement to a free public education as there was in 1975. During the period from 1988 to 1989, more than 4 million students were served under special education programs (U.S. Department of Education, 1990). Procedural and due process rights are now guaranteed to these students and their families in every state of the United States. With the newest amendments to the Education of the Handicapped Act (EHA) enacted in 1986 (PL 99-457) and 1990 (PL 101-476), which changed the name of the

EHA to the Individuals with Disabilities Education Act (IDEA), new rights are now guaranteed to infants who are identified as disabled and their families, and to students 16 years of age and older who need transition planning for the provision of adult services.

Despite the progress made in less than 20 years, in large part because of the EHA and later amendments, school systems are still very far from "mainstreaming or including" students with disabilities into most typical neighborhood classrooms (Sailor et al., 1989). Statistics show that approximately the same percentage of students are now served in separate classes or schools (about 30%) as were in 1982 (Viadero, 1988; Walker, 1987). Other research data indicate that separate special education programs have not resulted in significant benefits to the students in terms of academic performance, graduation rates, self-esteem, or successful employment (Edgar, 1988; Madden & Slavin, 1983; Ysseldyke, 1987). In some cases the opposite has been indicated. Students with disabilities who were placed in regular classes have performed significantly better than students in separate classes in academics, self-esteem, and emotional stability (Madden & Slavin, 1983; Weiner, 1985).

Professionals and parents of students with severe disabilities now advocate for education in a regular classroom with some training in community settings because of the poor outcomes of separate special education programs (Sailor et al., 1989; Stainback, Stainback, & Bunch, 1989; Taylor, 1988). In fact, integrated education was named as a most crucial factor in providing quality services to students with severe disabilities in a nationwide survey of professionals (Meyer, Eichinger, & Park-Lee, 1987). Recognizing the importance of this issue, projects that address the needs of children with severe disabilities in integrated settings are targeted for funding under Section 624 of the IDEA (National Association of State Directors of Special Education [NASDSE], 1990). It is hoped that educators will work toward understanding the importance of replacing separate placements with strategies for merging special and regular education.

Models for Integrating A variety of approaches are now being used across the United States that include students with and without disabilities in a single educational environment (Lipsky & Gartner, 1989). One of the earliest models adopted is the *teacher consultant* approach (Huefner, 1988; Idol, 1986) in which experts, including special educators, work as consultants to the regular classroom teacher so that individual students with special needs can remain in or return to the classroom. Another regular education initiative is the *Adaptive Learning Environments Model* (ALEM) (Wang, 1989) in which regular and special educators provide direct instruction side-by-side to all students in the same classroom. A variety of assessment and instructional techniques can be utilized, depending upon the learning styles of the individual students.

For students with more severe or multiple disabilities, the *comprehensive local school* (CLS) model has been implemented successfully in several cities (Sailor et al., 1989). This approach involves starting all students in a regular classroom setting in their home communities and then, as they get older, pulling students from class for community-based training in work, domestic, and social/leisure settings. The educational base always remains a regular classroom in a local, public school.

It is imperative that these and other approaches be adopted so that data can be collected on the effectiveness of the *regular (or general) education initiative* (REI) that is currently supported by the Federal Department of Education, Office of Special Education and Rehabilitative Services (OSERS) (Will, 1986). More important, regardless of the outcomes of integrated education, it is society's moral and ethical approach to pursue the civil rights of all citizens (Peck, 1990). How can a country that passes the ADA bar these same citizens at a younger age from full access to an education with their peers?

Best Instructional Practices for Students with Disabilities

As society works to change the structure of existing systems, there are a number of curriculum methods that can be used to enhance the independent living and employment potential of students with disabilities. There is debate about whether or not students with developmental disabilities who are fully integrated in school programs may be deprived of practical skills training in the areas of employment, social skills, and community access. This is supported by recent findings that students with mild mental retardation fared significantly worse from 6 to 30 months after graduation than students identified as learning disabled, or those without disabilities, in terms of employment, postsecondary education, and independent living outcomes(Affleck, Edgar, Levine, & Kortering, 1990). These authors aptly point out that a pressing education issue is that of how to meet the practical needs of students with disabilities through in vivo and repeated skills training in real adult environments, while still trying to meet the legal and moral demands of an integrated education.

During the past 2 decades, proposals for restructuring secondary special education programs have centered on life and career demands and differ somewhat from the recent regular education proposals for school reform (Brolin, 1982, 1989; Clark & Kolstoe, 1990; Edgar, 1988; Kokaska & Brolin, 1985; Kolstoe, 1970). As Affleck et al. (1990) point out, these restructuring efforts include more opportunities outside the traditional classroom, although they do not preclude opportunities to participate in integrated activities. Some of the common features of these approaches include: 1) teaching goal setting and actual instruction across adult living areas (i.e., work, finances, social/sexual well-being, family/home life, use of community services); 2) infusing career education activities throughout the curriculum; 3) participating in work internships and paid employment prior to graduation; and 4) linking with adult service providers to ensure case management, employment, postsecondary education, and other options through formal transition planning.

Curriculum methods for students with severe disabilities, which include integration opportunities as well as functional skills training, are also readily available (Snell, 1987). As mentioned earlier in the chapter, a variety of quality program indicators for students with severe disabilities have been delineated by professionals and advocates in the field (Meyer et al., 1987). These 123 features, clustered into categories such as integration, home–school cooperation, staff development, functional skills training across adult domains, and data-based instruction, are now available as a program evaluation checklist through The Association for Persons with Severe Handicaps (TASH).

It is crucial that evaluation of the outcomes of education programs be based on the limited knowledge of best practices. Only then can it be decided what and how to teach students.

Evaluating Outcomes

Throughout the 1980s, researchers began to examine the postsecondary outcomes of students who exit the special education system. While employment and community adjustment outcomes vary by type of disability, several consistent factors have been identified. For example, the majority of students with disabilities exiting the school system continue to live with family members. For those individuals who obtain competitive employment, jobs are found through the self–family–friend network and tend to be entry-level positions (often part-time) with few opportunities for advancement or employee benefits that enhance self-sufficiency. Moreover, males with disabilities are employed with greater frequency than females (Affleck et al., 1990; Edgar, 1988; Hasazi, Johnson, Hasazi, Gordon, & Hull, 1989; Roessler, Brolin, & Johnson, 1990).

It has been suggested that the examination of postsecondary outcomes should assist professionals to evaluate the impact of special education programming and restructure secondary programs; however, in practice, it has been difficult to translate these outcomes into programmatic and curricular changes. As we enter the 1990s, it is important that we identify specific factors of education that positively affect employment success and community adjustment (Halpern, 1990; Roessler et al., 1990). In turn, emphasis must be placed on assisting local school systems to modify and restructure special education programs based on student outcomes specific to that geographical location (Adger, Neubert, McLaughlin, & Jamison, 1990; Bruininks, Wolman, & Thurlow, 1990).

Halpern (1990) offers the following advice for conducting future studies of postsecondary outcomes of students exiting special education programs:

1) studies need to be longitudinal (i.e, follow-along) to assess adjustment and outcomes over time; 2) a variety of outcomes need to be examined including employment, community integration, postschool education/training, and personal/social adjustment; and 3) appropriate subject sampling strategies need to be used. The importance of tracking students while they are still enrolled in the school system has been suggested as an important first step in assisting local education agencies (LEAs) design follow-along studies and in defining the sample, which will be contacted after exiting the school system. Hasazi et al. (1989) also suggest that outcome studies include comparison groups of students without disabilities to examine differences and similarities between the two groups in terms of employment and community experiences.

Outcomes for students in special education who drop out of school have also received increased attention. In a review of studies concerning students who exit school prior to graduation, Wolman, Bruininks, and Thurlow (1989) suggest the need for systematic evaluation of programs to prevent high-risk students from dropping out of school. Additional research is also needed to reflect the long-term adjustment of special education students who drop out of school. While initial studies pointed to poor employment outcomes for drop-outs when compared to graduates of special education programs (Zigmond & Thorton, 1985), two recent studies failed to confirm these initial negative outcomes (deBettencourt, Zigmond, & Thorton, 1989; Karpinksi, 1990). Studies documenting the outcomes of special education students after they leave the school system continue to be an important source of information for implementing and reforming current transition initiatives at the federal, state, and local levels.

TAKING RESPONSIBILITY FOR TRANSITION

In 1984, transition from school to work for students with disabilities became a major priority for OSERS (Will, 1984). Since then the emphasis has broadened from vocational transition to community adjustment in all areas of adult living (Halpern, 1985), and many models for achieving successful transition have been developed and field tested across the country (Wehman, Moon, Everson, Wood, & Barcus, 1988). The IDEA not only defines transition but also specifies that the needed transition services must be delineated by the students' IEPs no later than age 16 and responsible agencies must be designated to develop or deliver those services. Furthermore, when an agency fails to provide agreed upon services, the school must reconvene the IEP team to identify alternative strategies to meet the transition objectives. This new mandate, combined with the force of the ADA, should certainly help citizens with disabilities gain earlier access to work and community living options.

Unfortunately, empirical evidence supporting the transition practices that lead to successful adult outcomes is limited; however, there is some consensus regarding the elements of secondary programs for students with disabilities and transition planning practices that should lead to better outcomes (Sale, Everson, Metzler, & Moon, 1990). Some of these elements, identified by an extensive review of the literature and validation from a survey of professionals, parents, and advocates across the United States, are included in Table 9.1.

Legislative Mandates

Since the 1970s, important legislative mandates concerning equal access to education, employment/training, community services, and independent living have continually changed the scope of service delivery. A recognized competency needed by special educators and related service personnel at the secondary level is to understand legislative mandates from a number of disciplines (Baker & Geiger, 1988; Renzaglia & Everson, 1990). As students move from an entitlement system in education to an eligibility system in rehabilitation, employment/training, and human services, educators must work collaboratively with professionals and parents to identify appropriate postsecondary programs. Table 9.2 provides a review of pertinent legislation in each of these disciplines. Legislative mandates passed in 1990 continue to focus on the importance of equal access, cooperative planning, and transition service delivery. In addition to the landmark ADA, the IDEA and the reauthorization of vocational education legislation have important implications for educating students with disabilities.

Individuals with Disabilities Education Act of 1990 (IDEA) The IDEA contains important new language and provisions concerning the education system and related services aimed at children and youth with disabilities. For example, the definition of children with disabilities has been expanded to

Table 9.1. Secondary education practices that lead to successful adult outcomes

Community-Based Employment Training

1. Employment outcomes are included in the IEP/ITP.
2. Vocational training occurs in real job sites.
3. Students are placed into paid employment prior to graduation.
4. Students participate in regular vocational education programs.
5. The school hires employment specialists to place and train students in job internships and paid jobs.
6. Students in special education receive formal vocational evaluation after age 14.
7. A transition liaison is designated to initiate the ITP and monitor completion of objectives.
8. Detailed written schedules are in place that account for time spent in class and the community by students and staff.
9. Students receive community-based instruction in areas other than vocational preparation (e.g., money management, home/family care, and social skills).

(continued)

Table 9.1. (*continued*)

10. Special education classes are integrated into local, public schools.
11. The school system identifies how to promote equal access opportunities and supplemental services to students with special needs under the Carl D. Perkins Vocational and Applied Technology Education Act of 1990.
12. Teachers understand how to use Job Training and Partnership Act (JTPA) funds to supplement job training for students in special education.
13. The school sponsors job training programs for students in special education during summer months.
14. The school and other local agencies find a way to monitor the educational and employment outcomes for graduates of special education programs.

Parent and Consumer Involvement

1. Written materials are disseminated to families regarding school policies and programs, legislation, state/federal initiatives, and adult services.
2. Students and parents have access to peer support groups.
3. Parents and students actively participate in the development of individualized transition plans (ITP).
4. There is a systematic process of communication other than the IEP process between school and families.
5. The school has designated personnel to specifically work with families outside the school setting.
6. Family members participate in implementing IEP/ITP goals in home or community settings.
7. Student and family preferences are reflected in the IEP/ITP.

Interagency Coordination

1. Vocational educators, adult service case managers, and rehabilitation counselors attend ITP meetings.
2. A comprehensive local needs assessment of school and community services is conducted annually.
3. A local interagency agreement defines procedures for conducting ITP meetings, for delegating roles and responsibilities of professionals across agencies, for providing referrals, and for creating methods to develop needed services.
4. There is a local plan for cross-agency inservice training.
5. There is a local plan for funding and cost sharing.
6. Local businesses participate in transition planning.

Adult Service Options

1. Supported employment programs exist in the community.
2. There are transportation options in the community for people with disabilities.
3. Local case managers are assigned to transition-age youth with disabilities.
4. Self-advocacy groups are active in the community and get to know students before they graduate.
5. Integrated leisure options are available in the community.
6. Local colleges provide linkages/programs for recent school graduates with disabilities.

Table 9.2. Legislative mandates and initiatives

Year	Public Law #	Title
		Vocational Education
1963	PL 88-210	The Vocational Education Act of 1963
1968	PL 90-210	The Vocational Education Act Amendments
1976	PL 94-482	Education Amendments of 1976, Title II
1984	PL 98-524	The Carl D. Perkins Vocational Education Act
1990	PL 101-392	The Carl D. Perkins Vocational and Applied Technology Education Act of 1990
		Employment and Training
1962	PL 87-415	Manpower Development and Training Act (MDTA)
1964	PL 88-452	Economic Opportunity Act (EOA)
1973	PL 93-203	Comprehensive Employment and Training Act of 1973 (CETA)
1978	PL 95-524	Comprehensive Employment and Training Act Amendments
1982	PL 97-300	Job Training Partnership Act (JTPA)
1986	PL 99-496	Job Training Partnership Act Amendments of 1986
1992	PL 102-367	Job Training Reform Amendments of 1992 (amends PL 99-496)
		Rehabilitation Human Services
1973	PL 93-112	Rehabilitation Act of 1973
1975	PL 94-103	Developmental Disabilities Assistance and Bill of Rights Act of 1975
1978	PL 95-602	Rehabilitation, Comprehensive Services, and Developmental Disabilities Amendments of 1978
1983	PL 98-221	Rehabilitation Act Amendments of 1983
1984	PL 99-527	Developmental Disabilities Act of 1984
1986	PL 99-506	Rehabilitation Act Amendments of 1986
1987	PL 100-146	Developmental Disabilities Assistance and Bill of Rights Act Amendments of 1987
1990	PL 101-336	Americans with Disabilities Act of 1990 (ADA)
1992	PL 102-569	Rehabilitation Act Amendments of 1992
		Special Education
1975	PL 94-142	The Education for All Handicapped Children Act of 1975
1983	PL 98-199	The Education of the Handicapped Act Amendments of 1983
1986	PL 99-457	The Education of the Handicapped Act Amendments of 1986
1990	PL 101-476	Individuals with Disabilities Education Act of 1990 (IDEA)
1984	(Initiative)	Transition Initiative
1984	(Initiative)	Supported Employment Initiative
1986	(Initiative)	Regular Education Initiative
1992	(Guidelines)	Community-based educational placements on job sites for students with disabilities (guidelines from the Departments of Education and Labor)

Note: Initiatives from the U.S. Department of Education, Office of Special Education and Rehabilitative Services (OSERS) (Madeline Will, Assistant Secretary) include autism and traumatic brain injury (NASDSE, 1990). In addition, rehabilitation counseling and social work services are now included under the definition of related services, thereby increasing the opportunity for collaboration between school personnel and adult service providers during the transition planning process.

The definition of transition services in the IDEA expands on Will's (1984) definition of transition as an outcome-oriented process that includes postsecondary education, vocational training, integrated employment (including supported employment), continuing and adult education, adult services, independent living, or community participation. Most important, the definition specifies that "transition related activities be based upon the individual student's needs, taking into account the student's preferences and interests" (NASDSE, 1990, p.2). This should expand parental and student choice in terms of vocational programming in the schools and postsecondary options.

In addition to the focus on school-to-work transition, a provision has been added that addresses the multiple transitions that children with disabilities may face during the school years (e.g., transition from medical care to special education, between residential and community-based placements, between separate and integrated classroom settings) (NASDSE, 1990). The recognition of these transition points stresses the importance of collaborative relationships between educators and other service providers, as well as the need for service coordination.

The definitions of assistive technology device and assistive technology service contained in the Technology-Related Assistance for Individuals with Disabilities Act of 1988 (PL 100-407) have also been added to the IDEA. The rationale behind the addition of these definitions is that special educators and related service personnel understand new developments in technology and use this technology to mainstream students into the least restrictive educational and employment settings.

The Carl D. Perkins Vocational and Applied Technology Education Act of 1990   Recent projections indicate the majority of individuals entering the work force in the 1990s will be females, nonwhites, and immigrants (Hodgkinson, 1989; Hoyt, 1991). Overcoming race and sex stereotypes in educational program placement, employment, and postsecondary training opportunities takes on new importance in light of demographic and work force projections (Neubert & Leak, 1990). Educators must work with students and families to ensure access to training opportunities that will prepare them for semi-skilled or skilled jobs. The Carl D. Perkins Vocational and Applied Technology Education Act further strengthens the assurance of equal access concerning recruitment, enrollment, and placement activities related to vocational education programs for students with disabilities. The assurances in Sec. 118(B)(I) specify that: 1) equal access to a full range of vocational education programs be provided in the least restrictive environment; 2) vocational education be included on the IEP when appropriate; 3) planning activities be coordinated among vocational education, special education, and vocational rehabilitation representatives; and 4) the provision of vocational education be monitored to determine if it is consistent with the IEP. A number of additional assurances that promote integration of students with disabilities and disadvantages into regular vocational education programs include:

1. Assisting students who are members of special populations to enter vocational education and fulfilling the transitional service requirements of Section 626 of the IDEA
2. Assessing the special needs of students participating in programs with respect to their successful completion of vocational education in the least restrictive environment
3. Providing supplementary services to students who are members of special populations (i.e., curriculum modification, equipment and classroom modification, support personnel, and instructional aids and devices)
4. Providing guidance, counseling, and career development activities
5. Providing counseling and instructional services designed to facilitate the transition from school to postschool employment and career opportunities

Finally, the Carl D. Perkins Vocational and Applied Technology Education Act stipulates that LEAs must provide information concerning available opportunities in vocational education to students with disabilities and their parents no later than ninth grade. This provision of information is extended from the Carl D. Perkins Vocational Education Act of 1984 by requiring information on criteria for program eligibility, specific courses/services available, and employment opportunities. Again, this provision serves to increase student and parental choice in planning educational and vocational goals.

SUPPORTING AND EMPOWERING FAMILIES AND INDIVIDUALS

Legislative mandates and changes in family and social structures have altered and magnified the importance of partnerships between parents and the educational community (Chapman, 1990; Hodgkinson, 1989). For students with disabilities and their families, mandates for individual planning, care, advocacy, and coordination of services among diverse service delivery systems have changed the scope of educators' responsibilities and highlighted the importance of empowering parents and individuals with disabilities so that they can make informed choices (Gerry & McWhorter, 1990).

Supporting Parents

As Turnbull (1988) points out, society is entering a new era of family–professional relationships in which families of a young person with a disability must be supported rather than involved. This means "providing assistance to families in meeting their needs and maximizing their strengths. It does not mean a side focus on insuring the greatest degree of parent involvement in program activities" (p. 271). Opportunities for forging these new relationships are now possible for families with very young children with disabilities because of the Education of the Handicapped Act Amendments of 1986 (PL 99-457). This law mandates interdisciplinary service provision in the home so that the family can most positively meet the needs of their infants or toddlers. The thrust of the law is to prevent institutionalization and promote community integration at the earliest possible age.

This new type of service delivery, which emphasizes the whole family, will entail finding solutions to an array of existing problems. Some of these include: How do professionals across many disciplines work together to support a family and who can best coordinate these services? How can society empower families to seek the best professional help knowing that most available systems are inadequate? How do professionals learn to use unified methods across age spans and disciplines so that families do not have to start over at every transition stage? How do professionals learn to make assumptions about the weaknesses, roles, and responsibilities of families as they relate to their child with a disability and to society?

Currently, the answers to these and other questions are not based on a sound empirical framework (Turnbull, 1988); however, several authors have proposed ways in which professionals can improve the support process while gathering empirical evidence about best practices (see Table 9.3). At the very least, this list may serve as a guide for training new professionals across disciplines. It may also assist families in determining the value of their interactions with professionals.

Empowerment and Advocacy

Changes in our education and rehabilitation systems have highlighted the need for parents and consumers to take a more active role in planning services and identifying employment and community life goals. Empowering parents and consumers means educators must share up-to-date information on legislative mandates. Instructional techniques that facilitate self-advocacy and decision-making skills must also be included in instructional settings (Gould & McTaggart, 1988; Mithaug, Martin, & Agran, 1987). Teachers and related service personnel must become familiar with the provisions of the ADA in order to: 1) advocate effectively for students in work study and community-based settings, 2) educate parents to advocate for their offspring in terms of access to community services and employment opportunities, and 3) teach students how to advocate for themselves in community-based settings after they exit the school system.

For example, under Title I (Employment) of the ADA, employers will be obligated to make reasonable accommodations to the work site only if they are

Table 9.3. Improving the support process for families

1. Before planning activities, *find out what the family desires* for themselves and their child and what they know about existing and needed community services. Then decide how you can honestly assist the family, especially if you do not share their values and goals.
2. Try to *understand the needs of the entire family*, not just the perceived needs of the child with the disability. All service plans (IFSP, IEP, and ITP) should include goals and objectives that involve the whole family.
3. *Support to the family should be "future oriented,"* whenever possible, to prevent discontinuation of services. It is never too early to provide information on services that may be needed later in life. Assist families to learn generic skills that they can use at every stage of planning for their children.
4. *Keep updated* on best practices and the existing state of services in your community. Provide this information to the family so that they can develop and change their choices.
5. *Figure out practical ways to deal with concrete problems* (e.g., transportation, respite care, recreation options, interruption in social security and medical insurance payments, and housing). Prove your credibility and concern.
6. *Provide information to families* in as many formats as possible including directories, visits to programs, introductions to parent networks and support groups, and inclusion in professional training programs.
7. *Accept family participation in your "agency programs"* at whatever level they feel comfortable. This may range from extremely active to no involvement at all. Regardless, keep providing information and continue to offer assistance.
8. *Coordinate service to a family with all other agencies* so that a holistic approach can be taken. This is particularly important from ages 5 through 16 when the school system assumes most responsibility for providing support.
9. *Help families to take charge of their situation* and become effective advocates for decent community services. Do not desert them when they try to change the inadequate systems that pay your salary.
10. Do not assume that every family is always sad, stressed, or unable to cope positively with their situation. *Do assume that families can make the right choices* when they are informed and when professionals are providing good services.

Adapted from Everson and Moon (1987); Halvorsen, Doering, Farron-Davis, Usilton, and Sailor (1989); Sailor, Anderson, Halvorsen, Doering, Filler, and Goetz (1989); Turnbull (1988); Wehman, Moon, Everson, Wood, and Barcus (1988).

aware of an applicant's or employee's physical or mental disability. This means that the request for a reasonable accommodation will generally come from an applicant or employee (Brown & Bass, 1990). For students with less obvious disabilities (e.g., learning disabilities, emotional impairments) teaching self-advocacy skills takes on a new importance. Since these students often obtain employment through the self–family–friend network after exiting the school system (Hasazi et al., 1989; Roessler et al., 1990), they will need to be

188 / Neubert and Moon

able to express their needs (e.g., two-step directions, reorganized work station) in relation to their disability if accommodations are to be made. They will also need to be aware of their rights under the ADA and learn appropriate ways to confront employers if these rights are violated (Barnes, 1991).

For individuals with more severe or obvious disabilities, educators will need to provide students with varied experiences in community-based work settings to assess their skills and their needs in terms of accommodations. Educators can then play an important role in introducing employers and parents to examples of reasonable accommodations (e.g., reassigning job tasks, utilizing part-time or modified work schedules, modifying entrance exams, or modifying equipment or devices). In addition, educators and parents will have to work toward employer education concerning stereotypes of specific disabilities and the importance of identifying the essential functions of a job. Brown and Bass (1990) stress that "an employer should not assume that an accommodation is required without consulting the applicant or employee with the disability" (p. 2).

THE CHANGING ROLE OF SPECIAL EDUCATORS

As noted by Cosden (1990), special educators face new challenges that will expand their role in education and community-based settings. The changing demographic composition of school-age populations and their corresponding multicultural needs, the need for increased advocacy and collaboration with other professionals, the need to address dropouts and "at-risk" students, and the expanding interface between special and regular educators will obviously make an impact on how the education system trains teachers. These issues are discussed briefly in terms of updating teacher education programs.

Multicultural Needs

Demographic shifts in population trends underscore the need for trained personnel who can serve culturally and linguistically diverse students in school and community-based settings. By the year 2000, it is estimated that 53 cities will have a majority minority population (Hodgkinson, 1985). The overrepresentation of minority students in special education programs continues to be a pressing concern (Wyche, 1989) along with shortage of teachers from ethnic populations (American Speech-Language-Hearing Association et al., 1989). In light of these problems, a minority emphasis in discretionary programs and an outreach to minority institutions and organizations is a focus of the IDEA. The requirement specifies that applicants for grants, contracts, and cooperative agreements must demonstrate how they will address the needs of children with disabilities from minority backgrounds and how a plan for outreach services to minority institutions of education will be developed (NASDSE, 1990).

The changing ethnic composition of student populations, especially in urban areas, requires the implementation of alternative and diverse education programming that offers a holistic approach to serving the needs of students. Hodgkinson (1989) advocates for the ongoing service coordination of education, health, transportation, housing, and correction services to meet the increasingly diverse needs of all individuals in society. Similarly, Gerry and McWhorter (1990) advocate for an effective case advocacy system for individuals with disabilities throughout the life span to ensure effective coordination and provision of services.

Service Coordination

While coordination of services is the cornerstone of new social and education legislation (Lewis, 1991), problems related to interagency planning and limited fiscal resources continue to hinder a holistic approach to providing services. The lack of a designated person or agency to ensure coordination of services across community agencies also remains a persistent problem for many youth with disabilities and their families during the transition process (Gerry, 1989; Sailor et al., 1989) and to families with infants and toddlers entitled to services under Part H of PL 99-457 (Gerry & McWhorter, 1990).

Special educators must be able to share information with service providers, identify short- and long-term placement goals, involve parents in the planning process, advocate on the behalf of consumers, monitor placements, and identify changing service needs (Wehman et al., 1988). These planning, managing, and coordinating activities extend special educators' roles (Storey & Mank, 1989) and parallel many of the case management and caseload management techniques employed by adult service providers in vocational rehabilitation programs, social services, and agencies serving persons with mental disabilities (Greenwood, 1982; Intagliata & Baker, 1983; Marlowe, Marlowe, & Willets, 1983).

Training personnel to assume liaison, case management, or service coordination roles is critical if fragmented services are to be ameliorated. Such training requires an interdisciplinary focus on understanding varied service delivery systems (Kortering & Edgar, 1988; Snell, 1990; Szymanski, Hanley-Maxwell, & Asselin, 1990). Service coordination implies that practitioners be able to collect or use relevant assessment information, plan realistic employment and community life goals, link students to appropriate services, monitor the provision of services, and advocate for the student (and the family) on an ongoing basis.

At-Risk Youth

The term "at risk" has been used to identify divergent categories of children and youth from adverse economic conditions and specific geographical locations, those with physical disabilities, those with special healthcare needs, and those who speak English as a second language (Fradd & Correa, 1989). In a recent report, the William T. Grant Foundation (1988) identified four groups of youth and young adults who are particularly at risk in terms of becoming educated, employed, and self-sufficient adults. These include: 1) youth with disabilities, 2) adolescents in rural areas, 3) adolescents in inner cities concentrated in neighborhoods of poverty, and 4) homeless youth. Problems associated with dropping out of school, joblessness, and welfare dependency have recently been addressed for at-risk youth by both special and regular educators. Solutions for addressing these problems in regular education school reform initiatives parallel many of those proposed by special educators including increased service coordination, school–family partnerships, school–business partnerships, mentorship programs, instruction in appropriate social and personal behavior, and increased participation in community-based experiences (Chapman, 1990; deBettencourt & Zigmond, 1990; Hahn, 1987; Wolman et al., 1989).

It is important that, as society works toward full integration of students with disabilities, students who have met with marginal success in the education system and who are particularly at risk of exiting the education system without the full benefit of services they are entitled to under PL 94-142 are not overlooked. As personnel are trained, it is important to instruct teachers how to work with students who are likely to drop out of school and how to implement alternative instructional and community-based practices for at-risk youth. Hahn (1987) maintains that there is evidence pertaining to the reasons why students drop out of school. The following reasons have been identified. Students: 1) are behind in grade level and older than classmates, 2) experience poor academic performance, 3) dislike school, 4) are suspended or given detention frequently, 5) are pregnant, 6) are welfare recipients and/or members of single parent households, 7) view employment as an attractive alternative to school, and 8) have undiagnosed learning disabilities or emotional problems. Some have cautioned that increased academic course requirements may result in higher failure rates for special education students, thereby exacerbating the dropout problem (Wyche, 1989).

According to the Twelfth Annual Report to Congress (U.S. Department of Education, 1990), 27% of special education students drop out of school; however, Gerber and Levine-Donnerstein (1989) caution that the dropout rate among special education students in some local and regional studies is as high as 50%. Students with learning disabilities make up the largest group of students in special education (47%) and are more likely to drop out of school than those with disabilities. Minority students in special education are also particularly at risk of dropping out of school (Wyche, 1989). Gerber and Levine-Donnerstein (1989) point out that while 40% of general education students who drop out of school may return for a General Education Diploma (GED), there is currently no evidence to suggest that this same trend pertains to special education students. Therefore, the consequence of dropping out may be more serious for students with disabilities in terms of postschool adjustment.

Several recent studies have pointed to an emerging issue that special and regular educators must be aware of in designing programs for at-risk youth; that is, some students who drop out of special education programs may return to the school system several times (Adger et al., 1990; Blackorby, Edgar, & Kortering, 1991; Karpinski Neubert, & Graham, 1992). This brings into question the legal obligation of school systems to identify dropouts/re-enrollees from special education programs and to develop alternative approaches to providing educational and vocational opportunities.

Students with disabilities are also at risk in terms of their access to postsecondary education and training programs even if they graduate from the public schools. Since students with mild disabilities make up the largest group of individuals who receive special education services, it is important that they be linked with appropriate postsecondary opportunities that will expand their employment options beyond entry-level jobs. Using the National Longitudinal Transition Study of Special Education Students data base, Fairweather and Shaver (1990) found that youth with disabilities were much less likely to enroll in postsecondary education programs than youth without disabilities (15% versus 56%, respectively). Secondary educators must work with individuals who have disabilities and their families to ensure that they understand they are entitled to apply to these programs under Section 504 of the Rehabilitation Act of 1973 and the ADA.

MERGING GENERAL AND SPECIAL EDUCATION TEACHER PREPARATION PROGRAMS

A number of professionals in special education have recently advocated for combining personnel preparation tracts so that teachers learn to educate all students, regardless of their learning differences (Lilly, 1989; Lipsky & Gartner, 1989; Marshall & Herrman, 1990; Pugach, 1988; Sarason, 1982). This would appear to be a very sensible movement in light of the increased emphasis on integration and the acceleration of at-risk students being referred to special education programs in the schools today. Yet, while current school reform initiatives have addressed the need for alternative personnel preparation programs, it should be pointed out that the "regular education initiatives" proposed by special educators have not been promoted to the same extent in the regular education literature. Sarason (1982) points out that "what we see in our public schools is a mirror image of what exists in colleges and universities" (p. 258).

Changes in teacher education programs that emphasize increased collaborative efforts between regular and special education are difficult for many reasons including: 1) politics, power, and fear of job loss; 2) the belief by many educators that we do need separate systems of education; and 3) the need to train teachers according to inflexible state and local certification criteria (Lilly, 1989; Stainback & Stainback, 1989).

A few colleges and universities have begun the job of updating teacher training. As Lilly (1989) observed, the time to do so has never been better with the array of education reforms now calling for better education practices. For example, both the Holmes Group report (1986) and the Carnegie Forum on Education and Economy report (1986) call for teacher control and autonomy at the building level and for a new professional curriculum at the graduate level that would enable teachers to serve the diverse learning needs of today's student body. As several experts have noted, special education can either participate in this reform or inhibit it by clinging to separate systems of service delivery and professional development (Lipsky & Gartner, 1989).

One of the major elements that will have to change is the present acceptance of roles and responsibilities of teachers and other professionals working in schools. Pugach (1988) put it this way:

teacher educators in special education will prepare graduates to accept the role of working with students who do not readily fit classroom teachers' conceptions of whom they are prepared to teach, while general educators will agree to ensure that their graduates are prepared from the outset to seek out and expect the services special education provides. (p. 54)

Gartner and Lipsky (1987) see the problem as a "deal" between special and regular education that is promoted by: 1) funding channels; 2) lack of empowerment of regular classroom teachers burdened by huge class loads, low pay, and no decision-making authority; and 3) the referral and assessment process that is the basis of PL 94-142. Regular educators must be taught that they are responsible for all students, and special educators must move into the classroom to help with learning problems. Moving a student out of the classroom, except for training in the community or on a job, should not be the most acceptable alternative.

Stainback and Stainback (1989) delineated a number of steps that can be taken to merge teacher training programs. First, they suggest joint teaching, research, and service activities through which information, knowledge, and concerns can be shared. Restructuring organizational units is their second suggestion. This can involve whole departments, such as the special education department, curriculum, and instruction, or it can mean the joining of certain faculty to departments that match their area of expertise. It may simply mean renaming departments from special education to educational support personnel. A third and more practical step calls for reorganizing class offerings in all departments and changing requirements for graduation or certification so that all students take the same core courses. Of course, this would entail updating almost all courses and field experiences so that future teachers would be exposed to a variety of instructional situations. With core courses being the same for everyone, typical specializations or majors could be developed (e.g., history, reading, mathematics, and art), as well as new majors (e.g., employment training, community functioning skills, alternative communication, and adaptive academic learning instruction). Emphasis in early childhood, elementary, and secondary years could exist, but specialization in disability categories would not. Finally, school systems will need to coordinate with universities to change certification requirements, placement of personnel in classes, and inservice training for professionals who are already hired.

Merging and improving teacher training may be the most difficult aspect of the integration process since it is not really being advocated strenuously by either party. As demographic, societal, and work force changes continue to take place, the need for collaborative efforts in the schools and in training programs will become increasingly apparent. Parents, students, and advocates can contribute to this process by acting as change agents as society works to meet the diverse needs of all students in schools.

CONCLUSION

The advances made in educating children and youth with disabilities since 1975 have indeed been remarkable. The ADA, in concert with other recent legal mandates, provides even greater access to equal education, employment, housing, and recreation for individuals throughout their life span. Despite the progress, demands for better education outcomes for all students are being voiced from many sides, including employers, advocates, parents, education reformers, and former students. The challenge to educators is to identify effective practices for integrating students with disabilities into education programs while, at the same time, providing practical training in a variety of community-based settings across different life skill domains. The need for an increased emphasis on practical skills training is likely to become an important issue for many students given recent demographic, societal, and work force trends.

Policymakers, direct service providers, and the general public must understand that the separate systems of regular, special, remedial, or bilingual education are no longer viable in such a diverse society. Diploma tracks, curricula, and educational roles must be re-examined. Education programs must be expanded to include service coordination activities for students, job training opportunities, activities that promote career development, and academic requirements that prepare individuals for a changing work force. Obviously, this expansion requires new roles for educators who must not only provide effective instruction but advocate and prepare students for the challenges they will meet as adults. Educators will also play an important role in assisting students with disabilities and families to understand the rights guaranteed to them under the ADA and in providing opportunities that promote integration in community settings throughout the school years. The challenges are many but the opportunities are limitless if collaboration, especially among employers, parents, teacher educators, and policymakers, is the cornerstone of reform efforts in the education system.

REFERENCES

Adger, C., Neubert, D., McLaughlin, M., & Jamison, P. (1990). *A follow-along study of special education students who have exited secondary programs in Prince George's County, Maryland: Final report* (#H159A80001). College Park, MD: Institute for the Study of Exceptional Children and Youth.

Affleck, J.Q., Edgar, E., Levine, P., & Kortering, L. (1990). Postschool status of students classified as mildly mentally retarded, learning disabled, or nonhandicapped: Does it get better with time? *Education and Training in Mental Retardation, 25,* 315–324.

American Speech-Language-Hearing Association Council Administrators of Special Education, Council for Exceptional Children, Council of Graduate Programs in Communication Sciences and Disorders, Higher Education Consortium for Special Education, National Association of State Directors of Special Education, & Teacher Education Division. (1989). *A free appropriate education: But who will provide it?* Reston, VA: Council for Exceptional Children.

"Americans with Disabilities Act of 1990: What Should You Know?" *Exceptional Children, 57*(2), Supplement.

Baker, B., & Geiger, W.L. (1988). *Preparing transition specialists: Competencies from thirteen programs.* Vienna, VA: DISSEM/ACTION.

Barnes, A. (1991). *The Americans with Disabilities Act (ADA): What does it have to do with education?* Unpublished manuscript, The George Washington University, Department of Teacher Preparation and Special Education, Washington, DC.

Blackorby, J., Edgar, E., & Kortering, L.J. (1991). A third of our youth? A look at the problem of high school dropout among mildly handicapped students. *Journal of Special Education, 25,* 102–113.

Brolin, D.E. (1982). *Vocational preparation of persons with handicaps* (2nd ed.). Columbus, OH: Charles E. Merrill.

Brolin, D.E. (1989). *Life centered career education: A competency based approach* (3rd ed.). Reston, VA: Council for Exceptional Children.

Brown, S.J., & Bass, A.S. (1990). *The Americans with Disabilities Act of 1990: A guide to compliance.* Washington, DC: Arent, Fox, Kintner, Plotkin, & Kahn Law Office.

Bruininks, R.H., Wolman, C., & Thurlow, M.C. (1990). Considerations in designing survey studies and follow-up systems for special education service programs. *Remedial and Special Education, 11,* 7–17, 46.

Carnegie Forum on Education and the Economy. (1986). *A nation prepared: Teachers for the 21st century.* New York: Carnegie Corporation.

Chapman, W. (1990). The Illinois experience: State grants to improve schools through parent involvement. *Phi Delta Kappan, 72,* 355–362.

Clark, G.M., & Kolstoe, O.P. (1990). *Career development and transition education for adolescents with disabilities.* Boston: Allyn & Bacon.

Cosden, M.A. (1990). Expanding the role of special educators. *Teaching Exceptional Children, 22*(2), 4–7.

deBettencourt, L.U., & Zigmond, N. (1990). The learning disabled secondary school dropout: What teachers should know, what teachers can do. *Teacher Education and Special Education, 13,* 17–20.

deBettencourt, L.U., Zigmond, N., & Thorton, H. (1989). Follow-up of postsecondary age rural learning disabled graduates and dropouts. *Exceptional Children, 56,* 40–49.

Edgar, E. (1988). Employment as an outcome for mildly handicapped students: Current status and future directions. *Focus on Exceptional Children, 21,* 1–8.

Everson, J.M., & Moon, M.S. (1987). Transition services for young adults with severe disabilities: Defining professional and parental roles and responsibilities. *Journal of The Association for Persons with Severe Handicaps, 12*(2), 87–95.

Fairweather, J.S., & Shaver, D.M. (1990). Making the transition to postsecondary education and training. *Exceptional Children, 57,* 264–270.

Fradd, S.H., & Correa, V.I. (1989). Hispanic students at risk: Do we abdicate or advocate? *Exceptional Children, 56,* 105–110.

Gartner, A., & Lipsky, D.K. (1987). Beyond special education: Toward a quality system for all students. *Harvard Educational Review, 57,* 367–395.

Gerber, M.M., & Levine-Donnerstein, D. (1989). Educating all children: Ten years later. *Exceptional Children, 56,* 17–27.

Gerry, M.H. (1989). *The Danish approach to supporting the transition from school to adult and working life.* Washington, DC: Fund for Equal Access to Society, U.S. Department of Education, Health and Human Services and Labor.

Gerry, M.H., & McWhorter, C.M. (1990). A comprehensive analysis of federal statutes and programs for persons with severe disabilities. In L.H. Meyer, C.A. Peck, & M.L. Brown (Eds.), *Critical issues in the lives of people with severe disabilities* (pp. 495–525). Baltimore: Paul H. Brookes Publishing Co.

Gould, M., & McTaggart, N. (1988). Self-advocacy for transition: Indicators of student leadership potential today. *American Rehabilitation, 14*(4), 16–25.

Greenwood, R. (1982). Systematic caseload management. In R. Roessler & S. Rubin, *Case management and rehabilitation counseling: Procedures and techniques* (pp. 159–187). Baltimore: University Park Press.

Hahn, A. (1987). Reaching out to America's dropouts: What to do? *Phi Delta Kappan, 69,* 256–263.

Halpern, A. (1985). Transition: A look at the foundations. *Exceptional Children, 54,* 403–414.

Halpern, A. (1990). A methodological review of follow-up and follow-along studies tracking school leavers from special education. *Career Development and Exceptional Individuals, 13,* 13–27.

Halvorsen, A., Doering, K., Farron-Davis, F., Usilton, R., & Sailor, W. (1989). The role of parents and family members in planning severely disabled students' transition from school. In G.H.S. Singer & L.K. Irvin (Eds.), *Support for cargiving families: Enabling positive adaptation to disability* (pp. 289–314). Baltimore: Paul H. Brookes Publishing Co.

Hasazi, S.B., Johnson, R.E., Hasazi, J.E., Gordon, L.R., & Hull, M. (1989). Employment of youth with and without handicaps following high school: Outcomes and correlates. *Journal of Special Education, 23,* 243–255.

Hodgkinson, H.L. (1985). *All one system: Demographics of education. Kindergarten through graduate school.* Washington, DC: Institute for Educational Leadership, Inc.

Hodgkinson, H.L. (1989). *The same client: The demographics of education service delivery systems.* Washington, DC: Center for Demographic Policy, Institute for Educational Leadership, Inc.

Holmes Group. (1986). *Tomorrow's teachers: A report to the Holmes group.* East Lansing, MI: Author.

Hoyt, K. (1991). Education reform and relationships between the private sector and education: A call for integration. *Phi Delta Kappan, 72,* 450–453.

Huefner, D.S. (1988). The counseling teacher model: Risks and opportunities. *Exceptional Children, 54,* 403–414.

Idol, L. (1986). *Collaborative school consultation.* Reston, VA: Council for Exceptional Children.

Intagliata, J., & Baker, F. (1983). Factors affecting case management services for the chronically ill. *Administration in Mental Health, 11*(2), 75–91.

Karpinski, M. J., Neubert, D.A., & Graham, S. (1992). A follow-along study of postsecondary outcomes for graduates and dropouts with mild disabilities in a rural setting. *Journal of Learning Disabilities, 25,* 376–385.

Kokaska, C.J., & Brolin, D.E. (1985). *Career education for handicapped individuals* (2nd ed.). Columbus, OH: Charles E. Merrill.

Kolstoe, O.P. (1970). *Teaching educable mentally retarded children.* New York: Holt, Reinhart & Winston.

Kortering, L.J., & Edgar, E.B. (1988). Vocational rehabilitation and special education: A need for cooperation. *Rehabilitation Counseling Bulletin, 31,* 178–184.

Lewis, A.C. (1991). Coordinating services: Do we have the will? *Phi Delta Kappan, 72,* 340–341.

Lilly, M.S. (1989). Teacher preparation. In D.K. Lipsky & A. Gartner (Eds.), *Beyond separate education: Quality education for all* (pp. 143–158). Baltimore: Paul H. Brookes Publishing Co.

Lipsky, D.K., & Gartner, A. (1989). The current situation. In D.K. Lipsky & A. Gartner (Eds.), *Beyond separate education: Quality education for all* (pp. 3–24). Baltimore: Paul H. Brookes Publishing Co.

Madden, N., & Slavin, R. (1983). Mainstreaming students with mild handicaps: Academic and social outcomes. *Review of Education Research, 53,* 519–659.

Marlowe, H.A., Marlowe, J.L., & Willets, R. (1983). The mental health counselor as case manager: Implications for working with the chronically mentally ill. *American Mental Health Counselors Association Journal, 5*(4), 184–191.

Marshall, K.J., & Herrman, B.A. (1990). A collaborative metacognitive training model for special education and regular education teachers. *Teacher Education and Special Education, 13*(2), 96–104.

Meyer, L.H., Eichinger, J., & Park-Lee, S. (1987). A validation of program indicators in educational services for students with severe disabilities. *Journal of The Association for Persons with Severe Handicaps, 12,* 251–263.

Mithaug, D.E., Martin, J.E., & Agran, M. (1987). Adaptability instruction: The goal of transitional programming. *Exceptional Children, 53,* 500–505.

National Association of State Directors of Special Education. (1990). *Education of the Handicapped Act Amendments of 1990 (PL 101-476): Summary of major changes in parts A through H of the act.* Washington, DC: Author.

Neubert, D.A., & Leak, L.E. (1990). Serving urban youth with special needs in vocational education: Issues and strategies for change. *TASSP Bulletin, 2*(2), 1–3.

Peck, C.A. (1990). Linking values and science in social policy decisions affecting citizens with severe disabilities. In L.H. Meyer, C.A. Peck, & M.L. Brown (Eds.), *Critical issues in the lives of people with severe disabilities* (pp. 1–16). Baltimore: Paul H. Brookes Publishing Co.

Pipho, C. (1991). Business leaders focus on reform. *Phi Delta Kappan, 72,* 422–423.

Pugach, M. (1988). Special education as a constraint on teacher education reform. *Journal of Teacher Education, 39*(3), 52–59.

Renzaglia, A.M., & Everson, J.M. (1990). Preparing personnel to meet the challenges of contemporary employment service alternatives. In F.R. Rusch (Ed.), *Supported employment: Models, methods, and issues* (pp. 395–408). Sycamore, IL: Sycamore Publishing.

Roessler, R.T., Brolin, D.E., & Johnson, J.M. (1990). Factors affecting employment success and quality of life: A one-year follow-up of students in special education. *Career Development of Exceptional Individuals, 13* 95–108.

Sailor, W., Anderson, J.L., Halvorsen, A.T., Doering, K., Filler, J., & Goetz, L. (1989). *The comprehensive local school: Regular education for all students with disabilities.* Baltimore: Paul H. Brookes Publishing Co.

Sale, P., Everson, J., Metzler, H., & Moon, S. (1990). Quality indicators of successful vocational transition programs. In P. Wehman & S.J. Kregel (Eds.), *Supported employment: Research to practice, Volume III* (pp. 197–222). Richmond: Virginia Commonwealth University.

Sarason, S. (1982). *The culture of the school and the problem of change.* Boston: Allyn & Bacon.

Snell, M. (1987). *Systematic instruction of the moderately and severely handicapped.* Columbus, OH: Charles E. Merrill.

Snell, M.E. (1990). Building our capacity to meet the needs of persons with severe disabilities: Problems and proposed solutions. In A.P. Kaiser & C.M. McWhorter (Eds.), *Preparing personnel to work with persons with severe disabilities* (pp. 9–24). Baltimore: Paul H. Brookes Publishing Co.

Stainback, S., & Stainback, W. (1989). Facilitating merger through personnel preparation. In S. Stainback, W. Stainback, & M. Forest (Eds.), *Educating all students in the mainstream of regular education* (pp. 121–130). Baltimore: Paul H. Brookes Publishing Co.

Stainback, W., Stainback, S., & Bunch, G. (1989). A rationale for the merger of regular and special education. In S. Stainback, W. Stainback, & M. Forest (Eds.), *Educating all students in the mainstream of regular education* (pp. 15–27). Baltimore: Paul H. Brookes Publishing Co.

Storey, K., & Mank, D. (1989). Vocational education of students with moderate and severe disabilities: Implications for service delivery and teacher preparation. *Career Development for Exceptional Individuals, 12,* 11–24.

Szymanski, E.M., Hanley-Maxwell, C., & Asselin, S. (1990). Rehabilitation counseling, special education, and vocational special needs education: Three transition disciplines. *Career Development for Exceptional Individuals, 13,* 29–38.

Taylor, S.J. (1988). Caught in the continuum: A critical analysis of the principle of least restrictive environment. *Journal of The Association for Persons with Severe Handicaps, 13*(1), 41-53.

Turnbull, A.P. (1988). The challenge of providing comprehensive support to families. *Education and Training in Mental Retardation, 23*(45), 261–272.

U.S. Department of Education. (1990). *Twelfth annual report to Congress on the implementation of the Education of the Handicapped Act.* Washington, DC: U.S. Department of Education, Office of Special Education Programs.

Viadero, D. (1988). Researchers' critique escalates the debate over "regular education" for all students. *Education Week, 7*(28), 20.

Walker, L.J. (1987). Procedural rights in the wrong system: Special education is not enough. In A. Gartner & T. Joe (Eds.), *Images of the disabled—disabled images* (pp. 97–116). New York: Praeger.

Wang, M. (1989). Adaptive instruction: An alternative for accommodating student diversity through the curriculum. In D.K. Lipsky & A. Gartner (Eds.), *Beyond separate education: Quality education for all* (pp. 99–120). Baltimore: Paul H. Brookes Publishing Co.

Wehman, P., Moon, M.S., Everson, J.M., Wood, W., & Barcus, J.M. (1988). *Transition from school to work: New challenges for youth with severe disabilities.* Baltimore: Paul H. Brookes Publishing Co.

Weiner, R. (1985). *P.L. 94-142: Impact on the schools.* Washington, DC: Capital Publications.

Will, M. (1984). *OSERS program for the transition of youth with disabilities: Bridges from school to working life.* Washington, DC: U.S. Department of Education, Office of Special Education and Rehabilitation Services.

Will, M. (1986). Educating children with learning problems: A shared responsibility. *Exceptional Children, 52,* 411–416.

William T. Grant Foundation. (1988). *The forgotten half: Pathways to success for America's youth and young families.* Washington, DC: Author.

Wirt, J.G. (1991). A new federal law on vocational education: Will reform follow? *Phi Delta Kappan, 72,* 425–433.

Wolman, C., Bruininks, R., & Thurlow, M.L. (1989). Dropouts and dropout programs: Implications for special education. *Remedial and Academic Special Education, 10*(5), 6–20, 50.

Wyche, L.G. (1989). The tenth annual report to Congress: Taking a significant step in the right direction. *Exceptional Children, 56,* 14–16.

Ysseldyke, J.E. (1987). Classification of handicapped students. In M.C. Wang, M. Reynolds, & H.J. Walberg (Eds.), *Handbook of special education: Research and practice, Volume I: Learner characteristics and adaptive education* (pp. 253–271). New York: Pergamon Press.

Zigmond, N., & Thorton, H. (1985). Follow-up of postsecondary age learning disabled graduates and dropouts. *Learning Disabilities Research, 1*(1), 50–55.

Chapter 10

Public Accommodation and Housing Reforms

John Kregel

Although the Americans with Disabilities Act (ADA) does not focus ex-tensively on nondiscriminatory housing practices, provisions of the act extend and build upon other recent federal legislation that does affect hous-ing facilities for individuals with disabilities. This combination makes it likely that more accessible housing will be available in the near future. For example, Title III of the act (Public Accommodations) expands the coverage of previously existing legislation to almost every public and private entity in the United States. Still, as a practical matter, finding affordable, accessible housing remains a tremendous challenge for millions of individuals with disabilities.

The purpose of this chapter is to describe the housing rights of these persons with disabilities under current federal and state legislation. First, the major federal statutes are discussed. Second, the specific provisions of the ADA's Title III are described in detail. Third, an overview of state legislation is provided to emphasize the importance of state activity and clarify the relationship between state and federal legislation. Finally, programs that pro-vide rental assistance and low interest loans are described in order to deter-mine the success rate of attempts to provide financial assistance to individuals with disabilities who are trying to acquire housing.

THE NEED FOR HOUSING REFORM

Persons with disabilities are less likely than other citizens to live on their own, in part because of the significant service gaps that exist in the network of services and supports available for individuals with disabilities. Some researchers, for example, using a prevalence estimate of 0.7% of the general population for individuals with both mental retardation and developmental disabilities, estimate that over 80% of these individuals are cared for or assisted by family members (Braddock, Hemp, Fujiura, Bachelder, & Mitchell, 1990). As family members age and become less able to assist the person with a disability, the family's concern for the future well-being of the individual intensifies. Many people are completely unable to obtain the assistance they urgently need to promote their independence, yet larger and larger numbers of people can be expected to request supervised assistance in the near future.

In addition to the adults who live at home due to the lack of services and supports, millions of other adults continue to live at home because they cannot obtain appropriate housing. The lack of clear legislative mandates and the inconsistencies in eligibility criteria for various programs make it impossible for many individuals with disabilities to obtain the needed rental assistance and residential support services. While affordable and accessible housing programs are available in numerous communities, these programs are not available in sufficient numbers to meet the existing need. Unfortunately, the size of many existing programs is woefully inadequate to meet the identified need; waiting lists that stretch for months or even years exist for some programs. As a result, many otherwise capable individuals are being prevented from leading independent, productive lives.

The magnitude of the housing problem can be expected to increase dramatically. Efforts at deinstitutionalization (Lakin, White, Hill, Bruininks, & Wright, 1990), which will result in more individuals with disabilities entering local communities through the residential service system, continue. Even more individuals will be in need of services as a result of the provisions of the Omnibus Budget Reconciliation Act of 1987 (OBRA) (PL 100-203), which requires that the necessary services are provided to individuals with disabilities in nursing homes. The large school-age population of children and adolescents will also put pressure on the already overburdened service system. With the cost of residential care rising rapidly, fundamental changes must be made to residential service systems to ensure that the housing and residential needs of individuals with disabilities are met.

FEDERAL LEGISLATION

After decades of disregard, a large amount of federal activity was seen during and after the 1960s. Four key federal statutes, which address housing transactions and accessibility, have been passed:

1. The Architectural Barriers Act of 1968
2. Section 504 of the Rehabilitation Act of 1973
3. The Fair Housing Amendments Act of 1988
4. The Americans with Disabilities Act of 1990

Prior to the passage of these federal statutes, many state legislatures had been active in passing legislation that addressed the housing rights of individuals with disabilities. However, considerable variability remains in the extent to which state civil rights legislation encompasses specific groups of individuals with disabilities.

The Architectural Barriers Act of 1968

The Architectural Barriers Act (PL 90-480) requires all buildings constructed, altered, or financed by the federal government to be accessible to individuals with physical disabilities. The Architectural and Transportation Barriers Compliance Board (ATBCB) was established in 1973 to promote compliance with the act. In 1978, the Board was authorized to establish "minimum requirements and guidelines and federal accessibility standards (29 U.S.C. 792[6][7]." These guidelines proved very controversial and, in 1983, the participating federal agencies (General Services Administration, Department of Housing and Urban Development, Department of Defense, and the U.S. Postal Service) jointly issued the UFAS guidelines to cover all buildings subject to the act.

While somewhat limited in its application, several components of the Architectural Barriers Act paved the way for future legislation. First, its primary purpose was to provide accessibility to public buildings. Existing structures were not covered under the Act, although in 1976 provisions were added to include buildings leased by the federal government. Second, "building" was defined very broadly in the Act to include structures 1) that were open to the public, or 2) where individuals with disabilities might be employed. This was intended to include recreational, educational, medical, and other structures, not just offices occupied by federal agencies. Third, the Act ultimately led to four key federal agencies issuing a single "federal" standard. The Uniform Federal Accessibility Standards, issued in 1984, eliminated variance that had previously existed across a number of federal agencies.

Major Provisions of the Architectural Barriers Act The Act requires that buildings and facilities owned, leased, or funded by the federal government be usable by and accessible to persons with disabilites. The Act is prospective in that it does not require "retrofitting" or extensive modifications of existing structures. Its major premise is that new buildings must be usable and accessible when they are designed and constructed. However, existing or older buildings must be made accessible when they are altered (if the building is subject to design and construction standards) or when a lease is renewed.

The Act's application to specific types of residential units is limited, although the UFAS regulations apply to Section 8 housing units (discussed later in the chapter) and housing structures leased by the federal government for use in subsidized public housing programs. Also exempt from the Act's mandate are structures designed that are primarily for use by nondisabled military personnel and are operated by the Department of Defense. Compliance sanctions are significant. For instance, federal agencies can withhold funds or suspend funds while corrective action is taken if noncompliance is found in a specific program. In addition, individuals may file complaints directly with the funding agency and, if necessary, the requirements of the act are enforceable through court action.

Section 504 of the Rehabilitation Act of 1973

Another crucial piece of federal legislation that directly affects housing programs for persons with disabilities is Section 504 of the Rehabilitation Act (PL 93-112). Adopted in 1977, this legislation does not cover the programs or activities of individuals or organizations in the public or private sector not receiving federal assistance; however, Section 504 does prohibit discrimination against qualified individuals with disabilities in any program or activity that receives federal financial assistance. Furthermore, in 1978, the prohibition of discriminatory practices was extended to programs and activities of federal executive agencies and the U.S. Postal Service.

While the nondiscrimination mandate of Section 504 comprises only a single sentence, its application in the areas of housing, employment, education, transportation, health services, and recreation programs made it the most wide-reaching and significant piece of disability legislation prior to the ADA. Similar to the functional definition found in the ADA, Section 504 applies to all individuals who have a physical or mental disability that substantially limits one or more major life activities, who have a history of such impairments, or who are considered to have such impairments.

Changes embodied in the Civil Rights Restoration Act of 1988 greatly expanded the application of Section 504. These changes state that if the agency receiving federal funds is a department or other unit of a state or local government, then Section 504 applies to all programs of that agency, not just those programs that receive federal funds. If the agency is a corporation, Section 504 mandates nondiscrimination in all aspects of the corporation's activities.

Major Provisions of Section 504   Final regulations implementing Section 504 were issued by HUD in June of 1988 and mandate **program accessibility** in housing programs covered under Section 504 if the individual meets all stated eligibility requirements (e.g., age, income) for a specific program. Program accessibility, when applied to housing, does not mean that all units of a specific structure must be completely barrier-free. Rather, individuals with disabilities must have full access to the same range of housing alternatives (e.g., types of units as well as all common areas) available to other tenants. Factors to consider in determining whether the full range of options is available include the size and location of the unit, the proximity of the unit to recreational and parking areas, various amenities offered with the unit, and so forth.

Section 504 requires a great deal more "retrofitting," or modification of existing facilities, than is required under the FHAA. Although program accessibility does not dictate total, massive retrofitting of existing structures, it does require an average of 5% of the units in a structure to be accessible, regardless of the structure's age. In addition, when a unit is altered or renovated with federal funds, the alteration must result in an accessible unit.

The technical standard for HUD's Section 504 regulations is the Uniform Federal Accessibility Standard (UFAS). To comply with the UFAS, new multi-family projects of five or more units (as opposed to four or more units under the FHAA) must be accessible, with at least 5%, or one unit, accessible to individuals with mobility requirements. At least 2%, or one unit, must be accessible to individuals with hearing or visual impairments.

The Fair Housing Amendments Act of 1988

Prior to the passage of the ADA, the Fair Housing Amendments Act of 1988 (FHAA) (PL 100-430) was the most recent piece of federal legislation affecting the rights of individuals with disabilities. The legislation, signed into law by President Reagan in September of 1988, became effective on March 12, 1989. The purpose of the FHAA was to modify, expand, and strengthen the nondiscriminatory enforcement mechanisms contained in Title VIII of the Civil Rights Act of 1968 (Bureau of National Affairs [BNA], 1990).

The FHAA added persons with disabilities as a new class of protected individuals. This marked the first time that discrimination based on "disability" was included in a major piece of federal civil rights legislation. Similar to the ADA, the FHAA defines the meaning of discrimination and imposes accessibility requirements for private activities that are not financed by the federal government.

Persons Covered Under the FHAA The FHAA contains a functional definition of "disability," very similar to the definition found in the ADA. Persons covered under the amendments include qualified persons with physical or mental disabilities whose impairment **substantially limits one or more major life activities,** who have a record of such impairment, or who are regarded as having such an impairment. Persons with AIDS and individuals who are HIV-infected are covered under the amendments if they are otherwise qualified, meaning that health and safety considerations in the ADA definition of disability are applicable. Alcoholics are covered under the FHAA, but persons addicted to controlled substances (e.g., drug users) are not. The amendments also prohibit discrimination against individuals who **associate** with individuals who have disabilities or who plan to have an individual with a disability reside in the residence that they intend to rent or purchase. In other words, it is illegal to refuse to rent or sell a housing unit to an individual simply because that individual has a spouse, child, parent, other relative, roommate, friend, or other associate who has a disability.

Major Provisions of the FHAA The Department of Housing and Urban Development (HUD) issued final regulations implementing the amendments on January 23, 1989. The regulations addressed both existing housing and new construction. In the area of existing housing, the regulations attempt to define the rights and responsibilities of both the buyer/tenant (the individual with a disability) and the seller/landlord. The individual with a disability has a right, at his or her own expense, to undertake **reasonable modifications** to existing premises that will provide him or her **full enjoyment** of the residence. The landlord cannot require that any modifications be completed by a specific contractor, or insist on the restoration of any modification that does not limit the use and enjoyment of the unit by future tenants (e.g., widened doorways); however, in some instances, the landlord may require the tenant to restore the premises to the state in which they existed prior to the modification (e.g., in the case of significant modifications made to kitchen or bath fixtures). The landlord can also demand a complete description of any work that will be done and assurances that the work will be completed in a competent manner, complying with all applicable local codes and regulations. Additional interest payments on the part of the tenant may also be required. The HUD regulations also apply to the concept of reasonable accommodation to the landlord's policies or operating procedures. Reasonable accommodation must be afforded to enable the individual with a disability to use and enjoy his or her residence, including all common areas. Access to lobbies, clubhouses, laundry facilities, swimming pools, and other recreational areas must be provided unless doing so would result in an undue hardship on the landlord. Reserved parking spaces must be provided when necessary. Policies regarding pets may need to be liberalized to accommodate seeing eye dogs for individuals with visual impairments.

The HUD regulations, as well as other regulations pertaining to the FHAA and the ADA, attempt to compromise between the provision of total access for the individual with a disability and the perceived burden that might be placed on a landlord to make extensive or costly renovations. Landlords must permit reasonable modifications in cases where the applicant can live successfully (i.e., experience full enjoyment) in the unit after the modifications are made. Frequently, modifications will not require any significant investment of resources by the landlord. It is possible that tenants may bear significant financial responsibility for any modifications. They cannot expect to be provided with supports or services that fall outside the scope of services offered to other tenants.

The FHAA provisions concerning new housing construction are perhaps the most innovative components of the entire act. Regulations regarding new construction cover all multi-family units built for first occupancy after March 13, 1991. Multi-family units that fall under these regulations include all ground floor apartments in buildings with four or more apartments if an elevator is not in the building, or all apartments in buildings that have both four or more apartments and an elevator. The regulations do not require that elevators be installed in any building designed and constructed as a "walk-up" building without an elevator. The following requirements apply to all covered multi-family units:

1. Common use areas must be accessible. The structure must have an accessible route, usable by individuals with disabilities, including persons in wheelchairs, that connects accessible public use and common use areas.
2. All doorways within housing units, including entry doors, must be wide enough to allow wheelchair passage.
3. All electrical outlets, power switches, thermostats, and other environmental controls must be in accessible locations. Kitchens and bathrooms must be designed to allow individuals in wheelchairs to comfortably maneuver in them. Technical accessibility guidelines follow the standards of the American National Standard Institute (ANSI).
4. All units must be **adaptable.** In other words, while not immediately accessible, units must be designed and constructed to enable rapid, appropriate modifications to be made. For example, grab bars may not need to be installed in bathrooms; however, bathroom walls must be reinforced to allow the future installation of adaptive equipment and devices.

The Americans with Disabilities Act of 1990

Although it does not focus extensively on housing issues, the ADA does add to nondiscrimination in housing programs by extending the principles of previous legislation to state and local governments and public accommodations. Title II prohibits discrimination in **housing programs funded by state and local governments.** Title II of the ADA prohibits discrimination on the basis of disability in services, programs, or activities of all state and local governments. Whereas Section 504 of the Rehabilitation Act of 1973 prohibited discrimination in all programs receiving federal assistance, Title II extends this prohibition to all activities, irregardless of whether they receive federal funding. All governmental activities of public entities are covered, even those carried out by contractors or agents working on behalf of the state or local government. For example, states would be obligated to ensure that the services and activities of a state park inn operated under contract by a private entity are in compliance with Title II's requirements. This mandate became effective in January of 1992.

In addition, Title III of the ADA focuses on all places of public accommodations, regardless of size. It mandates that the goods, services, privileges, and facilities of any public place be provided in the most integrated setting possible. It also prohibits discrimination in the "full and equal enjoyment" of the services and facilities; however, Title III does not apply in situations in which the individual poses a direct threat to the health and safety of others. The term *direct threat* refers to situations in which there exists a significant risk that cannot be eliminated by changes in procedures or through the provision of auxiliary aids.

Definition of Public Accommodations Public accommodations are broadly defined to include virtually all private commercial entities. The following list summarizes the types of entities defined by the ADA as places of public accommodation:

1. An inn, hotel, motel, or other place of lodging, except an establishment in which: 1) five or fewer rooms are rented, and 2) the proprietor actually resides
2. A restaurant, bar, or other establishment that serves food or drink
3. Places of entertainment (e.g., a movie theater, concert hall, or stadium)
4. An auditorium, convention center, lecture hall, or other place of public gathering
5. A bakery, grocery store, hardware store, shopping center, or other sales or rental establishment
6. Service establishments (e.g., laundromat, bank, beauty shop, funeral parlor, pharmacy, office of an accountant or lawyer, professional office of a healthcare provider, or hospital)
7. Public transportation terminals
8. A museum, library, gallery, or other cultural facilities
9. A park, zoo, amusement park, or other place of recreation
10. A nursery, school, college, university, or other place of education
11. Social service establishments (e.g., day care centers, senior citizen centers, homeless shelters, or food banks)
12. A gymnasium, health spa, bowling alley, golf course, or other place of exercise or recreation (ADA, Sec. 301[7][A–L])

Accessibility of Public Accommodations Title III also contains provisions designed to ensure the physical accessibility of all public accommodations. It is considered a violation of the act to fail to remove architectural or communication barriers in existing facilities if removing such barriers is readily achievable. New facilities are held to an even higher standard. They must be readily accessible and usable by individuals with disabilities unless it is impractical to do so.

The readily achievable standard for existing buildings and readily accessible standard for new construction are quite different. The ADA defines readily achievable as:

easily accomplishable and able to be carried out without much difficulty or expense. In determining whether an action is readily achievable, factors to be considered include
(A)   the nature and cost of the action needed under this Act;
(B)   the overall financial resources of the facility or facilities involved in the action; the number of persons employed at such facility; the effect on expenses or resources; or the impact otherwise of such action upon the operation of the facility;
(C)   the overall financial resources of the covered entity; the overall size of the business of a covered entity with respect to the number of its employees; the number, type and location of its facilities; and
(D)   the type of operation or operations of the covered entity, including the composition, structure, and functions of the workforce of such entity; the geographic separateness, and administrative or fiscal relationship of the facility or facilities in question to the covered entity. (ADA, Sec. 301[9][A–D])

In determining whether or not the removal of existing structural or communication barriers is readily achievable, factors such as the size and type of the business, the financial resources of the entity, and the type of cost required for the modification must be taken into consideration. If the removal of the barrier cannot be accomplished without a great amount of difficulty or expense, then the goods or services of the entity must be made available through alternative means, if such means are available.

Since it is far less costly to incorporate accessible design features into new buildings than to retrofit existing structures, a higher accessibility standard has been established for new construction and major alterations. This standard dictates that a building must be both readily accessible and useable by persons with disabilities. The FHAA made use of this same standard for common areas in newly constructed multi-family housing units. Although this standard does not mean total accessibility in every part of every area of a facility, it does mean a high degree of convenient accessibility.

Auxiliary Aids and Services   A public accommodation cannot deny an individual the right to participate in or benefit from its goods or services. Furthermore, services or accommodations that are separate or segregated are specifically prohibited, as is the provision of goods or services to a person with a disability that are not equal to those provided to others. In some circumstances, public accommodations must offer additional services to individuals with disabilities. For example, segregating available seating for individuals in wheelchairs in a movie theater or gymnasium to an inferior area of the facility is a clear violation of Title III. Wheelchair seating must be provided in such a way as to be "dispersed throughout the seating area" and "located to provide lines of sight comparable to those for all viewing areas" (Section 302[6][2][a][A][iii]).

When necessary, Title III requires that public accommodations provide "auxiliary aids and services" to ensure equal access to a facility's goods and services, unless doing so places undue burden on the entity or fundamentally alters the nature of the goods or services provided. Auxiliary aids include interpreters, readers, taped texts, and similar services. The type or types of aids that must be used are not specified; however, the effect of the aid must be to provide individuals with disabilities the opportunity to achieve the same results as individuals without disabilities. For example, a retail entity may be required to write down information that is normally spoken in order to accommodate the needs of individuals with hearing impairments. Unfortunately, the provision of an interpreter at all times may place an undue burden on the store. Similarly, if an individual is available to read the menu aloud for a customer with a visual impairment, a restaurant may not be required to provide menus in braille. Whether or not the requirement to provide a specific auxiliary aid under Title III poses an undue burden is based on a case-by-case assessment using criteria similar to those used to assess undue hardship under Title I.

Enforcement Under Title III   Title III may be enforced by an individual lawsuit or by actions of the Attorney General. An individual may bring a lawsuit for an injunction or for attorney's fees, although compensatory or punitive damages are not available under the statute. The Attorney General may bring suit in cases where a pattern of illegal conduct is involved or in cases of significant public importance. In instances where the Attorney General has initiated action, the court may order injunctive relief, award damages, or impose civil penalties.

STATE LAWS

To a large extent, the recent federal activity merely brought federal legislation into step with state law pertaining to the housing rights of persons with disabilities. State housing discrimination laws have played the dominant role of shaping the relationship between the buyer/tenant and seller/landlord, and will continue to be critical in the future. Although many states possess comprehensive nondiscriminatory legislation, a great deal of variability exists in the individuals covered by different state statutes and the activities regulated under the legislation.

Persons Covered Under State Legislation

Most state nondiscrimination or human rights laws prohibit discrimination in housing against persons with mental or physical impairments; however, a significant number of states do limit the individuals covered under their legislation. For example, some states only cover persons with physical disabilities and not persons with mental impairments. In contrast, several states (e.g., Virginia, Wisconsin) have recently expanded their legislation to add persons with mental impairments. Some states specifically cover in their statutes persons with AIDS. Others have interpreted their laws as extending coverage to individuals with AIDS. Unfortunately, some states do not even have a law prohibiting discrimination against individuals with disabilities.

In addition to provisions found in the nondiscrimination legislation of certain states, some states have specific pieces of legislation (termed "White Cane Laws"). Anachronistic in nature, these laws expressly require that individuals with disabilities have full and equal access to housing. These provisions, often found in state laws dealing with housing or public accommodations, usually protect only individuals with physical disabilities. Other states limit protection to persons with visual or hearing impairments.

Major Provisions in State Laws

The intent of incorporating nondiscrimination provisions into state civil rights laws is to add individuals with disabilities to the groups protected under the legislation. In state legislation, public accommodations and housing are frequently covered. Similar to federal legislation, many state laws require that a specific number (or percentage) of units within multi-family dwellings are accessible to individuals with disabilities when new housing is built. Few, if any, states require landlords or owners to devote significant resources to retrofitting existing housing units.

In nondiscrimination legislation, discrimination is also prohibited in all areas of the housing procurement process (e.g., advertising, sale, purchase, financing, and leasing a housing unit). Questions regarding an individual's disability are forbidden during the acquisition, financing, construction, or maintenance of a housing unit. Significant features of several state laws are the tax benefits that are sometimes provided for new or existing accessible housing. These benefits may take the form of either deductions or exemptions.

PROGRAMS PROVIDING FINANCIAL ASSISTANCE

In addition to the federal laws that prohibit housing discrimination against individuals with disabilities, several programs administered by the Department of Housing and Urban Development (HUD) provide financial assistance for individuals with disabilities and organizations (public and private) that provide housing to individuals with disabilities. Such programs and federal legislation include: 1) the Section 8 Rental Assistance Program, 2) the HUD Section 202 Program, 3) the Housing and Community Development Act Amendments, 4) the Stewart B. McKinney Homeless Assistance Amendments Act (Title IV), and 5) the Cranston-Gonzalez National Affordable Housing Act (Title VIII). The key provisions of each piece of legislation are summarized in this section.

Section 8 Rental Assistance Program

The parent legislation for the Section 8 Rental Assistance program is the Housing and Community Development Act of 1974 (PL 93-383). This act attempts to aid low income families, including qualified individuals with disabilities, to acquire suitable housing in private accommodations. However, there are specific income requirements that must be met for any individual to acquire services through the program. To be eligible, an individual's income generally must not exceed 80% of the median income for the area in which the individual intends to reside.

If individuals with disabilities meet the stated income eligibility criteria, they are specifically targeted for services in the Section 8 program. Individuals with disabilities are defined in the Section 8 regulations as persons who: 1) possess a physical or mental disability that substantially impedes an individual's ability to live independently, or 2) meet the federal definition of developmental disability. Emphasis is placed on serving individuals with disabilities who are involuntarily displaced at the time of application for services or who are spending more than 50% of their monthly income for rent.

Scope of Services   The rental assistance provided through this program can be directed toward either the tenant or the residence. In the **tenant-based** program, eligible individuals and their families receive certificates of participation that can be used to rent an apartment or home in the community, providing the residence meets certain quality standards and the landlord agrees to participate in the program. Existing housing units must generally fall within "fair market" rental limits, although rents up to 20% over the fair market rate can be subsidized through the program if it can be shown that the extra cost is associated with an accessible unit within a market area. The key advantage of the tenant-based program is that it allows the individual significant freedom of choice in selecting an appropriate residential unit.

In addition to tenant-based provisions for existing housing, the program also applies **project-based** assistance in moderate rehabilitation, substantial rehabilitation, and new construction. In project-based assistance, certificates are attached to the residential unit as opposed to the renter. Moderate rehabilitation provides assistance to owners of substandard housing, who may contract units that have been rehabilitated to meet program standards for a 15-year period. Rehabilitation must involve more than routine maintenance and involve an expenditure of over $1,000 per unit. Up to 5% of the units in this category may be renovated for accessibility alone. The fact that the subsidy is attached to the unit limits the ability of the individuals residing in these units to move.

In substantial rehabilitation and new construction projects, the owner agrees to provide a certain number of units prior to undertaking substantial rehabilitation or new construction. The owner (a public or private entity) may then use the Section 8 guarantee to obtain conventional financing for the project. The owner is then obliged to select eligible individuals to reside in the units. This program has the potential to alleviate the lengthy waiting period that frequently exists for tenant-based certificates. However, the demand for project-based units is usually quite large and waiting lists develop quickly after availability is announced. Much too often, the number of available units under this component of the program falls short of the number needed to serve all eligible individuals.

The HUD Section 202 Program

While the Section 8 program provides rental assistance to specific individuals or specific residential units, the intent of the Section 202 program is to provide direct federal loans to private, nonprofit corporations to construct new or substantially rehabilitated housing properties. The Section 202 program is specifically designed to support projects for persons who are elderly or persons with disabilities or the families of these two groups. Loans are available only to borrowers defined as private, nonprofit corporations or consumer cooperatives, which are incorporated at the time of application. Consumer cooperatives, religious or minority organizations, senior citizens' groups, or other similar entities are generally the types of nonprofit corporations that receive Section 202 loans. The legislation requires that 20%–25% of all Section 202 loans be awarded to organizations in rural areas.

Section 202's definition of disability is identical to that found in Section 8—an individual with a "handicap" is a person with an indefinite or long-term physical, mental, or developmental disability. This disability must also significantly impede the individual's ability to live independently. In addition, this ability must be expected to improve through suitable housing conditions. This definition significantly intertwines the Section 202 and Section 8 programs as does the fact that Section 8 rental assistance certificates are required for a minimum of 20% of the units in a project funded through Section 202.

Scope of Services Section 202 funds may be used by a successful applicant to construct new facilities, acquire existing facilities, or substantially rehabilitate existing facilities. Loans are awarded through a highly competitive rating and ranking process. Key criteria used in the rating process include:

1. The borrower's capacity to carry out a long-term housing project
2. The borrower's financial capacity
3. The location of the project

4. Modest design and cost containment within the construction or rehabilitation of the facility
5. The extent of displacement resulting from the project

Restrictions on both the size and the location of the facility are made by the program. For persons with physical or developmental disabilities, the size limit is 40 apartment units or independent living units, or 15 persons within a group home. A maximum of 20 units are allowed in independent living residences for persons with long-term mental illness. The preferred size for facilities serving individuals with developmental disabilities is no more than six to eight individuals. Residences should be scattered throughout a community and be in proximity to shops, recreational opportunities, jobs, and other community services. For instance, Section 202 housing should not be located next to institutions, sheltered workshops, special schools, or other similar facilities.

Another key provision of the program requires that each project develop and submit a management plan that outlines types of recreational, continuing education, transportation, and other services needed by residents. The plan must identify the means for the provision of services, the sources of funds identified to provide the services, and the management services offered by the borrower. This provision represents the first time within federal housing programs that the comprehensive, community-based support needs of individuals with disabilities are acknowledged in a housing assistance program.

The Housing and Community Development Act Amendments

In 1987, the Housing and Community Development Act Amendments (PL 100-242) were enacted to encourage disability representatives to participate in the development of Section 202 standards. Specific provisions ensure that Section 202 applications for individuals with disabilities are not in direct competition with projects for elderly individuals. New procedures and guidelines were developed to address the unique accessibility needs of individuals with disabilities. Allowable rents within projects serving individuals with disabilities are based upon the costs of **operating** the project as opposed to fair market values. A plan for supportive services that will enable the individual to remain in the community must be developed and implemented.

The Stewart B. McKinney Homeless Assistance Amendments Act

The Stewart B. McKinney Homeless Assistance Amendments Act (PL 100-628), Title IV (Homeless Housing Assistance) encompasses a permanent housing program for individuals with disabilities. Under the program, supportive housing funds can be used to assist in the operational costs of implementing projects for persons with disabilities who are permanently homeless. Title IV also allows the waiver of certain standards for individuals with disabilities, such as elimination of the eight-person limit on housing programs, if the programs serve primarily individuals with disabilities.

The Cranston-Gonzalez National Affordable Housing Act

Title VIII, Supportive Housing for Persons with Disabilities, of the Cranston-Gonzalez National Affordable Housing Act (PL 101-625), provides direct financial assistance to nonprofit entities providing housing to individuals with disabilities. As opposed to a loan, Title VIII enables HUD to provide a direct capital advance for the purchase of an existing facility or the construction of a new group home, independent residences, or apartments for individuals with disabilities. As long as individuals with disabilities are able to obtain units in the project, the nonprofit agency is not required to repay the capital advance. Under Title VIII, group homes are limited in size to no more than eight individuals.

CONCLUSION

The previously discussed federal and state programs represent the United States's efforts to eliminate housing discrimination based on disability and to provide the financial aid and supports necessary to enable individuals with disabilities to obtain available housing. While legislation has expanded the housing opportunities available for individuals with disabilities, the availability of affordable and accessible housing remains a key barrier for the independence of millions of individuals. Since the comprehensive needs of persons with disabilities are not yet assessed (the number of individuals in need of specific types of housing is yet unknown), it is impossible to determine the effectiveness of current efforts or to engage in long-range system planning. Fragmentation in the service delivery system and poor interagency collaboration lead to unnecessary duplication and significant gaps in services and supports.

A lack of knowledge on the part of human service professionals regarding the details of specific programs and strategies for obtaining available funds limits their applicability to various segments of the community. For example, service coordinators or case managers serving persons with mental retardation or developmental disabilities are generally poorly informed regarding housing assistance programs. In contrast, professionals working in psychosocial rehabilitation programs for persons with long-term mental illness or independent living centers for persons with physical or sensory disabilities are usually more knowledgeable of these programs or regulations. However, these latter groups tend only to serve a small segment of the overall populations, leaving literally millions of potentially eligible individuals unaware of available services and programs. Staff development efforts are needed at both the preservice and inservice level for all professionals who are involved in rehabilitation and day service programs for individuals with disabilities. These professionals must be provided the knowledge and skills necessary to enable them to assist the individuals they serve to obtain available and affordable housing. In addition, particular attention should be paid to staff training programs for special education personnel in secondary schools, as well as professionals providing services to students with special needs in post-secondary education institutions.

Finally, and perhaps most important, the size of the United States's housing program for individuals with disabilities remains woefully small in comparison to the overwhelming current need and the anticipated future need for such services. Many individuals are totally unable to access the assistance they urgently need to promote their independence. Hundreds of thousands of adults continue to live at home with their parents or other relatives, often because they cannot obtain appropriate housing. A lack of clear legislative mandates and inconsistencies in eligibility criteria for various programs make it presently impossible for many individuals with mental retardation, long-term mental illness, cerebral palsy, epilepsy, traumatic brain injury, orthopedic impairments, and other physical and sensory disabilities to obtain much-needed residential support services. The size of many existing programs is woefully inadequate to meet the identified need. While affordable and accessible housing programs are available in numerous communities, they are rarely available in sufficient numbers to meet existing needs. Waiting lists exist for some programs that stretch for many months or even years. As a result, many otherwise capable individuals are prevented from leading independent, productive lives.

The magnitude of the housing problem can be expected to increase dramatically over time. The majority of adults with severe disabilities are living with their parents or other relatives. As family members age and become less able to assist the individual with a disability, the family's concern for the future well-being of the individual becomes greatly magnified. In the near future, larger numbers of individuals can be expected to request supervised and unsupervised housing assistance. It is imperative that funding agencies recognize that the availability of accessible housing will not by itself guarantee that the individual will be able to live independently in his or her community. For many individuals, financial and other supports are necessary to maximize their independence. For example, many individuals who are eligible for housing assistance cannot participate in these programs because of a lack of available personal assistant services. Other individuals, dependent on income maintenance programs and minimal earnings form sheltered employment programs, simple lack sufficient financial resources to enable them to live on their own. While the recent flurry of federal activity has attempted to address key shortcomings in the present system, the problem of program capacity remains a critical challenge for federal and state agencies.

REFERENCES

Americans with Disabilities Act, PL 101-336. (July 26, 1990). 42 U.S.C. 12101, et seq: *Federal Register, 56*(144), 00000–35756.

Architectural Barriers Act, PL 90-480. (1968).

Braddock, D., Hemp, R., Fujiura, G., Bachelder, L., & Mitchell, D. (1990). *The state of the states in developmental disabilities.* Baltimore: Paul H. Brookes Publishing Co.

Bureau of National Affairs. (1990). *The Americans with Disabilities Act: A practical and legal guide to impact, enforcement, and compliance.* Washington, DC: Author.

Cranston-Gonzalez National Affordable Housing Act, PL 101-625. (1990).

Fair Housing Amendments Act, PL 100-430. (1988).

Housing and Community Development Act, PL 93-383. (1974).

Housing and Community Development Act Amendments of 1987, PL 101-242. (1988).

Lakin, K.C., White, C.C., Hill, B.K., Bruininks, R.H., & Wright, E.A. (1990). Longitudinal change and interstate variability in the size of residential facilities for persons with mental retardation. *Mental Retardation, 28,* 343–351.

Omnibus Budget Reconciliation Act, PL 100-203. (1987).

Section 504 of the Rehabilitation Act of 1973, PL 93-112. (1977).

Stewart B. McKinney Homeless Assistance Amendments Act, PL 100-628. (1988).

Chapter 11

Recreation and Leisure Lifestyle Changes

Ronald Reynolds

The Americans with Disabilities Act (ADA) will not only improve employment opportunities, access to public services, and telecommunications capabilities for more than 43 million citizens, but it will also greatly expand the recreational and leisure opportunities available to these individuals and create an environment conducive to an independent leisure lifestyle. This chapter explores the potential impact of the ADA on the leisure of persons with disabilities from both an historical and current perspective. The benefits of play, recreation, and leisure for individuals in general are overviewed, a brief historical perspective on leisure and recreational opportunities for persons with disabilities in the United States in the pre–World War II era is provided, and recent trends are discussed. Also addressed is the professionalization of leisure services for individuals with disabilities since the 1950s. Finally, this chapter attempts to look beyond current approaches of providing leisure services and opportunities, emphasizing the potential effects of the ADA.

RECREATION AND THE SATISFACTION OF PERSONAL NEEDS

All individuals possess the same basic needs and desires, which are physically, biologically, and socially determined. A plethora of researchers in the social, psychological, and leisure service fields have documented how individuals achieve their basic needs through play and recreation. The majority of these researchers believe that leisure enhances life. For example, several theories have been developed to explain why children and adults seek play and leisure experiences. Classical theories of play include: surplus energy, relaxation, instinct, preparation for life, and recapitulation. More recent theories include task generalization, compensation, catharsis, psychoanalysis, and arousal-seeking explanations. Whatever the motivation, recreation is integrally related to other life activities and has several potential benefits. It is proven that active recreational pursuits can have a positive effect upon a person's health. Physiologists and physicians agree that participation in activities involving exercise is essential to the development and maintenance of fitness for living. Children naturally require physical activity to meet physiological needs. Emotional well-being, likewise, is enhanced through recreational and leisure pursuits. According to some physicians, as many as 50% of all office visits may be induced by various types of stress. To maintain positive mental health it is important for individuals to supplement their daily routine with some form of recreation. Recreational activities also provide persons with the opportunity to develop rewarding and satisfying relationships with others. The social development of both children and adults can be enhanced through recreative experiences. Unfortunately, persons with disabilities have not had ready access to leisure services and opportunities, as the following illustrates:

> Leisure and recreation activities are an important part of American life. They promote physical health, social interaction, skill development and self-esteem. Unfortunately, these activities have historically received relatively low priority in programs for persons with developmental disabilities. This longstanding neglect is deteriorating because appropriate participation in leisure/recreation activities is associated with development of collateral skills important in daily life, such as independent living and work skills. The possession of these skills can play an important role in the successful community adjustment of individuals with disabilities. (Institute on Community Integration and the Research and Training Center on Community Living, 1989, p. 1)

RECREATION AND LEISURE SERVICES FOR PERSONS WITH DISABILITIES: 1900–1940

The early 1900s marked a gradual trend toward the development of recreation services for persons with disabilities in institutional settings. These settings included federal and state hospitals for persons with mental illness and mental retardation, some medical and surgical hospitals, and prisons. While some community-based programs were developed to serve special populations, they were few in number and limited in scope. Some of these community-based programs included public schools, which often offered recreation programs for children with disabilities, and organizations such as the American Red Cross, which assumed responsibility for the provision of recreation services for personnel in military hospitals during World War I.

In the 1920s and 1930s, recreation services were greatly expanded in state hospitals for persons with mental illness and persons with mental retardation. While these programs (e.g., sports, music, special events) were largely diversional in nature, hospital personnel became increasingly aware of the benefits that recreation could have for persons with special needs. In 1930, the White House Conference on Child Health Protection spawned interest in the use of recreation as a medium for working with citizens with mental retardation. For the first time, individualized recreation programs were developed to improve functional skills necessary for community living (Witt, 1970). Recreation services were provided to other groups of persons with disabilities; however, the services tended to be scattered and sporadic.

It is important to note that community recreation services for persons with special needs did not keep pace with institutionally based services during this time frame. As one author notes:

> The recreation movement was born with a social conscience. It grew up with the settlement house movement, the kindergarten movement, and the youth movement that fostered the great youth agencies of this nation. Its earliest practitioners had a human welfare motivation in which the social needs of human development, curbing juvenile delinquency, informal education, cultural environment, healthy improvement and other objectives were central. Gradually the social welfare mission weakened and a philosophy which sees recreation as an end in itself was adopted; this is the common view in public recreation agencies throughout the country. (Gray, 1977, p. 23)

This decline in the provision of municipal recreation services for persons with special needs continued throughout the first half of the twentieth century. The reason for this trend has been expressed as follows:

> it could be said that at its highest point of success, the recreation profession unwittingly allowed the prime focus of its mission to shift from the delivery of specialized human services to professional development and facility management. Unfortunately, it appears that the provision of services to people became a means to broaden goals, purposes, and professional status, rather than remaining a vital and satisfying end into itself. (Hutchison, Stein, & Sessoms, 1975, p. 327)

Unfortunately, public recreation agencies provided few programs for those with special needs; therefore, volunteer agency associations were formed to provide such services. A few of these associations include: The Association for the Aid of Crippled Children, the Easter Seal Societies, and The Lighthouse (a service center operated by the New York Association for the Blind). These organizations provided day and residential camps, clubs, and assistive devices for persons with special needs. In many cases, this was the only form of recreation available. Overall, the period from 1900 to 1940 saw organized recreation for persons with disabilities dominated largely by institutional services and, to a lesser extent, philanthropic services.

RECREATION AND LEISURE SERVICES
FOR PERSONS WITH DISABILITIES: 1940–PRESENT

World War II prompted a tremendous expansion of recreation services in military hospitals (again provided by the Red Cross) and in hospitals managed by the Veterans Administration. In hospitals run by the federal government, the emphasis placed on recreation services resulted in an expansion of services in state residential facilities as well as a growing recognition that recreation could be therapeutic for persons with disabilities. It was also recognized that activities learned through such services could be used to develop skills that could be used after discharge. This view, that recreation could be used as a tool to bring about positive physical, social, and emotional change in persons with disabilities, was in sharp contrast to the philosophy of providing diversional recreation. Recreation was more than just a way to occupy one's free time.

By the 1950s, a few community-based centers were well-established to offer recreation services to people with physical and mental disabilities. Two of the most noted centers were The Recreation Center for the Handicapped in San Francisco and The Greater Kansas City Council on Recreation for the Handicapped. This decade also marked the beginning of the professionalization of leisure services for persons with disabilities. For example, the National Therapeutic Recreation Society was formed from the merger of the Hospital Recreation Section of the American Recreation Society; The Recreation Therapy Section of the American Association for Health, Physical Education, and Recreation; and the National Association for Recreation Therapists. The early membership of this organization was comprised largely of individuals who provided leisure and recreation services in large hospitals and residential facilities. Municipal recreation departments also began to employ personnel to organize and administer special recreation services for persons with physical, social, or emotional difficulties.

The 1950s and 1960s also saw a large increase in the number of national volunteer and service organizations that provided recreation services for people with special needs. Some of these organizations and their affiliates include: 1) the United Cerebral Palsy Association; 2) the Muscular Dystrophy Association; 3) the National Multiple Sclerosis Association; 4) Goodwill Industries; 5) the Kennedy Foundation; 6) the American Foundation for the Blind; 7) the National Association for Retarded Citizens; 8) the Kiwanis, Elks, Lions, Moose, and Eagles; and 9) the Junior Chamber of Commerce. Additionally, volunteer youth associations arose to include the YMCA and the

YWCA, the Boy and Girl Scouts, and the Boys' and Girls' Clubs, which have been involved with programs for persons with disabilities.

In the 1970s, the federal government, specifically, the National Park Service, Department of Interior, established the Division of Special Programs and Populations. This division was established to develop a comprehensive access plan to ensure that parks are accessible to all visitors. Such issues as historic site accessibility, wilderness experiences, expansion of interpretive programs to enable participation of persons who are deaf and blind, exploration of technological approaches, and accessible transportation systems are being addressed by the division. In addition, policies and guidelines relative to persons with special needs are formulated, employment opportunities within the service are reviewed, specialized training is recommended, technical assistance is provided to park areas to aid in the elimination of programmatic and physical barriers, and special demonstration projects are coordinated (National Park Service, Division of Special Programs and Population, Department of Interior, n.d.).

The next 20 years saw three trends, which markedly influenced the provision of recreation services for those persons with special needs. These three trends include the passage of nondiscriminatory legislation, the continued professionalization efforts in the field of therapeutic recreation, and the normalization movement.

Legislation

The first trend occurred in the area of legislation, specifically with Section 504 of the Rehabilitation Act of 1973. This provision, which addresses program accessibility, has been referred to as the handicapped Bill of Rights. Its implications for recreation services are summarized in the following passage:

> No otherwise qualified handicapped individual in the United States shall, solely by reason of his handicap, be excluded from participation in, be denied the benefits of or be subjected to discrimination under any program or activity receiving federal financial assistance. (*Federal Register*, August 23, 1973, p. 163)

The Education for All Handicapped Children Act of 1975 (PL 94-142) may well be the most important piece of legislation affecting children with disabilities. This law, which is designed to ensure a free and appropriate public education for all children between the ages of 3 and 21, identifies recreation as a related or supportive service. Specifically, the law outlines the assessment of leisure function, the provision of recreation programs in schools and community agencies, and leisure education.

Professionalization

The second trend of the 1970s and 1980s that affected the provision of leisure services to persons with disabilities was the continued professionalization efforts in the field of therapeutic recreation. For the first time, consensus was achieved concerning the development of a Philosophical Position Statement. Previously, practitioners and educators had a difficult time reaching an agreement on a definition for therapeutic recreation. This statement was developed to reach a consensus concerning the purpose and practice of the field. The following passage depicts this purpose:

> The purpose of therapeutic recreation is to facilitate the development, maintenance, and expression of an appropriate leisure lifestyle for individuals with physical, mental, emotional, or social limitations. Accordingly, this purpose is accomplished through the provision of professional programs and services which assist the client in eliminating barriers to leisure, developing leisure skills and attitudes, and optimizing leisure involvement. Therapeutic recreation professionals use these principles to enhance clients' leisure ability in recognition of the importance and value of leisure in the human experience. (National Therapeutic Recreation Society, 1982)

Three major areas of service are assumed under this approach in order to facilitate appropriate leisure lifestyles. They are: 1) therapy, which results in the improvement of specific functional behaviors; 2) leisure education, which results in the acquisition of skills, knowledge, and attitudes related to leisure involvement; and 3) recreation participation, which includes voluntary participation in interest and activities. There are now approximately 13,000 therapeutic recreation specialists who are nationally certified at a professional or paraprofessional level.

Normalization

The final trend, which has had a profound effect upon the philosophy of leisure service delivery for persons with disabilities, is the normalization movement. This movement dictates that persons with disabilities should receive the same opportunities to participate in recreation and leisure services as the general public. They should not be isolated in segregated, "special" recreation programs and facilities. To illustrate the power of this trend, the reader is asked to compare the current societal approach to rehabilitation with this statement, which appeared in the literature in the late 1960s:

> If we integrate the ill, the disabled, the handicapped into normative settings, we remove them from the therapeutic and rehabilitative milieu. They have gone about as far as they can go in the treatment milieu and that the main objective should be fun. In most instances, however, the ill, the disabled, the handicapped (in their ever changing needs at each age level, etc.) can best be served in a clinical setting. That is, where they can have access to many rehabilitative services in one setting, and where the recreation is therapeutic; that is, addressed to the amelioration of the changing aspects of the disease or disability. (Goodzeit, 1967, p. 31)

Leisure service professionals have shifted dramatically from this outdated approach in favor of self-sustained leisure participation in community settings. The following normalization principles serve as guidelines for many of the leisure opportunities afforded to persons with disabilities (Reynolds & O'Morrow, 1985). The first principle, integration, is similar in nature to educational mainstreaming in that it supports leisure services for persons with disabilities in generic settings utilized by the general public. For example, a remedial swim class for persons with cerebral palsy would best be conducted at a facility that also serves persons without disabilities. Likewise, facilities that are easy to access via public transportation, are near other major services, and encourage social integration should be chosen. The concepts of labeling and building perception also figure greatly in the principle of integration. Programs and classes for persons with special needs should not be referred to as "handicapped" events. Recreation centers should not be designated as "special" and buildings that have an undesirable external appearance or image should be avoided. The second principle, deviancy juxtaposition, is based on the premise that mixing or pairing various groups of persons with disabilities results in the learning of inappropriate behaviors on the part of those involved and, generally, results in a negative perception being acquired by the general public. For example, sponsoring a special event for separate groups of persons who have physical disabilities, mental retardation, or who exhibit emotional problems violates the principle. The last principle, dignity of risk, is based upon the belief that persons with special needs are often overprotected by others, including family and human services professionals. As a result of the overprotection, recreational events or activities aimed at challenging the individual are avoided for fear of failure. Consequently, persons with disabilities may not be afforded the dignity of risk allowed others in society.

Reviewing these trends has helped to trace the evolution of leisure services for persons with disabilities from the scattered diversional offerings of residential facilities to the point where they are now the concern of all citizens. A shift in the approach taken by leisure service professionals from that of the provision of segregated programs and services to a concern for the development of an "independent leisure lifestyle" on the part of those they serve has also been revealed. However, also vital to success in the provision of leisure and recreational services is the selection of appropriate instructional techniques.

APPROPRIATE INSTRUCTIONAL TECHNIQUES

Persons who assist individuals with disabilities to learn activity skills must be careful to select techniques that can be used with peers who do not have disabilities. In addition, activities that are age-appropriate and enjoyed by the participant should be selected. The person with special needs should also participate directly in determining his or her goals and strategies. Furthermore, it is important that the appropriate role models and reinforcement techniques are utilized. Recreation specialists assisting persons with disabilities may assume one, several, or all of the following roles as described by Nesbitt and Edginton (1973):

1. *Initiator/organizer* This role may be played by an individual with a disability or an "outside" individual who will design strategies for improving the recreational services received by persons with disabilities.
2. *Investigator/ombudsman* This person becomes involved in fact finding, data gathering, and identification of the current status of recreational services received.
3. *Mediator/negotiator* This person deals with situations in which no response has been received from the recreation service delivery system.
4. *Lobbyist* The lobbyist gains attention for the leisure concerns of the group and persuades appropriate decision makers.
5. *Counselor* In this role, the professional offers guidance regarding the quality of leisure and recreation services.
6. *Resource assistant* The professional is responsible for coordinating logistics associated with the process of improving the quality of recreational services.
7. *Educator* This person calls for improvement in the level of society's awareness of the recreational needs of persons with disabilities.
8. *Critic/evaluator* The professional assists persons with disabilities in determining whether or not they have met the goal of improving the quality of leisure services received.

The models and techniques should be modified only enough to meet the needs of persons with disabilities. Whenever possible, generic services, such as those offered to the general public, should be utilized.

RECREATION AND LEISURE PROGRAMS: DEVELOPMENT AND IMPLEMENTATION

Despite the passage of PL 94-142 and its amendments, "special populations, including persons with severe handicaps, autism, mental retardation and physical and learning disabilities are still not fully or effectively integrated into our school, community or recreational settings" (Schleien, Krotee, Mustonen, Kelterborn, & Schermer, 1987, p. 53); however, programs attempting to promote and study integration in the leisure and recreational settings are, nonetheless, being developed and implemented.

Promoting Integration

Following the previously outlined principles of normalization, the Montgomery County Recreation Department in Maryland launched an initiative to assist general recreators to serve individuals with disabilities in community settings (Richardson, Wilson, Wetherald, & Peters, 1987). After an initial needs assessment, the following program goals were developed:

1. Provide the range of options necessary to meet individual needs of all recipients in areas of recreation.
2. Provide access to non-segregated recreation services for all citizens with disabilities appropriate to their chronological age.
3. Promote access to recreation services that encourage interaction with non-disabled peers, using, whenever possible, the principle of normalization. The ratio of disabled persons to non-disabled persons is 1–10.
4. Develop strategies for the meaningful participation of citizens with disabilities in recreation and leisure activities.
5. Provide a coordinating staff committed to high quality services, activities and programs and the enhancement of cooperation at all levels of the service system which would monitor the provided services.
6. Promote meaningful participation of all consumers, especially in the determination of programs and services and their development and evaluation. (Richardson et al., 1987, pp. 11–12)

Utilizing a mainstreaming supervisor, volunteers, coordinators, and a group home specialist, the recreation department designed four "challenging levels" or degrees of integration. To date, 262 persons with disabilities have been fully integrated. Overall, completion rates, positive evaluations by companions and leaders regarding interaction with participants who do not have disabilities, and feelings of success felt by parents and advocates are indicators of the program's success.

In an interesting empirical study, Hedrick (1985) sought to determine whether participation in wheelchair tennis and mainstreaming would improve the perceived competence of adolescents with disabilities. After completing a 4-week instructional tennis program with their peers, the majority of wheelchair athletes experienced an increase in their perceived tennis ability accompanied by an increase in their overall perceived physical competence. The author of the preliminary study suggests that

the findings support the notion that improvement in a disabled individual's level of sport skill and the concurrent enhancement of his or her sport specific efficacy perceptions can promote a significant change in his or her more general (though still domain specific) perceptions of personal competence. (Hedrick, 1985, p. 43)

Schleien et al. (1987) studied the effects of integrating children with autism into a recreational setting. Utilizing a small N subjects design, two autistic children with severe disabilities were observed interacting with peers who did not have disabilities in a structured 3-week physical activity and recreation program involving cooperative sports and games, swimming, gymnastics, and open recreation. At the conclusion of the program, the authors found evidence of an increase in appropriate play behavior and orientation to play objects and peers on the part of the autistic children. Additionally, there was some improvement in the acceptance of the participants with disabilities by their peers without disabilities.

Pollingue and Cobb (1986) have developed a model for integrating adults with severe mental retardation into community recreation activities. This model features two basic components: 1) community-based training, and 2) interagency collaborating. Community-based training refers to the teaching of leisure skills under the same conditions that exist in the natural environment, while interagency collaboration emphasizes the utilization of existing resources rather than the creation of special services. In addition to these two basic components, the model also follows three basic phases. The first, an assessment phase, includes an analysis of the individual's leisure patterns and leisure choices and of the availability of community resources. Phase two, implementation, involves training the individual for the skills that will be needed at the actual site of the leisure activity. The final evaluation phase involves telephone contact with the parent/caregiver to ensure ongoing participation in the activity. This approach has proven successful in assisting adults with mental retardation to acquire social skills and to use leisure facilities independently.

A unique approach to family leisure programming involving children with disabilities has been developed (Monroe, 1987). This approach focuses upon the enhancement of family relationships through participation in leisure activities. Its goals are to pursue the improvement of integration and parenting skills and the development of leisure skills for families with a member who has a disability. While designed for use in a psychiatric setting, this program is applicable to any population. Utilizing a multi-family group, limited to four families or 16 participants, a therapeutic recreation specialist assesses family needs and develops a plan including goals and objectives. This plan is followed by a program of communication skills, parenting skills, and leisure education. Community recreation involvement is also stressed throughout the intervention.

Eliminating Social Stigma

There is an increasing body of knowledge related to removing the social stigma encountered by various groups of persons with disabilities attempting to use community recreation facilities. One such study (West, 1984) has focused on the degree to which perceptions of community stigma restrict participation by persons with disabilities in community recreation. A sample of 180 in-depth interviews of persons with physical disabilities, mental retardation, and mental illness from a metropolitan region in the midwest was taken. These individuals were questioned as to whether or not the reactions of the general public had made them hesitant to use public park and recreation areas. The results indicated that over one-half of the respondents felt that they had experienced some type of negative response. Those with highly visible impairments and persons with mental retardation reported experiencing even greater stigmatizing interactions. As more research is conducted in this area, a greater understanding of ways to achieve acceptance of persons with disabilities by their peers without disabilities can be achieved.

In an attempt to dispel the previously described negative attitudes toward persons with disabilities, Dattilo and Smith (1990) suggest several ways in which recreation specialists can utilize terminology that communicates positive attitudes toward persons with disabilities. This terminology is also extremely relevant when identifying programs and services for persons with disabilities. A few of the author's suggestions include: 1) not identifying individuals as being "special," and 2) avoiding the use of labels and medical diagnoses and using terms such as *a person with mental retardation* rather than *the mentally retarded person*. Another suggestion deals with modes of transportation. For example, it is more accurate to state that a person "uses a wheelchair" than "he or she is confined to a wheelchair." Similarly, phrases that infer pain and suffering such as "afflicted with" or "a victim of" should also be avoided (McAvoy, Schatz, Stutz, Schleien, & Lais, 1989).

Providing Outdoor Recreation

Perhaps the most pervasive trend in providing leisure opportunities for persons with disabilities has been in the area of outdoor recreation. Capitalizing on this trend, McAvoy et al. (1989) have demonstrated the positive benefits that can accrue from a wilderness experience involving persons with and without disabilities. These authors conducted 4- to 12-day canoe trips in Minnesota, Maine, Montana, and Ontario, Canada. Along with 180 adults without disabilities who were on the trip, other participants included persons with a variety of disabilities (e.g., head injuries, cerebral palsy, multiple sclerosis, osteoporosis, blindness, paraplegia, amputation, and Parkinson's disease). Based upon survey instruments and standardized interviews, the trip leaders found that outdoor adventure programs can result in "positive attitude and lifestyle changes including: attitudes toward persons of varying abilities; interpersonal relationships; confidence levels; willingness to take risks; feelings about self; goal-setting abilities; leisure skills; tolerance of stress; and, in some participants, an increased ability to live independently" (McAvoy et al., 1989, p. 62).

In a less intense day camp setting with a small number of children having a variety of disabilities, Edwards and Smith (1989) found preliminary support for the theory that such an environment can increase appropriate social interactions. Using a time-sampling technique, these authors found an increase in positive interactions, such as smiles, vocal tone, verbal content, and nonverbal vocalizations.

Many municipal park departments have initiated concentrated efforts to accommodate persons with disabilities. One such example is A.D. Barnes

Park in Florida, operated by the Metro-Dade County Park and Recreation Department (King, Richards, & Gregg, 1989). Some of the features of this facility include a specially constructed swimming pool with a hydraulic floor, which raises and lowers to accommodate wheelchair users, and an accessible nature center and sensory nature trail. There are also daily programs that offer camping experience for persons with disabilities who would not ordinarily be able to participate, a weekend respite care camp for children with severe disabilities, and an adapted equestrian program.

THE ADA AND INDEPENDENT
RECREATION PARTICIPATION

Thus far, the discussion of leisure for persons with disabilities has been limited. The chapter has dealt almost exclusively with agencies designed to provide specialized leisure services, public and quasipublic recreation facilities, volunteer service organizations, and public areas and facilities where the inclusion of persons with disabilities is mandated by law. Furthermore, there has been no discussion of the private sector in which recreational opportunities abound. The effects of the ADA will not only extend far beyond making many more facilities architecturally accessible, but because of its scope, the ADA will stimulate the following trends.

Resources Necessary for Leisure Participation Will Increase

The ADA directly affects all factors that determine whether or not persons with disabilities will be able to participate in recreational activities. In addition to the factor of physical accessibility, financial resources, communication, and transportation must also be considered. As access to employment opportunities increases dramatically, there will be a corresponding increase in the amount of discretionary income available to persons with disabilities. Much of this income can be spent in the United States's multi-billion dollar leisure industry, thus benefitting both the public and private sectors of its economy. Improvements in communication and transportation will also greatly expand leisure opportunities for persons with disabilities. As telecommunications innovations (e.g., TDD voice) are developed, more and more Americans can obtain information concerning recreational opportunities, contact family and friends to plan activities, and arrange transportation and accommodations for trips and vacations. Transportation innovations are especially evident in the field of travel. In the United States and abroad, there are several travel agencies that specialize in group and individual travel for persons with disabilities.

Accessible Leisure Opportunities Will Expand

The previously discussed laws have only made a fraction of recreational opportunities accessible for persons with disabilities. As the private sector complies to regulations concerning accessibility, more and more facilities such as theaters, museums, auditoriums, stadiums, playgrounds, hotels, and restaurants will become accessible for persons with disabilities. As a result, the tourism and entertainment industries will be direct beneficiaries.

Already, there is evidence that this trend is occurring. Not only do many travel agencies cater exclusively to persons with disabilities, but airports and airlines also provide needed accommodations and services. Many major cities publish "access guides," which include information concerning regulations related to accessibility, descriptions of accessible attractions, and listings of available transportation and referral services.

The Recreational Patterns of Families Will Be Directly Affected

The ADA will greatly improve the leisure lifestyles of all members of a family having a member with a disability. The interaction skills, parenting skills, leisure awareness, and leisure skills and abilities previously described can best be achieved in accessible settings. Such settings are already becoming more common. For example, the development of playgrounds consistent with the concept of "reasonable accommodation" as outlined in the ADA has already become a major topic of the National Recreation and Park Association's 1990 National Conference. Defining access as "a physical situation modified by environmental factors, not as a series of ramps," the presenters made suggestions to facilitate the play of children and parents in outdoor areas (Hadley & Hadley, 1990). Some of these suggestions follow: 1) providing slides wide enough to accommodate a child and a parent, 2) providing teeter totters with room for two on each end, 3) designing swings that can be operated solely by using the arms, 4) using platforms and connecting bridges between play houses, and 5) placing rubber tiles on the ground so that children with disabilities can interact with peers. It was also suggested that table heights be adjusted so that a parent who uses a wheelchair can eat and play with his or her child.

The Roles of Leisure Service Providers Will Shift

As recreational facilities are altered and constructed to invite access, the traditional roles played by park and recreation professionals will greatly expand. In addition to providing and maintaining facilities, leisure service professionals will take a much more active role in facilitating the involvement of persons with disabilities. Examples of these duties will include: 1) modifying and adapting facilities and equipment; 2) consulting with architects to ensure accessibility; and 3) working with independent living centers, state rehabilitation agencies, and volunteer advocacy associations. In the future, therapeutic recreation professionals will not only rethink their approach to providing services, but they will also spend much of their efforts training community recreation personnel to work with individuals exhibiting special needs. Hadley and Hadley (1990) suggest that recreation professionals serve as "play

facilitators" for children with disabilities by taking small toys and other articles to parks. In this case, play leaders who can set themes and assist the
children to evolve the action are needed. The authors' philosophy is echoed in
the statement that "not every child can play baseball, but every child can be a
pirate" (Hadley & Hadley, 1990).

The Range of Disabilities Served Will Greatly Expand

Prior to the passage of the ADA, the concept of disability generally extended
only to physical disability (most frequently thought of in terms of wheelchair
users) and, to some extent, persons with visual impairments. The current law
extends protection to *all* individuals with physical or mental impairments
affecting one or more life activities; thus, leisure service providers will have to
consider previously overlooked groups of individuals including people with
learning disabilities and individuals with mental retardation. For the first
time, programmatic accessibility will have to be considered in addition to
physical accessibility. Some challenges might include: 1) making a nature trail
illustrated with signs interpretable to a person with a learning disability,
2) explaining the rules for the use of a swimming pool to a person with mental
retardation, and 3) providing large print travel brochures for persons with
visual impairments.

Social Attitudes Will Change as Persons with
Disabilities Participate Successfully in Sports and Recreation

The two recreation activities with the highest visibility for persons with disabilities have probably been wheelchair sports and the Special Olympics for
persons with mental retardation. Both activities are exclusively for athletes
with disabilities. While these activities have already benefitted participants
and improved societal attitudes, the ADA has the potential to build even more
upon these efforts. For the first time, the general public will have the opportunity to observe persons with disabilities enjoying leisure activities and
sports in generic settings. With the implementation of the principles of normalization, physical and social integration can become a reality as *all* Americans share the same recreational resources. Dignity of risk will occur when
persons with disabilities are given the opportunity to participate and compete.
Furthermore, issues such as the perception of special buildings and deviancy
juxtaposition will be resolved as persons with disabilities enjoy community-
based activities.

Unique Challenges and Opportunities
to Leisure Service Providers Will Be Fostered

As the provisions of the ADA take effect, recreational service providers who
work with persons with disabilities will face a number of challenges. To
comply with the law, more extensive planning of facilities and programs will

be required. As previously indicated, consumers with disabilities will provide increased input in the planning process. In certain situations, leisure service professionals will have to provide more resources, such as personnel and capital outlay. Hard choices may have to be made when developing a facility that is accessible, yet less resistant to vandalism. Likewise, overadapation of programs and facilities will have to be avoided if the essence of the recreational experience is to be preserved. For example, wilderness areas should be accessible to persons with disabilities, yet the integrity of the area should be preserved. Farbman and Ellis (1987) submitted the following recommendations to the President's Commission on Americans Outdoors concerning the challenge of wilderness area preservation:

1. That the Architectural and Transportation Barriers Compliance Board (ATBCB) promulgate minimum guidelines and requirements for outdoor recreation facilities
2. That curriculum modules concerning accessible design be developed and made mandatory in colleges that prepare architects, landscape architects, engineers, and recreation planners and professionals
3. That studies be conducted on the impact of technological advances in equipment including wheelchairs, communication devices, etc., on access to outdoor recreation opportunities

Bork (1989) has met the challenge of exposing persons with severe disabilities to remote areas through his "Trail Partners" program. In this program, persons with disabilities are joined with volunteers who help to guide and assist individuals with mobility and sensory impairments as they visit wilderness areas. This cost-effective approach has been extremely effective in making the outdoor environment accessible while, at the same time, preserving its natural beauty. Innovative interventions, such as "Trail Partners," will optimize the effects of the ADA.

CONCLUSION

This chapter explores the role of recreation in the satisfaction of basic human needs and traces the development of organized recreation and leisure services to the present, emphasizing that individuals with disabilities have a *right* to leisure opportunities.

The ADA, which will have a dramatic impact on the leisure lifestyles of millions of persons with disabilities, will play a strong part in ensuring this right. It will result in an increase in discretionary income, expand the scope of leisure pursuits, positively affect the family unit, cause a shift in the roles of leisure service professionals, and improve societal attitudes toward those with disabilities. When successfully implemented, the ADA may well result in a new era of leisure service provision, an era in which *all* Americans can work and *play* together.

REFERENCES

Bork, K. (1989). Easy access to trail partners. *Parks and Recreation, 24*(12), 22–26.
Dattilo, J., & Smith, R.W. (1990). Communicating positive attitudes toward people with disabilities through sensitive terminology. *Therapeutic Recreation Journal, 24*(1), 8–17.
Edwards, D., & Smith, R. (1989). Social interaction in an integrated day camp setting. *Therapeutic Recreation Journal, 23*(3), 71–78.
Federal Register. (August 23, 1973). *41*, 163.
Farbman, A.H., & Ellis, W.K. (1987). Accessibility and outdoor recreation for persons with disabilities. *Therapeutic Recreation Journal, 21*(1), 70–76.
Goodzeit, J.M. (1967). Therapeutic recreation vs. recreation for the handicapped. *Therapeutic Recreation Journal, 1*(2), 31.
Gray, D.E. (1977). The case of compensatory recreation. *Parks and Recreation, 12*(11), 23.
Hadley, P.A., & Hadley, R.G. (1990, October). *Developing accessible playgrounds.* Paper presented at the Research Symposium at the National Recreation and Parks Association Annual Congress, Phoenix, AZ.
Hedrick, B.N. (1985). The effect of wheelchair tennis participation and mainstreaming upon the perceptions of competence of physically disabled adolescents. *Therapeutic Recreation Journal, 19*(2), 34–46.
Hutchison, I.J., Stein, T., & Sessoms, D. (Eds.). (1975). *Recreation and racial minorities in recreation and special populations.* Boston: Holbrook Press.
Institute on Community Integration and the Research and Training Center on Community Living, University of Minnesota. (1989). *Impact, 2*(3).
King, J., Richards, V., & Gregg, M. (1989). The wonder of A.D. Barnes Park. *Parks and Recreation, 24*(12), 34–39.
McAvoy, V., Schatz, E.C., Stutz, M.E., Schleien, S.J., & Lais, G. (1989). Integrated wilderness adventure: Effects on personal and lifestyle traits of persons with and without disabilities. *Therapeutic Recreation Journal, 23*(3), 50–64.
Monroe, J.E. (1987). Family leisure programming. *Therapeutic Recreation Journal, 21*(3), 44–51.
National Park Service, Division of Special Programs and Populations, Department of Interior. (n.d.). Brochure
National Therapeutic Recreation Society. (1982, May). Philosophical Position Statement.
Nesbitt, J.A., & Edginton, R. (1973). *A conceptual framework for consumerism and advocacy in parks, recreation, leisure and cultural services.* Paper presented at the Urban Recreation Conference, Montclair State College, Upper Montclair, NJ.
Pollingue, A.B., & Cobb, H.B. (1986). Leisure education: A model facilitating community integration for moderately/severely mentally retarded adults. *Therapeutic Recreation Journal, 20*(3), 54–62.
Reynolds, R.P., & O'Morrow, G.S. (1985). *Problems, issues and concepts in therapeutic recreation* (pp. 154–158). Englewood Cliffs, NJ: Prentice Hall.
Richardson, D., Wilson, B., Wetherald, L., & Peters, J. (1987). Mainstreaming initiative: An innovative approach to recreation and leisure services in a community setting. *Therapeutic Recreation Journal,·11*(2), 9–19.

Schleien S., Krotee, M.L., Mustonene, T., Kelterborn, B., & Schermer, A.D. (1987). The effect of integrating children with autism into a physical activity setting. *Therapeutic Recreation Journal, 21*(4), 52–62.

West, P.C. (1984). Social stigma and community recreation participation by the mentally and physically handicapped. *Therapeutic Recreation Journal, 18*(1), 40–49.

Witt, P.A. (1970). *A history of recreation for the mentally retarded.* Unpublished, personal copy.

Appendix A

Suggested Readings on Integrated Leisure and Recreation

Bender, M., Brannan, S., & Verhoven, P. (1984). *Leisure education for the handicapped: Curriculum goals, activities, and resources.* San Diego: College-Hill Press.

Musselwhite, C.R. (1986). *Adaptive play for special needs children: Strategies to enhance communication and learning.* San Diego: College-Hill Press.

Robb, G., Havens, M., & Witman, J. (1983). *Special education . . . naturally.* Bloomington: Indiana University.

Rynders, J., & Schleien, S. (1991). *Together successfully: Integrating community activities for persons with and without disabilities.* Arlington, TX: Association for Retarded Citizens-United States and National 4-H.

Schleien, S.J., & Ray, M.T. (1988). *Community recreation and persons with disabilities: Strategies for integration.* Baltimore: Paul H. Brookes Publishing Co.

Wehman, P., & Schleien, S. (1981). *Leisure programs for handicapped persons: Adaptations, techniques, and curriculum.* Austin, TX: PRO-ED.

Wilcox, B., & Bellamy, G.T. (1987). *The activities catalog: An alternative curriculum for youth and adults with severe disabilities.* Baltimore: Paul H. Brookes Publishing Co.

Wuerch, B., & Voeltz, L. (1982). *Longitudinal leisure skills for severely handicapped learners: The Ho'onanea curriculum component.* Baltimore: Paul H. Brookes Publishing Co.

Appendix B

Manufactures of Modified Recreation Equipment

Childcraft Education Company
20 Kilmar Road
Edison, NY 08817
(201)572-6100

Constructive Playthings
1227 East 119th Street
Grandview, MO 64030
(815)761-5900

Developmental Learning Materials and Teaching Resources
P.O. Box 2000
Allen, TX 75002
(214)727-3346

Discovery Toys
619 Atlantic Hill Drive
Eagan, MN 55123
(612)454-7326

Flaghouse, Inc.
150 North Macquesten Parkway
Mt. Vernon, NY 10550
(914)699-1990

Fred Sammons, Inc.
Box 32
Brookfield, IL 60513
(800)323-5547

J.A. Preston Corporation
60 Page Road
Clifton, NY 07012
(800)631-7277

Richard Katz and Associates, Architects
1103 Westgate
Oak Park, IL 60301
(708)524-1000

Salco Toys
R.R. 1, Box 59
Nerstrand, MN 55053
(507)645-8720

Skill Development Equipment Co.
P.O. Box 6300
Anaheim, CA 92807
(714)524-8750

Sportime
2905 East Amwiler Road
Atlanta, GA 30360
(800)241-9884

Theraplay Products
P.C.A. Industries, Inc.
2924 40th Avenue
Long Island City, NY 11101
(718)784-7070

Appendix C

Bibliography

In addition to the references cited in the text of this chapter, the author found the following resources related to the provision of leisure and recreation services and to the ADA.

Accessibility: A Guide to Open Environments, published by the National Recreation and Park Association, 3101 Park Center Drive, Alexandria, VA 22302.

This booklet informs persons with disabilities about what to expect in the way of facilities and barriers in a variety of outdoor environments.

Access to Parks and Recreation: Disabled People Speak (Catalogue #12).

Discusses the importance of accessibility, the personal value of recreation, various common access problems and solutions, and the process of conducting evaluations. Contact: Technical Training Videotapes, National Park Foundation, P.O. Box 57473, Washington, DC 20037.

Access to Park and Recreation Facilities (Catalogue #13).

Focuses on architectural/physical access to buildings, facilities, and outdoor recreation activities. Contact: Technical Training Videotapes, National Park Foundation, P.O. Box 57473, Washington, DC 20037.

Wheelchair Vagabond, by J.G. Nelson.

Nelson, a seasoned wheelchair traveler, recounts his experiences and gives camping pointers from his travels in a VW bus. Topics include: choosing the right vehicle, what to take and where to put it, planning your trip, where to stop, gourmet cooking, camping equipment, and hundreds of hints to help the traveler with a disability. Contact: The Disability Bookshop, P.O. Box 129, Vancouver, WA 98666. (206) 694-2462.

Sports and Recreation for the Disabled: A Resource Manual, by M.A. Paciorek and J. Jones.

This 400-page manual contains information about equipment, medical considerations, national and local governing bodies, contact persons, sport adaptations, equipment modifications, and supplies for some 50 individual and team sports in seven major disability groups as represented by the Committee on Sports for the Disabled. Contact: Benchmark Press, 701 Congressional Boulevard, Suite 340, Carmel, IN 46032. (317) 573-6420.

Part IV

The ADA and Societal Acceptance

The concept of ADA and societal acceptance can occur best through the empowerment of persons with disabilities. People with disabilities and their advocates must hold major key positions in all levels of government, business, and industry. The placement of people into only "appropriate disability-specific" positions is not enough. People with disabilities must hold important positions (e.g., at least at subcabinet levels) in HUD, Transportation, SBA, OPM, Labor, Trade Affairs, Treasury, and so forth; furthermore, people with disabilities must become aides on key congressional committees and run for office. The ceiling on jobs in key management and civic positions in business and the community must be erased for people with disabilities.

Individuals in society will never accept people with disabilities if they do not work with them, recreate with them, and live in the same neighborhoods. Inclusion and acceptance can only occur as people with disabilities gain more influence and power, not only over their own lives, but also over important activities in the community and workplace. ADA is one positive step in the right direction for this to occur.

Chapter 12

Increased Access to Community Resources

Pamela S. Wolfe

$$\longleftarrow\!\times\!\longrightarrow$$

Although the ADA is patterned after Section 504 of the Rehabilitation Act, its provisions extend the rights of individuals with disabilities in both public and private sectors. The provisions of the ADA cover all but the smallest employer, prohibit discrimination, and negate the use of generalizations in hiring and employment decisions (Golden, 1991). Furthermore, the ADA serves to make individuals with disabilities an integral and important part of the work force by ensuring that employees perform essential functions of a job rather than marginal duties.

The ADA has been structured as a tenable means to induce change within a range of organizations and individuals. The ADA takes into account such factors as the size of the business, the type of operation, and the nature and cost of accommodation. Although the cost of the changes needed to effectively implement the ADA are difficult to assess, the benefits are readily visible. Each year the United States spends approximately $300 billion on disability-related costs. By placing two-thirds of the persons with disabilities who are currently unemployed in the workplace, the amount of money paid in disability payments will decrease while the valuable knowledge, talent, and expertise that these individuals will bring to their jobs will simultaneously

The author wishes to gratefully acknowledge the expertise and information provided by Sister Sundhardi Cole, Independence Resource Center, Charlottesville, Virginia, and by April Holmes, Region X Community Service Board, Charlottesville, Virginia. Without their guidance, this chapter would not have been possible.

241

increase (The President's Committee on Employment of People with Disabilities, 1990). The ADA succeeds in providing a strong legislative backing for the rights of these persons with disabilities, especially those who are unemployed, and serves as a firm investment that will yield high returns in both individual and economic growth.

The need for disability rights legislation such as the ADA is apparent. A poll conducted by Louis Harris and Associates (1986) revealed that 69% of working-age individuals with disabilities did not work due to access and attitudinal difficulties. Overall, the Louis Harris and Associates (1986) poll found that being an American with disabilities typically meant having less money, education, and access to jobs. In order for these persons to obtain increased access, integration must first be achieved.

FROM INTEGRATION TO INCREASED ACCESSIBILITY

The importance and value of integration has been emphasized and evidenced in efforts undertaken in school, work, and community settings. Community integration, in particular, has been the guiding principle and the final objective for legislation, policies, and ideologies for individuals with disabilities (Laski, 1991). However, efforts to achieve integration have clearly illustrated that mere physical proximity or access does not ensure true integration (Brinker & Thorpe, 1986). The distinction between living *in* the community and truly being *part of* the community is an important one (Kregel, Wehman, Seyfarth, & Marshall, 1986). True community integration, which encompasses physical and emotional factors, has been the most difficult to achieve.

Both qualitative and quantitative components are involved in community integration (Crapps, Langone, & Swaim, 1985). Certainly such quantitative aspects as physical access and the opportunity for participation are necessary, but qualitative aspects such as a sense of belonging and ownership of decisions are pivotal as well.

Access to information and to evolving technology are also important to community integration. These aspects have the power not only to enhance the quality of life of individuals with disabilities, but also to allow these individuals to have a more active and integral role in the community. Without physical and ideological access, persons with disabilities do not have an equal opportunity to achieve full community integration.

The Influence of Normalization

A glance at the historical evolution of the field service provision for individuals with disabilities reveals considerable variability and change (Heal, 1980). Ideological and attitudinal shifts have had a profound influence on the treatment and services accorded to these individuals. One example of such a shift is the concept of normalization. The principle of normalization has increased the integration of individuals with disabilities into society by removing many architectural and attitudinal barriers. One direct result of the normalization principle was the deinstitutionalization of persons with disabilities into the community. Although deinstitutionalization permitted many individuals with disabilities to have access to the community, relatively little attention was, or has been paid to an equally important aspect of successful community integration—the aspect of societal change.

Heal (1980) questions whether or not true community integration can be achieved through normalization. Heal postulates that a more egalitarian approach may aid in the true integration of individuals with disabilities and suggests that the quality of "humanness" should supersede all other qualities as a basis for valuation in society. It is important that, as a society, Americans begin to value uniqueness and individuality. As service providers, Americans must be responsible for according respect to individuals with disabilities and strive to display the value of unique talents and individuality.

Empowerment through Advocacy

Being involved in community decision-making makes all community members part of a vested interest in the outcome of events. The premise that individuals should have a right to be a part of the development and execution of the policies and decisions that will affect their lives seems like a simple idea. Yet, it has only been recently that professionals have begun to acknowledge the importance of empowering individuals with disabilities through active partnership and choice-making. The provisions set forth in the ADA influence the empowerment of individuals with disabilities in a variety of ways. Individuals with disabilities will become an integral part of planning and instituting changes that will affect their integration and participation in society. By working with others in the community to make their needs known, suggesting necessary changes, and participating in finding solutions, fuller participation within the community can occur.

Advocacy has been one venue used to empower individuals with disabilities. Advocacy is the support provided to help people protect and promote their rights, benefits, and services (Virginia Department of Medical Assistance Services, 1990). Ludlow and Herr (1988) suggest that advocacy efforts must encompass systems advocacy, individual advocacy, and self-advocacy. For example, systems advocacy, which is defined as an organized effort to influence policy-making (Eklund, 1976), can include advocacy at the federal level (e.g., lobbying for legislation), state level (e.g., advocating for state policy), and local level (e.g., advocating for change in public and private agencies within a local community). Individual advocacy is defined by Ludlow and Herr (1988) as a case-by-case effort to help individuals with disabilities to obtain their rights and services. Self-advocacy, defined as representation of interest by individuals with disabilities, places the individual in the role of consumer with a voice in the available services. Ludlow and Herr (1988) suggest that all three types of advocacy may be necessary to induce change in a system. Through such advocacy efforts, individuals with disabilities will be empowered to effect change in the issues and actions that influence their lives.

Although not yet achieved in many cases, the importance of community integration of individuals with disabilities has been emphasized. The ADA will serve as a strong catalyst for integration, yet legislation alone cannot achieve true integration; that is, although the ADA will serve as a guiding force, ultimately, each individual must work to fulfill its goals for themselves. Components of community integration such as access, acceptance, interdependence, and decision-making are all part of a larger solution that can only be achieved through belief in the importance of the goal.

OBTAINING SERVICES

To a person with a disability, empowerment is greatly fostered by knowledge of what services are available and of how to obtain those services. Effective use of services can not only increase an individual's access and quality of life, but also expand that person's knowledge. Yet, use of community services requires an understanding of three elements: 1) one's own needs, 2) how to locate and contact the appropriate agency or individual, and 3) assessment of the services rendered. These elements require decisions to be made prior to contacting a service agency and after contact has been established. The following questions were designed to help individuals contacting a service agency pinpoint their needs prior to actual contact. The ADA has influenced the accessibility of services by both broadening the number and type of services available, and by creating governing legislative bodies to oversee their compliance. The ADA extends into both the public and private sectors. Additionally, it requires specific governing agencies, such as the EEOC, and other agencies to be responsible for compliance and to provide a means through which to voice complaints.

Decisions Made Prior to Contact

What are my specific needs?
What are the timelines under which I am working (i.e., immediate crisis or long-term intervention needs)?
How much intervention do I desire?

Established Contact

Can this agency give me the appropriate information or assistance?
If not, are names of contact persons or additional referrals available?
Do I need to apply for the service?
What are the eligibility requirements of the agency?
Is there a fee for the service?

What documentation is required to obtain the service?
What are the age requirements?

In summary, to obtain services effectively, an individual must first be aware of his or her needs, know how to locate services, and once located, how to obtain the available services. Questions asked both before and during contact with service agencies may be helpful in the location and use of needed services.

ENFORCEMENT AGENCIES

One of the most important aspects of the ADA will be its forum for follow-along and enforcement of regulations. Several different federal agencies will be responsible for the regulation and enforcement of the ADA. These agencies are sources from which individuals affected by the ADA can gather information, receive clarification, or voice complaints concerning enforcement or implementation of regulations. In addition, areas of agency responsibility and contact information for each agency are as follows:

Employment   The Equal Employment Opportunity Commission (EEOC) regulates and enforces employment discrimination laws. The EEOC will accept complaints and offer available remedies to disputes, such as back pay and court orders, to stop discrimination.

Public accommodations   The Architectural and Transportation Barriers Compliance Board (ATBCB) will issue minimum guidelines for accessibility of new or remodeled structures. The Department of Justice will issue and enforce regulations.

Transportation   The ATBCB will issue minimum guidelines for accessibility of new or remodeled depots. The Department of Transportation will issue and enforce regulations.

Telecommunications   The Federal Communications Commission (FCC) will define and enforce regulations. (The President's Committee on Employment of People with Disabilities, September, 1990.)

The remainder of this chapter discusses some of the difficulties individuals with disabilities may face in obtaining services within their community. To illustrate the effects of the ADA and typical community resources that may be helpful, three case studies are presented. In each case study, the effects of the ADA are discussed and potential challenges and possible solutions to typical problems are offered. It is important to note that all names of persons appearing in the case studies are fictitious. The characters serve only to represent real-life persons and situations.

For information on organizations dealing with issues of disability, consult the *Directory of National Information Sources of Handicapping Conditions and Related Services* (1986) available from the U.S. Department of

Health, Education, and Welfare, Office of Human Development Services, Office of Handicapped Individuals, Washington, DC.

CASE STUDY 1: JIM AND CONSTANCE ROWE

Similar to many Americans, Jim, age 35, is working to provide a better life for himself and his family; however, Jim is not typical. As a result of an infection that occurred at birth, he has severe spastic cerebral palsy. He has only limited use of his arms and legs and, as a result, he uses a motorized wheelchair. Jim is considered to be generally unintelligible by those who are not familiar with his speech patterns. To facilitate communication with others, he uses a portable computer that attaches to his wheelchair. This computer is equipped with a sensor that reveals a printed message on the computer screen.

After graduating from college with a business degree, Jim began working as a marketing executive at the corporate headquarters of a large company in a nearby metropolitan area. While he was in college, the Department of Rehabilitative Services (DRS) helped to provide the funds for some of Jim's tuition as well as for his transportation expenses to and from the university. However, even with this assistance, Jim's student loan was sizeable. In addition, Jim recently purchased a new home. Although it is spacious and close to work, it is still in need of some structural modifications to make access by wheelchair easier. His student loans, coupled with the cost of a new home, have caused him to put off the purchase of a new van. Although Jim plans to purchase a van in the future, he currently uses the public bus system.

Jim met his wife, Constance, while in college. The couple agreed early in their marriage to hire an attendant to help Jim with his personal needs. They felt that this decision would strengthen their marriage by not forcing them into the roles of attendant/caregiver and patient. By advertising, Jim found a personal attendant who not only helps him with personal needs, but also helps him travel to and from work each day. Although Jim must pay for the attendant himself, he feels that the assistance he receives has offered him a sense of independence that he considers worth the expense.

Potential Effects of the ADA on the Rowes

A major component of the ADA that may affect the lives of the Rowes is Title I. Title I prohibits discrimination in employment, and requires both public and private employers to make reasonable accommodations in the workplace for their employees with physical and/or mental disabilities. Since he has the ability to perform the essential functions of his job, Jim clearly met the criterion of "qualified individual with a disability." The ADA did not really affect his hire since he had already been placed prior to its passage; however, it may affect subsequent promotions and all types of employment activities such as employee compensation, job training, or other privileges of employment (Golden, 1990).

An important component of Title I is the provision of reasonable accommodation. Accommodation can encompass both facilities and job restructuring, which can include eliminating nonessential elements of the job, re-delegating assignments, or redesigning procedures for undertaking a task (Golden, 1991). For example, Jim requires a modified work schedule due to stamina restraints. Rather than the typical 8-hour day, Jim only works for about 5 hours. Jim leaves work at 3 o'clock rather than 5 o'clock and completes some work at home on the weekends. His management position also entails occasional travel, an aspect of the job that is difficult for Jim. To accommodate Jim's difficulty with travel, any out of the office business has been delegated to another worker. In return he has taken on some other duties at the home office. The changes in job duties reflect Jim's opinion of the best use of his talents and those of his co-workers.

Under the ADA, technical assistance will be made available from all agencies responsible for regulations of the bill. For example, agencies such as the EEOC will be required to offer employment training programs as well as provide technical assistance (Linthicum, Cole, & D'Alonzo, 1991). Assistive technology can also be used to help an employee complete a job. Under the ADA, employers may be required to buy or modify equipment or devices that are job-related. At Jim's request, his company paid for a device allowing a portable computer to be attached to his chair. Additionally, he was supplied with a gooseneck receiver for his phone and a mechanical page turner. Jim's company also invested in equipment for a teleconference room. The company modified the tables and chairs so they were accessible to his wheelchair and lowered the controls for audiovisual equipment. Additionally, his office and the teleconference room were equipped with a light sensor device to activate the lights when someone entered the room. Although the company could have chosen the least expensive option of two equally effective modifications, they felt that these modifications would also be beneficial to clients.

Of course, another broad implication of the ADA that will affect virtually every aspect of Jim's life is accessibility to public accommodations. Title II of the ADA requires public accommodations to provide auxiliary aids and services, and to remove existing physical barriers; therefore, all new facilities will have to be accessible. Once enacted, Jim should be able to negotiate buildings without facing accessibility barriers.

Methods and means of transportation will also change as a result of the new legislation. These changes should make it possible for Jim to travel independently to and from work and to other places in his community. Both publicly and privately funded bus and rail systems must be accessible to individuals with disabilities. For example, if Jim is unable to reach the bus stop due to fatigue, the public bus system may need to provide a supplemental paratransit system for him (Golden, 1991).

CASE STUDY 2: MICHELLE AND CARL DEGEORGE

Forty-year-old Michelle DeGeorge has been deaf since birth. In addition to her deafness, Michelle's eyesight has been rapidly deteriorating over the past 20 years due to glaucoma. This gradual loss of sight demands that Michelle and her husband, Carl, prepare for the time when Michelle's vision becomes completely impaired.

Michelle and Carl met during high school as they were both enrolled in special education classes. The school years were a particularly hard time for both individuals. Due to an undetected hearing loss, Carl had been placed in a class for persons with behavior disorders for the duration of his elementary and junior high school years. It was Carl's frustration with his placement that led him to "act out" the special education label. Both Carl and Michelle felt the sting of being labelled "special education students," and both were more than anxious to leave the school setting and move into the real world. Although Michelle had been taught sign language early in her life, Carl did not learn to sign until his high school years; however, signing has now become the primary means of communication between the DeGeorges and among other friends with hearing impairments.

After high school, Michelle and Carl began entry-level jobs in their hometown. Although the couple aspired to a career in farming, Carl took a job in a print shop and Michelle worked on the household staff of a hotel. Their first experience with the real world was harsh. The couple required a great amount of support from government programs, specifically programs such as Social Security and the DRS. When their two children were born, they received assistance from Aid to Dependent Children (ADC) and housing was provided through their local Housing Authority. Despite their dependence, Michelle and Carl managed to save money and to secure a loan through the Farm Home Association with Carl's brother cosigning the loan. By working at the print shop and on his farm, Carl managed to get a good start on his farming future. Eventually, Carl was able to quit the print shop and focus all his energy on making the farm a success. As vocations and incomes have changed, the services available to the couple have varied. In addition, the inability to negotiate the seeming maze of requirements and qualifications has also resulted in some frustration.

The couple's children both attend a nearby community college, yet, they visit home rather infrequently. The reason for these infrequent visits is that the couple has tried to foster in their children a strong sense of independence and self-reliance. True to their beliefs, Michelle and Carl have tried to solve their own problems independently as well. Fortunately, both rely strongly on each other (i.e., Carl drives Michelle to work) and the community resources at their disposal (i.e., both love to socialize and take part in community events). Michelle is an avid churchgoer and has become, through the years, a vocal political activist for the rights of individuals with disabilities.

The degenerative nature of Michelle's eyesight has resulted in her enrollment in mobility classes; in addition, she uses a cane that is available to her through her state's Department of the Blind. Michelle also found this organization to be helpful in supplying informative catalogs and items useful in helping her maintain her independence (e.g., the cane).

Potential Effects of the ADA on the DeGeorges

One of the provisions of the ADA that will most directly affect the DeGeorge family is Title IV, which requires that companies who offer telephone service to the general public also offer intra- and interstate telephone relay services to individuals who use such devices as TDDs or telecommunication devices. These services must be offered 24 hours a day, 7 days a week, at regular rates by July 26, 1993. The provision also requires state and local governments to make 911 emergency systems directly accessible to TDD users. Telephone relay services will enable Michelle to communicate with a wide variety of individuals rather than only a limited number of individuals as with a similar TDD system. In addition, if Michelle or Carl need to call for emergency assistance, their call will be translated directly rather than through relay services. Federally funded public service announcements that are broadcast on television will also be required to be closed-captioned for those with hearing impairments.

The DeGeorges will also feel the effects of the ADA in the area of public accommodations. The ADA prohibits discrimination in all private, public and commercial organizations and activities. The provision will require public accommodations (e.g., restaurants, theaters, and hotels) to provide auxiliary aids and services to individuals with disabilities. Similar to other provisions of the ADA, employers have the right to decline such services if undue hardship would result and have the right to select the required auxiliary aid or service. For example, in a restaurant, the owner could choose to have a braille menu available or to have a waiter read the menu choices. Such aids or services also include TDDs, TV decoders, and visible alarm systems, which would need to be provided by large hotels. Owners of stores with a "no pets" policy would have to accommodate service animals such as a seeing eye dog.

The DeGeorges may also feel the effects of the ADA in the area of employment. Michelle works for a large hotel chain that is expanding its operation base and opening a second chain in a nearby town. When Michelle applied for a new position as a Co-Training Coordinator of Staffing in the new hotel being opened, the regulations of the ADA stipulated that Michelle could not be asked about her medical conditions during interviews for her new position. Under the ADA, at the pre-job offer stage, employers can not ask whether Michelle has a disability but rather only if she would be able to complete necessary job-related functions.

Furthermore, under the ADA Michelle cannot be discriminated against in hiring, promotion, or demotion. Like coordinators of other departments,

Michelle will be entitled to receive job training. Michelle's new job will also require some job restructuring, a feature of the ADA. For example, she will be working to staff and train additional employees of the new hotel chain. Due to difficulties with hearing and eye sight, Michelle will be planning and structuring training activities although much of the direct training will be provided by another employee. Michelle and her new employers feel that these job restructuring changes make the best use of Michelle's talents and expertise. Furthermore, because the ADA stipulates that Michelle's employer must post notices describing the ADA in an accessible manner, Michelle and other employees working with her will be made aware of the ADA.

Although public accommodations must provide services to individuals with disabilities, private clubs and religious organizations are exempt. Under the ADA, Michelle's church does not have to comply with nondiscriminatory practices; however, the church she attends has chosen to provide an interpreter for translating the weekly sermons.

CASE STUDY 3: THE THOMASES

Kurt Thomas was diagnosed as having severe mental disabilities and epilepsy as the result of a birth injury. For most of his educational career, he has been enrolled in classes for individuals with severe disabilities. At age 21, Kurt is finally through school. His teacher, who is very concerned about integration and the opportunity for social interaction with peers who do not have disabilities, has pursued efforts to teach outside the classroom setting.

Although Kurt is ambulatory, his speech is often difficult to understand. Because he has never learned to sign adequately or to use a communication board, much of his communication is done through gestures. In addition, Kurt wears a helmet to protect himself from injury due to fairly frequent drop seizures. Though his seizures often look alarming to others, he usually requires only some time to rest before being able to resume his activities. Results from IQ tests conducted during Kurt's educational programming yielded scores in the low 20s; however, his parents and teachers attest that his IQ score does not tell the whole story. Despite his low score, Kurt has excellent social skills and enjoys being with people.

Presently, Kurt is living at home, but he plans to move into a group home or supervised apartment in the near future. Kurt's parents have had a difficult time adjusting to his adult status. His impending move from home and the issue of guardianship have forced his family to look at the future and make some difficult decisions.

Vocationally, Kurt has been placed at an individual supported employment work site as a busperson in a local fast food restaurant. Although his current employer has been satisfied with Kurt's work, other potential employers expressed some concern over his epilepsy. These employers initially felt that

Kurt would be absent from work a great deal or that their insurance rates would increase; however, his present employer felt confident that Kurt would be able to maintain an adequate work schedule and would not incur further costs.

Kurt generally works 10–20 hours per week in order to maintain his Medicaid coverage, although he is thinking of increasing his hours because he so greatly enjoys his work. A job coach, who first trained Kurt, is slowly being faded out as Kurt becomes confident with his job duties. The job coach and transportation to and from work were both supplied by the local community service board. Working toward greater independence, Kurt is currently being taught to use the bus system.

Even though work has been fulfilling for Kurt, he still lacks a social life. Kurt is involved in a local church group and some activities organized by his local parks and recreation program; however, a lack of transportation has restricted other opportunities for socializing. Both Kurt and his parents hope that he will become involved in other activities, and that more opportunities will emerge as he becomes more proficient in his public transportation skills.

Potential Effects of the ADA on the Thomases

Kurt will probably feel most of the ADA's impact in the area of employment. As mentioned in reference to the Rowe case study, Title I of the bill prohibits discrimination in employment. Even though Kurt is now successfully placed in a job, earlier in his job search, Kurt encountered discrimination due to his epilepsy. Under the ADA, an employer cannot deny employment to an individual based on generalized fears about safety or absenteeism (Golden, 1991).

At his new job, Kurt experienced adaptations in scheduling and equipment to help accommodate his needs. Due in part to his epilepsy, Kurt functions better with a fixed schedule rather than a rotating schedule that is subject to frequent change. Kurt's employer has adapted her own schedule to accommodate this factor. Relatively minor but important adaptations in the workplace have also enabled Kurt to better perform his job. In order to cue Kurt to a sequence of tasks he needs to complete each day, the job coach has posted laminated cards of the tasks so that Kurt can mark off each job after it has been completed. This simple and inexpensive accommodation has meant that Kurt can fulfill the job requirements successfully, thus proving that reasonable accommodations are not only realizable, but also effective for both the employer and the employee.

Because Kurt is employed by a fast food restaurant that is part of a large national chain that provides excellent fringe benefits, Kurt will be able to use several services if he increases his hours to full-time status. Even though health and dental insurance are covered by an agency other than the employer, under the ADA, the insurance carrier cannot discriminate against Kurt regarding such benefits. Furthermore, under the ADA, employers cannot discriminate against individuals with disabilities in employer-sponsored activities, such as social or recreational programs. This provision means that Kurt will have the same access as other employees to employer-sponsored membership in a local health club.

Kurt will also benefit from changes in public transportation under the ADA. Because he will be reliant on the bus for transportation after learning how to use it, Kurt may benefit from paratransit eligibility. Even though Kurt can use an accessible fixed bus route, if he is required to work at a time that is not served by an accessible bus, according to the ADA, the bus company may be required to provide paratransit services.

CONCLUSION

From an early age, the individual begins his or her role as a consumer of goods and services. This role typically entails the identification of needs and the subsequent use of a variety of methods and means to achieve the desired outcomes. Inherent in the role of consumer is the incumbent responsibility of identifying one's needs and gaining access to the necessary services.

Individuals with disabilities are also consumers. Many individuals with disabilities, however, have unique and varied needs that many products and services are not able to meet. Parents and professionals have long complained of the bureaucratic and fragmented nature of many service agencies. Such fragmentation has often served to make their role as consumers difficult and time-consuming. As the case studies illustrate, there are a variety of available resources and methods to aid in the achievement of satisfactory outcomes, to induce change, and to improve the overall quality of life for individuals with disabilities. Effective use of community resources often entails creativity in identifying existing resources and locating new services. By utilizing community resources effectively, individuals with disabilities have the opportunity to meet their needs.

Integration encompasses far more than simple physical proximity. The distinction made between being in a community and being part of the community is an important one. Central to integration is a sense of belonging and ownership of decisions. The ADA provides important impetus for creating a sense of belonging and partnership in decision-making for individuals with disabilities. However, a large part of the success of the ADA depends on individuals with disabilities making their needs known. Additionally, individuals with disabilities will need to problem-solve for solutions that meet their needs and that of the business or organization as well as become cognizant of venues of action for enforcement.

As the case studies illustrate, the ADA will directly affect individuals with disabilities and their families. Families like the Rowes, the DeGeorges, and the Thomases illustrate how the ADA will affect aspects of daily life in such broad areas such as employment, transportation, public accommodations, and telecommunications. The case studies also illustrate that enactment of the ADA regulations will require active participation by both individual citizens and organizations to work. Some provisions may be easily identified and remedied, other provisions may require extensive restructuring and change. Whatever the amount of change necessary, it is apparent that the ADA will mean that individuals such as Jim, Michelle, and Kurt are given greater opportunities for access to, and integration in, the community.

The ADA represents an important moral and legal impetus for change that will affect the lives of countless individuals with disabilities, their families, and their friends. The ADA allows the opportunity for change in all aspects of society. Through successful utilization of community resources, the full intent and nature of the ADA may be realized.

REFERENCES

Brinker, R.P., & Thorpe, M.E. (1986). Features of integrated educational ecologies that predict behavior among severely mentally retarded and non-retarded students. *American Journal of Mental Deficiency, 91*, 150–159.

Crapps, J.M., Langone, J., & Swaim, S. (1985). Quantity and quality of participation in community environments by mentally retarded adults. *Education and Training of the Mentally Retarded, 20*, 123–129.

Eklund, E. (1976). *Systems advocacy.* Lawrence: University of Kansas.

Golden, M. (1991). The Americans with Disabilities Act of 1990. *Journal of Vocational Rehabilitation, 1*, 13–20.

Heal, L.W. (1980). Ideological responses of society to its handicapped citizens. In A.R. Novak & L.W. Heal (Eds.), *Integration of developmentally disabled individuals into the community* (pp. 35–42). Baltimore: Paul H. Brookes Publishing Co.

Kregel, J., Wehman, P., Seyfarth, J., & Marshall, K. (1986). Community integration of young adults with mental retardation: Transition from school to adulthood. *Education and Training of the Mentally Retarded, 21*, 35–42.

Laski, F.J. (1991). Achieving integration during the second revolution. In L.H. Meyer, C.A. Peck, & L. Brown (Eds.), *Critical issues in the lives of people with severe disabilities* (pp. 409–421). Baltimore: Paul H. Brookes Publishing Co.

Linthicum, E., Cole, J.T., & D'Alonzo, B.J. (1991). Employment and the Americans with Disabilities Act of 1990. *Career Development for Exceptional Individuals, 14*, 1–14.

Louis Harris and Associates. (1986, February). *A Survey of the unemployment of persons with disabilities.* Washington, DC: Author.

Ludlow, B.L., & Herr, S.S. (1988). Advocacy and adult rights to habilitation. In B.L. Ludlow, A.P. Turnbull, & R. Luckasson (Eds.), *Transition to adult life for people with mental retardation: Principles and practices* (pp. 233–256). Baltimore: Paul H. Brookes Publishing Co.

The President's Committee on Employment of People with Disabilities. (September, 1990). *The Americans with Disabilities Act in brief.* Washington, DC: Author.

Virginia Department of Medical Assistance Services. (1990). *Planning ahead: A guide for Virginians with Disabilities.* Richmond, VA: Author.

U.S. Department of Health, Education, and Welfare. (1986). *Directory of national information sources on handicapping conditions and related services.* Washington, DC: U.S. Department of Health, Education, and Welfare. Office of Human Development Services, Office for Handicapped Individuals.

Chapter 13

Promises Made and Promises To Be Broken

Steven J. Taylor and Robert Bogdan

Over 15 years have elapsed between the passage of Section 504 of the Rehabilitation Act and PL 94-142, both of which were heralded as landmark civil rights laws, and the passage of the ADA, a law that promises to be a rival to such previous legislation. It is now time to look at how persons with disabilities are faring in America today. In this chapter, the authors reflect on some of the changes that have occurred since the early and mid-1970s and discuss challenges for the future.[1] Specifically, the status of integration, societal acceptance, and the ADA are examined.

Preparation of this chapter was supported in part by the National Institute on Disability and Rehabilitation Research for the Research and Training Center on Community Integration through Cooperative Agreement #H 133 B0000-90 awarded to the Center on Human Policy at Syracuse University. The opinions expressed herein are solely those of the authors and no endorsement by the U.S. Department of Education should be inferred.

[1]This chapter looks at the ADA from the vantage point of persons with disabilities. The authors have refrained from commenting on the implications that the ADA might have for other groups that are discriminated against. In the political compromises surrounding the passage of the ADA, Congress inserted language to ensure that drug users, transvestites, and homosexuals would *not* be protected from discrimination. The attention devoted to these groups is conspicuous. One section (508) is devoted to transvestites and another section (511) makes reference to homosexuals and bisexuals in one clause and to "pedophilia, exhibitionism, voyeurism . . . kleptomania, or pyromania" in another. Obviously, homosexuality and bisexuality, as

INTEGRATION

Segregation represents the most extreme form of discrimination against persons with disabilities; therefore, one of the most hopeful trends since the 1970s has been the decline in the number of persons with disabilities who are physically segregated from other people. Significant progress has been made toward the successful physical integration of persons with disabilities into communities, schools, and workplaces. The populations of public institutions continue to decline at a steady pace as increasing numbers of adults and children with disabilities are integrated into regular work places and schools. In fact, the number of persons with developmental disabilities in public institutions has declined from 195,000 in 1967 to 88,000 in 1989 (Lakin, 1991). A number of states are on the verge of not having any persons with developmental disabilities living in institutions. Segregated settings are dying—a slow death, perhaps, but dying nevertheless. As Biklen and Knoll (1987) point out, institutionalization is "handicapism writ large" (p. 7).

Physical integration is not always, or even usually, accompanied by social integration. The most important lesson of recent history is that integration is vastly more complex than anyone imagined in the 1970s. Many persons with disabilities, although physically integrated into the community, schools, and work places, remain isolated and cut off from interactions with others who do not have disabilities (O'Brien, 1987). Limited social participation is a common experience among persons with disabilities even when they are present in neighborhoods, public schools, and regular work sites. For many persons with developmental disabilities who live in community intermediate care facilities for persons with mental retardation (ICFs/MR), group homes, and other facilities, life in the community is as restricted as life in large institutions. A sobering study by Bercovici (1983) found that many disinstitutionalized persons are enmeshed in a subculture separate from the rest of society. In "mainstreamed" public schools, special education students often have extremely limited contact with students who do not have disabilities. Even when adults and children participate in regular community, school, and work settings, friendships and meaningful relationships with people who do not have disabilities may be nonexistent (Stainback, Stainback, & Forest, 1989).

Social integration does not always occur spontaneously. It is impossible for people to be part of the community if they are segregated in institutions, special schools, or sheltered vocational and training centers. People need opportunities to participate in regular neighborhoods, schools, and work places, but opportunities do not ensure full integration and participation.

---

well as other behaviors or orientations, are not disabilities. What is significant is that Congress went out of its way to make sure that certain groups would not have a legal measure against discrimination.

Furthermore, integration is not a passing fad, it has weathered strong opposition. For example, a number of years ago, the authors visited an institution in which people with severe retardation were being prepared to leave an institution. An attendant at the institution was skeptical about the move and predicted that all of the residents would be returned to the institution as soon as the deinstitutionalization fad passed. She turned out to be wrong; however, deinstitutionalization, normalization, and integration continued to face significant opposition throughout the 1970s and into the 1980s. Unfortunately, many professionals, public employee unions, and parents waged a bitter battle against these trends (Taylor & Searl, 1987). In the mid-1970s, a group of professionals joined together to oppose a federal court order in the landmark *Wyatt v. Stickney* (1972) case that mandated a right to treatment under the least restrictive circumstances for institutionalized persons. In a memorandum prepared for the court, they advocated for a return to institutional custodial care for persons with severe disabilities (Taylor & Searl, 1987).

In addition, the American Federation of State, County, and Municipal Employees (AFSCME), a public employee union representing 250,000 mental health workers nationally, released a scathing report that denounced the policy of deinstitutionalization. The report, entitled *Out of Their Beds and into the Streets,* presented deinstitutionalization as a sinister plot to relieve state governments from caring for elderly people and those with disabilities and to put money in the pockets of private profiteers (Santiestevan, 1979). Many parents experienced what Turnbull and Turnbull (1980) call "jet lag" and feared that their sons and daughters with disabilities would be abused and neglected in the community and in regular schools.

As part of a backlash against deinstitutionalization and integration, politicians, civic leaders, and the general public voiced stiff opposition to efforts to confer full citizenship status on persons with disabilities. "Sometimes equality just costs too much," wrote Starr (1982), a member of the *New York Times* editorial board. According to Starr (1982), laws such as Section 504 and PL 94-142 demanded too much too fast:

> no matter how savage it sounds, spending money on the handicapped must be measured against the wealth produced by the nation's economy, and against other demands for help that similarly return a smaller amount of money to the national treasury than they cost. (p. 14)

Similar statements were made by some sectors of the business community in opposition to the passage of the ADA.

Almost every state in the United States experienced strong resistance to the presence of persons with disabilities in neighborhoods and community homes throughout the 1970s and 1980s. In an excellent article addressing this resistance, Keating (1979) wrote that "bomb threats, vandalism, violence, and phone threats have become our newest treatment for the mentally retarded"

(p. 87). Quoting one prospective neighbor of a group home, Keating wrote, "We don't want them. Put them back in Willowbrook" (1979, p. 87).

A central New York paper, *The Catholic Sun,* reported a bizarre story in 1976 (cited in Taylor & Searl, 1987). Alarmed by the number of former residents of mental hospitals and of institutions for persons with mental retardation who were wandering around the city, Mayor Edward Hanna of Utica banned all former hospital/institution residents from entering a city park without supervision. The mayor charged that there had been instances of panhandling, disrobing, and assaults by former residents. In opposition to the mayor's ban, two local priests and two nuns protested. Mocking the mayor's decree, they set up an IQ booth at the entrance to the park and asked visitors, "Do you have all of your mental faculties?" Eventually, the decree was withdrawn.

Despite the opposition, deinstitutionalization, integration, and related concepts have achieved widespread acceptance. As evidenced by the passage of the ADA, the segregation of individuals with disabilities is no longer considered tolerable. The statement of findings and purposes of the ADA reads:

> the Congress finds that . . . historically, society has tended to isolate and segregate individuals with disabilities, and, despite some improvements, such forms of discrimination against individuals with disabilities continue to be a serious and pervasive social problem. (42 U.S.C. 12101)

In short, Congress has declared that segregation is a form of discrimination; therefore, as a policy direction, integration is here to stay.

SOCIETAL ACCEPTANCE

The ADA also highlights contrasting themes in American culture. For example, there is long-standing discrimination against a range of groups in America. Persons with disabilities, in particular, continue to be subjected to stereotyping, segregation, and other forms of prejudice and discrimination (Biklen & Knoll, 1987). Congress noted in the statement of findings in the ADA that "discrimination against individuals persists in such critical areas as employment, housing, public accommodations, education, transportation, communication, recreation, institutionalization, health services, voting, and access to public services" (42 U.S.C. 12101).

While society can applaud the steady progress made in returning individuals with disabilities to their rightful place in the community, a significant number of people remain in public institutions and mini-institutions within the community. When the populations of public institutions are added to the number of persons with developmental disabilities in nursing homes and large private institutions, the total approaches 200,000 (Laski, 1991). In spite of a growing number of integrated school programs across the country, over one million students with disabilities are in segregated special education programs (U.S. Office of Special Education and Rehabilitative Services, 1989). People with certain disabilities, such as persons labelled mentally ill and those with severe disabilities, are especially vulnerable to discrimination in the form of segregation.

Cultural Discrimination

Institutionalization and other forms of segregation reflect deep-seated prejudice and discrimination against persons with disabilities on a cultural level. Biklen and Bogdan (1977) coined the term "handicapism" to characterize these negative forces:

> handicapism can be defined as a theory and set of practices that promote unequal and unjust treatment of people because of apparent or assumed physical or mental disability. Handicapism manifests itself in relationships between individuals, in social policy and cultural norms, and in the helping professions. (p. 206)

According to Biklen and Bogdan (1977), the popular media has reinforced stereotyped images of persons with disabilities in movies, news stories, and comic strips. Horror movies establish a link between physical and mental disabilities and violent acts. Comic characters use terms like "stupid," "idiot," and "dummy" as general epithets. Newspaper stories and editorials blame urban homelessness and street crime on deinstitutionalization of persons with mental illness and mental retardation. The conservative columnist, George F. Will, the parent of a son with Down syndrome who is well-known for his sympathetic views toward individuals with disabilities, cited with approval a proposal to put persons who are labelled mentally ill back in institutions. "Take back the streets," wrote Will, "Begin by reinstitutionalizing the mentally ill, who communicate an infectious, demoralizing ambience of disorder" (Will, 1991, p. 70).

Blatant discrimination runs counter to the American ethos of justice and fairness for all; therefore, when evidence of discrimination is clear, a segment of American society tries to eliminate it. The passage of the ADA reflects a recognition that individuals with disabilities are a minority that is discriminated against and that continued discrimination is unacceptable. The view that persons with disabilities constitute a minority group represents a shift in focus from their presumed deficits, which have been used to justify discriminatory practices, to social and cultural forces that continue to subject them to unequal and unfair treatment. Biklen and Knoll (1987) point out:

> we need to foster the perception of disability as merely one of a wide range of possible human differences. This done, individuals with a disability can then be seen as members of one of the myriad minority groups that together equal the human community. From this perspective, denial of access to community living, whether through nursing home placement, institutionalization, or placement in

other large congregate residences, can be viewed not as a treatment option but as discrimination. (p. 21)

As the ADA attests, cultural views of persons with disabilities are slowly changing. Cultural values and beliefs are reflected in legislation as well as in the popular media. Until the late 1960s, laws and court decisions were based on images of people with disabilities as being either objects of pity or menaces to society. Reflecting the dominant views of the early 1900s, the U.S. Congress passed laws to prevent the immigration of "idiots," "insane persons," "paupers," and other supposedly undesirable groups (Taylor & Searl, 1987). In the famous case of *Buck v. Bell* (1927), the U.S. Supreme Court upheld the involuntary sterilization of an 18-year-old woman deemed feeble-minded:

> it is better for all the world, if instead of waiting to execute degenerative offspring for crime, or let them starve for their imbecility, society can prevent those who are manifestly unfit from continuing their kind . . . three generations of imbeciles are enough! (Cited in Scheerenberger, 1983, p. 192)

Just as the passage of the ADA indicates that cultural views of individuals with disabilities are changing, the mass media also provides an indicator of cultural beliefs and values. In the 1980s, it was unusual to see anything in the mass media about individuals with disabilities other than pity-provoking stories or other negative portrayals. In contrast, the early 1990s have seen the production of popular television series, movies, and stage shows that depict people with disabilities as complex persons with pasts and futures, hopes and dreams, problems and joys—and not as unidimensional characters. One sign of the times is the controversy surrounding the question of whether or not the leading character of the award-winning film, *My Left Foot,* should have been played by a person with a disability rather than a person who did not have a disability. Notwithstanding the controversy, the popularity of this film, with its sensitive and humanizing portrayal of a person with a severe disability, is significant.

Social Stigma

Prejudice and discrimination against persons with disabilities are real, but are not inevitable. Yet, in passing the ADA, Congress found that people with disabilities "occupy an inferior status in our society" and have been faced with restrictions and limitations "resulting from stereotypic assumptions not truly indicative of the individual ability of such individuals to participate in, and contribute to, society" (42 U.S.C. 12101).

As can be seen, prejudice against persons with disabilities runs deep in American culture. These individuals are stigmatized and subjected to stereotyping. A stigma is not merely a difference, but a characteristic that deeply discredits a person's moral character (Goffman, 1963). According to Goffman (1963), people with demonstrable stigma are seen as "not quite human" and "reduced in our minds from a whole and usual person to a tainted, discounted one" (p. 5). Sociological and anthropological studies have documented the stigma associated with deafness (Higgins, 1980), blindness (Scott, 1969), epilepsy (Schneider & Conrad, 1983), chronic facial pain (Lennon, Link, Marbach, & Dohrenwend, 1989), mental retardation (Bogdan & Taylor, 1982; Edgerton, 1967), mental illness (Estroff, 1981; Scheff, 1966), and physical disabilities (Davis, 1964; Zola, 1982).[2] Edgerton (1967), who has provided one of the clearest analyses of stigma among persons with disabilities, states:

> the label of mental retardation not only serves as a humiliating, frustrating, and discrediting stigma in the conduct of one's life in the community, but it also serves to lower one's self-esteem to such a nadir of worthlessness that the life of the person is scarcely worth living. (p. 145)

Persons with disabilities have been subjected to stigmatization, rejection, and exclusion in the society at large; however, people without disabilities can and do accept, like, and love people with disabilities, including those with the most severe disabilities. Stigma and rejection represent only one side of the story.

A small, but growing number of studies and reports document instances in which individuals with disabilities are accepted and included by communities and their peers who do not have disabilities (Bogdan & Taylor, 1987; Groce, 1985; Lutfiyya, 1990; Taylor & Bogdan, 1989). Groce's (1985) book, entitled *Everyone Here Spoke Sign Language,* is a striking example of a study of a community in which people with a demonstrable difference, in particular, deafness, were not stigmatized or rejected by other community members. Groce's study is an anthropological/historical account of Martha's Vineyard, Massachusetts prior to the turn of the 20th century. A much higher than average number of people living in some of the towns on Martha's Vineyard happened to have hereditary deafness. As a consequence, everyone, both the hearing and those persons who were hearing impaired, knew sign language. People with hearing impairments were not viewed as disabled or different and were accepted as full fledged members of the community. When surviving members of the community of that era were interviewed, they did not distinguish between hearing and hearing impaired people. Analysis of tax ledgers and other historical documents indicated no differences between people with and without hearing impairments in social status or wealth.

The authors' own research has documented numerous examples of positive relationships between people without disabilities and those with the most severe disabilities (Bogdan & Taylor, 1987; Taylor & Bogdan, 1989). People

---

[2]The stigma associated with the labels of mental retardation and mental illness seems especially strong. Discrimination against these groups runs especially deep. Although the ADA does apply to persons with mental and physical disabilities, it seems particularly designed for persons with sensory or mobility impairments. Accessibility requirements and accommodations are almost exclusively directed toward physical disabilities. In Section 509 of the ADA, the U.S. Senate reaffirms its commitment not to discriminate on the basis of an individual's "race, color, religion, sex, nation of origin, age of state or physical handicap [emphasis added]."

without disabilities form close relationships with people who have severe disabilities for a host of reasons (family bonds, humanitarian concern, religious commitment, feelings of friendship), but the common ingredient is the "delabeling" of the persons with a disability. In such relationships, the disability does not bring stigma and the person is viewed in terms of his or her full humanity (Bogdan & Taylor, 1989). Therefore, the ADA will be successful in the extent to which it helps to create a society in which such legislation is not needed; in other words, a society in which people with disabilities are unconsciously accepted as undifferentiated members.

THE LAW

There are limits to the changes that can be brought about through the law. Nevertheless, the 1970s and early 1980s were times in which smashing legal victories were won on behalf of persons with disabilities. Federal courts handed down far-reaching orders mandating deinstitutionalization, the right to education, and other rights. Congress enacted such legislation as PL 94-142 and Section 504 in addition to a myriad of other laws and programs designed to benefit persons with disabilities. For a time, it seemed that both the courts and Congress would put a rapid end to segregation and discrimination. However, just as racial discrimination and segregation have persisted for over 35 years after the Supreme Court's landmark ruling outlawing "separate but equal" in *Brown v. Board of Education* (1954), discrimination based on disability is also stubbornly resistant to legal challenges.

The dual problems of prejudice and discrimination are complex and defy simple solutions. Laws cannot change hearts and minds, as Judy Heumann (1991), a well-known disability rights activist, stated in a recent address on the ADA:

> when I examine the past and look critically at the present, I realize that the challenge to be faced is much deeper than simply legislating discrimination away. We must all look at our own prejudices, our own roles in the systematic oppression that disabled people face. Only by rooting out our own bias will a future of true equality be possible. (p. 2–3)

This quote should not be interpreted as denigrating the importance of the ADA. The ADA will undoubtedly open some of the doors to societal participation that have long been closed to persons with disabilities; however, partially open doors do not automatically lead to equality and justice.

Ambiguity in the ADA, Section 504, and PL 94-142

There will be set-backs in the efforts to implement the spirit of the ADA, yet the spirit of the ADA is clear and unambiguous. "It is the purpose of this ACT . . . to provide a clear and comprehensive national mandate for the elimination of discrimination against individuals with disabilities" (42 U.S.C.

12101). This is not the first time federal law has aspired to lofty goals for individuals with disabilities. Both Section 504 and PL 94-142 were widely heralded civil rights laws that challenged society's treatment of both adults and children with disabilities. The federal regulations implementing Section 504 read:

> Section 504 thus represents the first Federal civil rights law protecting the rights of handicapped persons and reflects a national commitment to end discrimination on the basis of handicap. . . It establishes a mandate to end discrimination and to bring handicapped persons into the mainstream of American life. (*Federal Register,* May 4, 1977, p. 22676)

Unfortunately, similar to Section 504 and PL 94-142, and their accompanying regulations, the language of the ADA is filled with ambiguities and can be interpreted in ways that run counter to its spirit. PL 94-142 incorporated concepts like "free appropriate public education" and "least restrictive environment" and made reference to "full educational opportunity." The ADA's language is taken directly from the Section 504 regulations. Public and private entities (e.g., governments, employers, businesses) must make "reasonable accommodations" for "a qualified individual with a disability" unless these impose an "undue hardship," although what is viewed as reasonable from one perspective may be unreasonable or undue from another.

Federal courts will be the final arbitrators of the meaning of the ADA's provisions. In contrast to most of the 1970s, federal courts have increasingly adopted a narrow view of the requirements of civil rights laws. Beginning in 1979, the U.S. Supreme Court has sent a message to lower federal courts to refrain from handing down far-reaching decisions on behalf of people with disabilities and other groups. The Supreme Court's decisions in *Southeastern Community College v. Davis* (1979) and *Board of Education of the Henrick Hudson Central School District v. Rowley* (1982) stand out as examples of the Court's narrow view of equal opportunity and nondiscrimination requirements in federal laws.

Southeastern Community College v. Davis Frances B. Davis was a licensed practical nurse with a hearing impairment who desired to be a registered nurse. When she applied for admission into a nursing program operated by Southeastern Community College in North Carolina, she was turned down based solely on her disability. Southeastern argued that it would be impossible for Davis to participate safely in its nurse training program. Davis subsequently filed suit in federal court alleging a violation of Section 504's prohibition against discrimination. The case eventually ended up being heard by the Supreme Court. In June of 1979, the Court handed down a unanimous decision siding with Southeastern Community College.

The Supreme Court's decision in the *Davis* case centered on the meanings of the concepts of "otherwise qualified handicapped individual" and "reasonable accommodation." Davis argued that she was qualified to participate in the nursing program. An accomplished lip reader, she maintained that she met the academic and technical qualifications for admission into the training program. She further argued that Section 504 required "reasonable accommodations" for her disability. These might include modifications in program requirements (i.e., waiving certain clinical requirements), the provision of a sign language interpreter, or individual clinical supervision. The Supreme Court was unpersuaded.

According to the Supreme Court, a "qualified handicapped" person is one who meets all of the requirements for participation in a program *in spite of* his or her disability. Southeastern required nursing students to participate in clinical situations in which medical personnel wore surgical masks. Because Davis obviously would not be able to read lips in these situations, according to the Supreme Court she was not able to meet all program requirements. In addition, the Supreme Court also rejected Davis's arguments that Southeastern was required to make accommodations in its training program to enable her to participate. According to the Court, Section 504 did not require a program to undertake "affirmative action" or make "substantial modifications" to accommodate persons with disabilities.

Board of Education of the Henrick Hudson Central School District v. Rowley   It was not until 1982 that PL 94-142 was to be interpreted by the Supreme Court. The *Rowley* case involved a bright young girl named Amy Rowley who happened to be deaf. Integrated into a regular elementary school class, Amy was doing quite well. She was performing better than the average child in her class and was advancing easily from grade to grade, but her parents thought that she could be doing much better. Although she was an excellent lip reader, she could understand much less of what went on in the classroom than the other children. Amy's parents, who were also deaf, asked the school district to provide a sign language interpreter so that she would have the same opportunity to learn as other children. The school district refused and a hearing officer and the state commissioner of education upheld this decision. Amy's parents filed suit in federal court alleging a violation of PL 94-142. Two lower federal courts sided with the Rowleys. Petitioned by the school district, the Supreme Court agreed to hear the case.

The *Rowley* case hinged on the meaning of "free appropriate public education" guaranteed by PL 94-142. Amy's parents argued that the right to a "free appropriate public education" meant equality of opportunity. A majority of the Supreme Court disagreed. Writing for the majority, Justice William Rehnquist reasoned that PL 94-142 merely requires that states provide students with disabilities with "access" to a school program. The meaning of "free appropriate public education," according to the majority, is the requirement that "the education to which access is provided be sufficient to confer some educational benefit upon the handicapped child" (*Board of Education v.*

Rowley, 1982, p. 200). Since Amy was advancing from grade to grade, she was receiving "some educational benefit." It was irrelevant that Amy would probably achieve much more if she were provided with a sign language interpreter. In an admonition to lower courts, the majority added that "courts must be careful to avoid imposing their view of preferable educational methods upon the States" (*Board of Education v. Rowley,* 1982, p. 207).

Disability rights groups greeted the *Davis* and *Rowley* cases with dismay and anger. The Supreme Court's decisions seemed to reflect long-standing prejudice against persons with disabilities and violate the spirit of Section 504 and PL 94-142, which were meant to halt discrimination. It would be surprising if similar disappointments do not await attempts to implement the spirit of the ADA.

Shortcomings of the ADA

The ADA leaves untouched federal laws and programs that perpetuate segregation and discrimination against persons with disabilities. The ADA calls on public and private entities to end discrimination against these persons, but does not address federal laws and programs that perpetuate segregation and discrimination. In passing the ADA, it is as though Congress is suggesting to "do as we say, not as we do."

Many of the most formidable barriers to societal participation for individuals with disabilities are rooted in federal programs. Medicaid, specifically the ICF/MR program, continues to encourage institutionalization and placement in segregated facilities in the community. As of 1988, 84% of the $3.38 billion ICF/MR program was devoted to state institutions and large private facilities (Braddock & Fujiura, 1991). Repeated proposals for Medicaid reform have been thwarted by vested interests both inside and outside of government. Federal disability programs, Social Security Disability Insurance, and the Supplemental Security Income (SSI) program serve as disincentives to economic advancement (Berkowitz, 1987).

The spirit of the ADA will not be fulfilled as long as federal laws and programs continue to encourage segregation, discrimination, and dependence. As DeJong and Batavia (1990) argue, "Even if the legal requirements of ADA are enforced vigorously, as we hope they will be, the law cannot adequately substitute for other policy changes that need to be made" (p. 71).

THE SOCIETY

The elimination of discrimination will not automatically lead to a meaningful life for persons with disabilities. For any minority that is discriminated against, the pursuit of equality and nondiscrimination is an important struggle. If and when the last vestiges of discrimination are eliminated, people with disabilities will still be faced with the problems confronting other people. As this group slowly achieves integration into the society at large, they will experience the same educational, housing, and vocational opportunities, and quality of life experienced by other members of American society. Unfortunately, many will be disappointed.

The ADA places a high value on productivity and economic self-sufficiency; however, the strongest justification of the ADA is that nondiscrimination is right and just, not that persons with disabilities can be productive and economically self-sufficient. According to the statement of findings in the ADA, discrimination and prejudice "costs the United States billions of dollars in unnecessary expenses resulting from dependency and nonproductivity" (42 U.S.C. 12101). Supporters of the ADA have pointed to economic grounds to justify the law. DeJong and Batavia (1990) write:

> in this key period of enhanced international competitiveness, all persons who can contribute to our society must be encouraged to do so. The disabled population is perhaps our nation's most untapped economic resource. . . With supportive public policy, people with disabilities are likely to contribute substantially to the nation's productivity. (p. 73)

Beyond dispute is the fact that persons with disabilities *can* contribute significantly to the society, but have been systematically prevented from doing so. With artificial barriers removed, many individuals with disabilities will compete successfully in the economic marketplace. Others will contribute to society in other ways and will continue to depend on the government for basic support (Ferguson & Ferguson, 1984). Whether or not the ADA will help the economy or save the government money is irrelevant. Nondiscrimination *is* right and just. Our common humanity, *not economic productivity,* is the strongest argument in favor of breaking down the barriers to societal participation.

CONCLUSION

If the recent past is any indicator of the future, the ADA, like civil rights laws before it, will meet with mixed outcomes. Continued progress in the integration of persons with disabilities into society, as well as new and unexpected forms of segregation, can be anticipated. Blatant acts of discrimination and prejudice will be confronted and overcome, but less subtle acts will take their place. Some legal challenges to discrimination will meet with success and others with failure. The community of persons without disabilities will sometimes shock individuals who have disabilities with their prejudicial attitudes and sometimes surprise them with their kindness and acceptance. The disability rights movements will profit from the victories of other groups that experience discrimination, but suffer from their defeats. There will be not only unanticipated challenges to meet, but also new controversies to debate.

REFERENCES

Americans with Disabilities Act, PL 101-336. (July 26, 1990). 42 U.S.C. 12101, et seq: *Federal Register, 56*(44), 35544–35756.

Bercovici, S. (1983). *Barriers to normalization.* Baltimore: University Park Press.

Berkowitz, E.D. (1987). *Disabled policy: America's programs for the handicapped.* Cambridge: Cambridge University Press.

Biklen, D., & Bogdan, R. (1977). Handicapism in America. In B. Blatt, D. Biklen, & R. Bogdan. (Eds.), *An alternative textbook in special education.* Denver, CO: Love Publishing Co.

Biklen, D., & Knoll, J. (1987). The disabled minority. In S. Taylor, D. Biklen, & J. Knoll (Eds.), *Community integration for people with severe disabilities* (pp. 3–24). New York: Teachers College Press.

Board of Education of the Henrick Hudson Central School District v. Rowley, 458 U.S. 176. 102 S. CT. 3034, (1982).

Bogdan, B., & Taylor, S. (1982). *Inside out: The social meaning of mental retardation.* Toronto: University of Toronto Press.

Bogdan, B., & Taylor, S. (1987, Fall). Toward a sociology of acceptance: The other side of the study of deviance. *Social Policy, 34–39.*

Bogdan, B., & Taylor, S. (1989). Relationships with severely disabled people: The social construction of humanness. *Social Problems, 36,* 135–148.

Braddock, D., & Fujiura, G. (1991). Politics, public policy, and the development of community mental retardation services in the United States. *American Journal on Mental Retardation, 95,* 369–387.

Brown v. Board of Education, 347 U.S. 483 (1954).

Buck v. Bell, 274 U.S. 200. 47 S. Ct. 584 (1927).

Davis, F. (1964). Deviance disavowal: The management of strained interaction by the visibly handicapped. In H.S. Becker (Ed.), *The other side* (pp. 119–38). New York: The Free Press.

DeJong, G., & Batavia, A.I. (1990). The Americans with Disabilities Act and the current state of U.S. disability policy. *Journal of Disability Policy Studies, 1,* 65–75.

Edgerton, R. (1967). *The cloak of competence.* Berkeley: University of California Press.

Estroff, S.E. (1981). *Making it crazy.* Berkeley: University of California Press.

Federal Register. (May 4, 1977). *42*(86), 22676.

Ferguson, D.L., & Ferguson, P.M. (1984). The new victors: A progressive policy analysis of work reform. *Mental Retardation. 24*(6), 331–338.

Goffman, E. (1963). *Stigma: Notes on the management of spoiled identity.* Englewood Cliffs, NJ: Prentice Hall.

Groce, N.E. (1985). *Everyone here spoke sign language: Hereditary deafness on Martha's Vineyard.* Cambridge, MA: Harvard University Press.

Heumann, J.E. (1991, May 1). *The Americans with Disabilities Act: A civil rights victory—A national challenge.* Address before the Employment Law Center of San Francisco's annual luncheon.

Higgins, P. (1980). *Outsiders in a hearing world.* Berkeley, CA: Sage Publications.

Keating, R. (1979, September 17). The war against the mentally retarded. *New York,* 87–92.

Lakin, K.C. (1991). Foreword. In S.J. Taylor, R. Bogdan, & J.A. Racino (Eds.), *Community participation series: Vol. 1. Life in the community: Case studies of organizations supporting people with disabilities* (pp. xiii–xv). Baltimore: Paul H. Brookes Publishing Co.

Laski, F.J. (1991). Achieving integration during the second revolution. In L.H. Meyer, C.A. Peck, & L. Brown (Eds.), *Critical issues in the lives of people with severe disabilities* (pp. 409–421). Baltimore: Paul H. Brookes Publishing Co.

Lennon, M., Link, B., Marbach, J., & Dohrenwend, B. (1989). The stigma of chronic facial pain and its impact on social relationships. *Social Problems, 36,* 117–134.

Lutfiyya, Z. (1990). *Affectionate bonds.* Syracuse, NY: Center on Human Policy.

O'Brien, J. (1987). Embracing ignorance, error, and fallibility: Competencies for leadership of effective services. In S.J. Taylor, D. Biklen, & J. Knoll (Eds.), *Community integration for people with severe disabilities* (pp. 85–108). New York: Teachers College Press.

Santiestevan, H. (1979). *Out of their beds and into the streets.* Washington, DC: American Federation of State, County, and Municipal Employees.

Scheerenberger, R.C. (1983). *A history of mental retardation.* Baltimore: Paul H. Brookes Publishing Co.

Scheff, T. (1966). *Being mentally ill.* Chicago, IL: Aldine.

Schneider, J., & Conrad, P. (1983). *Having epilepsy: The experience and control of illness.* Philadelphia: Temple University Press.

Scott, R. (1969). *The making of blind men.* New York: Russell Sage.

Southeastern Community College v. Davis, 442 U.S. 397, 99 S. Ct. 2361, 60 L.Ed. 2d 980 (1979).

Stainback, S., Stainback, W., & Forest, M. (Eds.). (1989). *Educating all students in the mainstream of regular education.* Baltimore: Paul H. Brookes Publishing Co.

Starr, R. (1982, January). Wheels of misfortune: Sometimes equality just costs too much. *Harper's,* p. 14.

Taylor, S., & Bogdan, R. (1989). On accepting relationships between people with mental retardation and non-disabled people: Towards an understanding of acceptance. *Disability, Handicap, & Society, 1,* 21–36.

Taylor, S.J., & Searl, S.J. (1987). The disabled in America: History, policy, and trends. In P. Knoblock (Ed.), *Understanding exceptional children and youth* (pp. 5–64). Boston: Little, Brown.

Turnbull, H.R., & Turnbull, A. (1980). *Parents speak out: Then and now.* Columbus, OH: Charles E. Merrill.

U.S. Office of Special Education and Rehabilitative Services. (1989). *Eleventh Annual Report to Congress on the Implementation of the Handicapped Act.* Washington, DC: Author.

Will, G.F. (1991, June 17). Nature and the male sex. *Newsweek,* p. 70.

Wyatt v. Stickney, 344 F. Supp. 373 and 387 (D. Ala. 1972).

Zola, I.K. (1982). *Missing pieces.* Philadelphia: Temple University Press.

Appendix

Annotated Bibliography

R. G. Rayfield

Boothroyd, A. (1990). Impact of technology on the management of deafness. *Volta Review, 92*(4), 73–82.

This article explores the powerful influence of technological advances on the management of deafness and discusses some reasons for the delay between the development of new technologies and their application to the needs of special populations. Key areas of consideration include surgical treatment, prosthetic treatment (including implants and microphones), speech training, computer-assisted instruction, and telecommunications.

Bruyere, S. (1985). An existentialist approach to rehabilitation counseling. *Journal of Applied Rehabilitation Counseling, 16*(3), 36–40.

One of the key responsibilities of practitioners who advocate for consumer self-empowerment is to actively engage the individual's will in all facets of the rehabilitation process. This article provides an overview of the existential philosophy as it might be applied in the practice of vocational rehabilitation counseling. Featured are key terms and concepts, as well as details on the evolution of existentialism as a philosophy and as a form of psychotherapy, its parallel in the area of rehabilitation, and its application as a counseling intervention strategy for individuals with disabilities. The study asserts that existentialism as both a philosophy and as an approach to counseling is consistent with and can positively contribute to vocational counseling (e.g., its fundamental belief in the relevance of developmental history of the individual, its focus on the importance of psychological health and social integration, its criteria for consumer change, and its consumer-centered intervention strategies). Taken from an existentialist view, every person is empowered to choose his or her own existence and is thereby ultimately responsible for him- or herself. The focus of counseling interventions should be to restore in consumers a sense of freedom and personal responsibility. To do so would enable consumers to discover for themselves the meaning of their existence and would encourage them to make it a reality. Counselors would then be in a better position to set more meaningful vocational goals, as well as larger life goals with consumers, ensuring the provision of effective rehabilitation services.

Buddy, J.F., & Bachelder, J.L. (1986). The concept, model, and methodology. *Journal of The Association for Persons with Severe Handicaps, 11*(4), 240–245.

Part of a special issue on the national network of University Affiliated Facilities, the article defines independent living (IL) and discusses the development and application of the IL concept. An IL model that focuses on improving the community environment and offering assistive devices to persons with severe disabilities is presented.

Carrell, M.R., & Heavrin, W.T., Jr. (1987). The "handi-capable" employee: An untapped resource. *Personnel, 64*(8), 40–45.

The authors discuss terms that should not be used when dealing with employees with disabilities. They report on positive steps that some employers have taken in hiring and accommodating such persons and on some of the innovative adaptive equipment available for employees.

Cooper, A., & Mank, D. (1989). Integrated employment for people with severe physical disabilities: Case studies and support issues. *American Rehabilitation, 15*(3), 16–23.

Identifying successful competitive job placements for consumers with severe disabilities is a challenging and multi-faceted undertaking. The present article focuses on the nature of support services provided to individuals with severe physical disabilities within a program of supported competitive employment. Specifically, the research examines five case studies, each describing services provided to individuals placed by a Seattle, Washington employment service. Types of service were grouped into two categories (individual training and direct services, or systematic and external coordination) and gave specific examples of the responses made by the service provider to address issues and service needs. For those consumers having difficulty with transportation to and from work, the agency responded by: 1) providing travel and safety training; 2) using taxis and specialized transportation services; and 3) working with the city to have curbcuts, lights, crosswalks, and signs installed. Identified health problems were addressed through: 1) working with the client on self-care at home, 2) planning intervention to gradually increase work time, and 3) working with individuals to understand the impact of fatigue on their bodies and their disabilities. Although the authors utilized rehabilitation technologies, they were not completely persuaded that these strategies represented the cure-all for employment success. Perhaps the key ingredient to successful placement is making a job match that highlights an individual's strengths rather than requiring extensive modifications. Family or residential support was also important for job success. In addition, the success of the five cases was linked to the receptiveness of the employers and coworkers to hire individuals with severe and multiple disabilities and their commitment to acceptance and integration. The report also underscores the enormous expense associated with technology and support services; however, the relatively short duration of the project (approximately 16 months) does not provide a clear indication as to whether or not service costs will decrease with time and experience.

Cottone, R., Handelsman, M., & Walters, N. (1986). Understanding the influence of family systems on the rehabilitation process. *Journal of Applied Rehabilitation Counseling, 78*(2), 37–40.

The critical impact of family dynamics can no longer be overlooked when rehabilitation practitioners formulate strategies aimed at consumer empowerment. The writers of this article assert that the family social systems theory is an effective means of conceptualizing a number of the problems rehabilitation counselors encounter in their practices. An analysis of the influences of the family on the vocational rehabilitation process as well as the implications of a systems perspective for rehabilitation practitioners are discussed. Taken from a family systems perspective, the consumers and their problems must be viewed within a social context. The family systems approach underscores the importance of valued communication, of the family control over homeostasis, of the influence of role structures within families, and of how the observation of interfamily behaviors can serve as a good predictor of consumer outcomes. Utilization of family systems strategies can serve to restructure the maladaptive family in such a way that natural development can be facilitated. In contrast, the medical model and various psychological perspectives seek linear causality (A causes B) as a treatment focus.

Crisp, R. (1990). Return to work after spinal cord injury. *Journal of Rehabilitation,* January–March, 28-35.

On balance the return-to-work tract record for individuals with spinal cord injuries (SCI) has been mixed. This article reviews 12 recent studies that focused on return to work following SCI. The author selected only those studies that had been published within the past 10 years, having at least 50 respondents who were followed for at least 12 months after the injury. While evidence from the studies may be conflicting, some general conclusions about post-SCI employment may be drawn; 1) education has been associated most frequently with employment after SCI; that is, individuals with higher levels of education appear to undergo fewer changes in their value systems, occupations, leisure activities, and interests; 2) congruity between preinjury vocational interests and postinjury physical capabilities appears to be an important predictor of employment success; 3) there are conflicting reports linking severity of disability to employment and medical problems associated with disability; 4) individuals injured early in life (prior to age 30) appear more likely to become employed than those injured later in life, due to reduced adaptability of the older injured worker or the reluctance of employers to hire or rehire persons with limited work life; 5) gender also appears to influence return to work and the types of occupations into which individuals return; and 6) some studies have reported that some individuals with SCI choose to remain unemployed in order to retain benefits. The authors caution that the return-to-work research is of limited use to vocational rehabilitation service providers and propose that more research is needed to identify the events and learning experiences that enable individuals to face and overcome barriers to employment.

Elting, S. (1988). Become an informed technology consumer. *Exceptional Parent, 18*(7), 34–35.

This article for parents and teachers of nonverbal children describes information sources identified by the Center for Special Education Technology including general print information as well as information on school and community services, technology use with specific disabilities, software and hardware, assistive devices, and funding sources.

Emener, W. (1991). An empowerment philosophy for rehabilitation in the 20th century. *Journal of Rehabilitation, 57*(4), 7–12.

Rehabilitation practitioners dedicated to supporting independence and freedom on behalf of persons with disabilities must consider the issue of empowerment as a critical component and as a guiding operational value within rehabilitation's systems, agencies, facilities, companies, and professional service delivery personnel. In this article, Dr. Emener strongly recommends that consumer empowerment be the key focus of all rehabilitation interventions. He defines rehabilitation (helping consumers move from community dependence to a position of independence in the community of their choice) and discusses relevant philosophical beliefs pertinent to the field of rehabilitation (e.g., importance of individual's worth and dignity, maximization of potential, societal acceptance, positive development, and individual choice). His approach also underscores the importance of simultaneous consideration of both internal and external factors in four areas of rehabilitation service delivery: 1) rehabilitation systems (e.g., agencies, facilities, and companies); 2) rehabilitation professionals (e.g., rehabilitation counselors, supervisors, managers, and administrators; 3) families of individuals with disabilities; and 4) rehabilitation clients. Conclusions and recommendations identify specific strategies for facilitating a self-empowerment approach to rehabilitation service delivery. Practitioners are urged to maximize every opportunity they have to facilitate each consumer's self-empowerment.

Garner, J.B., & Campbell, P.H. (1987). Technology for persons with severe disabilities: Practical and ethical considerations. *Journal of Special Education, 21*(3), 122–132.

Issues related to technological advances for persons with severe disabilities are discussed. These include: obstacles to the use of adaptations and technological devices; strategies for selection, design, and use of technological devices; an approach for incorporating technology into the integrated team planning process; and ethical/philosophical concerns that should guide technological applications.

Goldberg, A.M. (1978). An evaluation of braille translation programs. *Journal of Visual Impairment and Blindness, 81*(10), 487–488, 490, 492.

This article might be of key interest to an employer who has considered adapting the work environment for a blind candidate. Three braille translation programs, which translate computerized text files into new files of ASCII representative grade 2 braille, are evaluated, including "Braille-Talk," "PC Braille," and "The Duxbury Translator." For each program, documentation, ease of operation, formatting, embedded commands, customer support, program errors, and manufacturer's comments are reviewed.

Guess, D., Benson, A., & Siegel-Casey, E. (1986). Concepts and issues related to choice-making and autonomy among persons with severe disabilities. *Journal of The Association for the Persons with Severe Handicaps, 10*(2), 79–86.

Advocates for consumer empowerment will need to address a variety of issues related to preferences and choice making among persons with severe disabilities. Following an analysis of various reasons why choice making has received relatively little attention as a treatment strategy, this article identifies a conceptual framework that offers various practical suggestions for teachers of persons with severe disabilities. Interestingly, preliminary findings show that few parents of adolescent students labeled severely or even moderately disabled have ever considered choice making and decision making as viable options. The authors contend that abilities and opportunity to express preferences, make decisions, and exercise choices are profoundly influenced by an individual's adaptive behaviors and that this factor ought to be considered when developing educational intervention for individuals with disabilities. It is concluded that the provision of consistent opportunities for consumers with severe disabilities to choose and express preferences might well have a positive impact on the learning process and on various aspects of more long-term personal development. The study also identifies various areas of analysis for researchers who may be interested in teaching choice-making skills. Suggestions for quantitative research included independent variables (e.g., choice of instructional materials, place of instruction, tasks to be learned) and dependent outcome measures (e.g., rate of acquisition, generalization, and maintenance of the learned skills over time). Use of qualitative research techniques to investigate choice- and decision-making opportunities also appears to be a viable extension of the methodology according to the researchers.

Henke, C. (1990). Funding to make wheels turn around. *Exceptional Parent,* *20*(2), 8, 10, 12.

This article presents an abundance of tips on financing the purchase of wheelchairs and other adaptive equipment for persons with physical disabilities. Of particular focus are parent/dealer cooperation, parental health insurance coverage, governmental programs, doctors' prescription letters, and community resources. In addition, a variety of potential funding sources are listed along with contact information.

Horne, R. (1989). *Assistive technology. NICHCY News Digest #13*. Interstate Research Associates, Inc., Washington, DC: National Information Center for Handicapped Children and Youth.

This newsletter analyzes six articles concerned with providing varied information on available assistive technology devices for persons with disabilities. *Technology: Becoming an Informed Consumer,* by Elizabeth Lahm and Sue Elting, reviews the history of technology for persons with disabilities with emphasis on assistive technology, offers case studies on technology applications, and provides guidelines for making informed choices when purchasing home computer software and selecting assistive technology equipment. *Assistive Technology: A Parent's Perspective,* by Julie Fleisch, underscores the many problems parents have experienced trying to keep up with available technology and with identifying financial resources needed to obtain the assistive devices. *Federal Legislation and Assistive Technology,* by Roxanne Rice, summarizes the provisions and requirements pertaining to assistive technology under federal guidelines. *Effective Use of Technology with Young Children,* by Mary L. Wilds, discusses the skills needed for interactive use of computers, selection of battery-operated toys and switches, and introducing young children to computers. *Integrating Technology into a Student's IEP,* by Ruth Bragman, reviews technology in the context of students' individualized education programs (IEPs), discussing hardware adaptations, student assessment/evaluation and considerations, traditional and technological considerations, and selection of devices and software and identification of their operational characteristics. *Starting the Funding Process,* by Suzanne Ripley, offers families suggestions for acquiring funding for assistive technology. Included among selected supplemental listings of additional informational sources were relevant books, reports, and magazine articles; magazines and newsletters; and an assortment of related organizations.

Karp, A. (1988). Reduced vision and speechreading. *Volta Review, 90*(5), 61–74.

This article outlines the eye disorders most likely to be experienced by a hearing impaired person, with an explanation of the impact these disorders will have on speechreading performance. Recommendations are also offered to assist visually impaired speechreaders, through consideration of optimal viewing angles, lighting conditions, use of low vision aids, and so forth.

Lynch, M.R. (1990). Tactile speech indicator: Adaptive telephone device for deaf–blind clients. *Journal of Visual Impairment and Blindness, 84*(1), 21–22.

This article explores many basic applications of an adaptive telephone device for deaf–blind persons with speaking voices. Using this device, the deaf–blind caller poses questions requiring one-word answers, and the device vibrates in response to touch-tone pulses from the other party. Discussed at some length are specific suggestions for such uses as making appointments and executing emergency calls.

Nichols, J. (1990). The new decade dawns: The search for quality and consumer empowerment converge. *Journal of Rehabilitation Administration, 15*(4), 69–70.

The trend toward consumer empowerment appears to have spurred renewed efforts by many companies and agencies to improve the quality of their products and services as well. The author explores these two issues believed to be dominating factors in rehabilitation delivery systems of the 90s and recaps how the focus has shifted over recent decades (e.g., the 50s and 60s featured various expansions of human services spurred by the passage of the Hill-Burton and Rehabilitation Acts; the 1970s were a decade of service access both for individuals with physical disabilities and for racial minorities; and the 1980s emphasized expansion through the development of program satellites and diversification). As examples of the current consumer empowerment–product quality trend, the following are discussed: the U.S. automobile industry's heightened emphasis on service quality, the disability rights movement, the increased empowerment of consumers, and the increased emphasis on the value and importance of the consumer. The report concludes by describing how the current trends are beginning to converge as larger amounts of well-informed customers are making more and more decisions as to whether or not specific services are acceptable.

Parette, H. (1990). *A question of assistive technology and services for young children with physical disabilities.* Little Rock, AR: Center for Research on Teaching and Learning, Governor's Developmental Disabilities Planning Council.

This report is the result of a statewide survey that assessed the assistive technology needs of youth with physical disabilities. It was conducted in Arkansas as a component of the grant application process of PL 100-407 (the Technology-Related Assistance for Individuals with Disabilities Act of 1988). The key purpose of the survey was to analyze participant satisfaction with assistive technology devices and services, cost expenditures for assistive technologies, travel required to receive technology and services, and typical funding sources. The survey also identified and explored various unmet life functioning needs reported by participants and their families. Among these needs were specialized cars, vans, and buses; vision and hearing aids; reading, writing, and typing aids; building accessibility; independent living; and use of a telephone. Most were evaluated prior to obtaining assistive devices. The study recommends a need for more information on assistive technology and services as well as a need for increased transportation options for persons with disabilities. Interestingly, a significant proportion of families of participants reported a substantial need for the option of purchasing assistive devices on a credit plan.

Securing technology funding: Empowering parents. (1990). *Exceptional Parent, 20*(8), 6–8.

This is a very thorough investigation of resource funding for assistive technology devices for persons with disabilities. It addresses how to locate community funding sources, set priorities, increase people's awareness of technological applications, and encourage parental involvement. The report also includes an annotated bibliography that lists additional funding sources.

Vash, C. (1991). More thoughts on empowerment. *Journal of Rehabilitation, 57*(4), 13–19.

Dr. Vash responds to Emener's (1991) paper by chronicling her own writings (i.e., articles, reports, presentations) in which she validates the importance of various political, psychosocial, psychological, and psychospiritual aspects of consumer empowerment in the rehabilitation arena. Exploring a variety of examples, she differentiates power over others from power over oneself (*The Burnt-out Administrator* [1980]); recounts the psychological values of having sufficient political influence to protect one's fundamental, self-evident, inalienable rights, (*The Psychology of Disability* [1981]); champions the issue of "empowerment of women with disabilities" in a film, *The Dream's Not Enough* (1981), and in a monograph, *Women and Employment* (1982); clarifies why people with disabilities sometimes reject assistive devices ordered by professionals (*Psychological Aspects of Rehabilitation of Engineering* [1983]); resolves that practitioners can help consumers most by informing them of ways to sort what they can control from what they cannot (*The Results of Helping: Empowerment or Helplessness?* [1983]); stresses the importance of expecting people with disabilities to meet their responsibilities (*Families with Disabilities: A Mutual Adjustment Process* [1983]); distinguishes a "consulting model" of rehabilitation service opposed to a "boss model" (*Evaluation from the Client's Point of View* [1984]); reacts to the ethical belief among rehabilitation counselors that they should be doing advocacy, recommending instead that their emphasis should be on teaching consumers to advocate for themselves (*Fighting Another's Battles: When Is It Helpful? Professional? Ethical?* [1987]); talks about what it's like to have a disability to a west coast Humanist Club (*Mortal: Why Me, Lord? God: Why Not?* [1984]); and prepares a panel presentation focusing on the controversy over who has the power to say "when" (*The Right to Die: Whose Decision Is It?* [1990]). She has little dispute with Dr. Emener's approach and concludes by reinforcing the fact that empowerment issues suggest the importance of mutual empowerment in decision making at all levels and in all specialties of rehabilitation.

Index

Page numbers followed by "t" or "f" indicate tables or figures, respectively.

Reasonable accommodation, 89–114
  categories of, 91–92
  concept of, 7–9, 91–93
  cost of, 47
  employer survey on, 94–107
    comments on, 106–107
    development of, 95–97, 99t–100t
    participating employers in, 95, 96t,
      97t
    results of, 100–106, 101t–104t
    survey collection procedure for,
      98, 100
  history of, 6–7
  implementation of, 108–111
  questions asked about, 50t–51t
  and rights of employers, 111–112
  and rights of persons with disabil-
    ities, 111, 112
  see also Employment
Reasonable modification, 7, 10, 11, 14,
  204
Recreation and leisure activities,
  217–238
  effects of ADA on, 228–231
  end eliminating social stigma,
    226–227
  history of services for persons with
    disabilities, 218–223
    1900–1940, 218–220
    1940–present, 220–223
  and independent recreation participa-
    tion, 228–231
  instructional techniques for, 223–224
  legislation for, 221
  manufacturers of modified recreation
    equipment for, 235–236
  need for, 217–218
  normalization movement for,
    222–223
  and organizations for persons with
    disabilities, 219, 220–221
  and professionalization of services,
    221–222
  promoting integration in, 224–226
  and providing outdoor recreation,
    227–228
  resource books on, 237–238
Rehabilitation Act of 1973 (PL 93-112),
  91, 137
  Section 504 of, 6–7, 10, 202–203,
    221

Rehabilitation Act Amendments of 1974
  (PL 93-156), 137
Rehabilitation Act Amendments of 1986
  (PL 99-506), and assistive tech-
  nology, 118
Rehabilitation technologists, 119
Rehabilitation technology, see Assistive
  technology
Related services, under the IDEA,
  165–166
Relationship discrimination, 52t

School drop-outs, 190–191
Section 8 Rental Assistance Program,
  210–211
Self-advocacy, 243–244
Service coordination, and special educa-
  tion, 189
Severe disability, defined, 93–94
Sheltered workshops
  and job satisfaction, 33
  and quality of life, 27
  see also Vocational rehabilitation fa-
    cilities
Social integration, 256
Social stigma, 226–227, 260–262
Societal acceptance, 90, 258–262
  and cultural discrimination, 259–260
  and social stigma, 260–262
Societal attitudes, 90, 159–160, 230,
  265–266
Southeastern Community College v.
  Davis, 7, 14, 263–264
Special education
  and merging general and special edu-
    cation programs, 191–193
  reform of, 175–194
    curriculum methods for, 178–179
    evaluating outcomes of, 179–180
    and models for integrating, 177–178
    and transition from school to work,
      180–185, 181t–182t
  see also Special educators
Special educators
  changing role of, 188–191
    and at-risk youth, 189–191
    and multicultural needs of students,
      188–189
    and service coordination, 189
  see also Special education
Spinal cord injury, 271–272